Passages: CAPE HORN and BEYOND

SAILING THROUGH LIFE'S CHANGING CURRENTS

LIN PARDEY

Paradise Cay Publications
Arcata, California

PARADISE CAY
PUBLICATIONS
www.paracay.com

Book and Cover Design	**Stephen Horsley, Outline Design NZ**
Editor	**Michelle Elvy**
Proofreader	**Elaine Lembo**
Cover image	**Michael Bell, Tacoma WA**

Publisher's Cataloging-in-Publication Data
provided by Five Rainbows Cataloging Services

Names: Pardey, Mary Lin, 1944- author.
Title: Passages : Cape Horn and beyond, sailing through life's changing currents / Mary Lin Pardey.
Description: Bluelake, CA : Paradise Cay Publications, 2025. | Also available in ebook and audiobook formats.
Identifiers: LCCN 2024908266 (print) | ISBN 978-1-929214-80-8 (paperback)
Subjects: LCSH: Illustrated works. | Sailing. | Married people. | Adventure and adventurers. | Aging. | Autobiography. | BISAC: BIOGRAPHY & AUTIOBIOGRAPHY / Memoirs. | BIOGRAPHY & AUTIOBIOGRAPHY / Women. | BIOGRAPHY & AUTIOBIOGRAPHY / Adventurers & Explorers. / TRAVEL / Special Interest / Adventure.
Classification: LCC PN5596.D83 P37 2025 (print) | LCC PN5596.D83 (ebook) | DDC NZ828.209~dc23.

Library of Congress Control Number **2024908266**
ISBN: 978-1-929214-80-8 Print edition
ISBN: 978-1-929214-37-2 eBook edition

Published and distributed by:
Paradise Cay Publications
P.O. Box 29, Arcata, California 95518
120 Mondo Way, Bluelake, California 95525
Tel: 707-822-9063
Email: info@paracay.com
www.paracay.com

US Trade Distribution:
Cardinal Publishers Group
2492 N. Shadeland Ave. Suite A
Indianapolis, Indiana 46219
Tel. 1-317-352-8200

New Zealand Distribution:
Boat Books NZ
22 Westhaven Drive,
Auckland CBD, Auckland 1010
Tel. 64-9 358 5691

Printed in the USA

Dedicated to all the friends I've met
and all the friends I haven't met yet.
I feel like I have spent most of my life sailing on a sea
of your good wishes.

Contents

PASSAGES

To the reader

If we have not met before

I was 20 years old and bored with the life I was leading. I decided to buy a small dinghy and learn to sail. I still wonder at the whimsy that brought this idea into my head as I grew up closer to the California desert than the sea.

Within a day of starting my search, I met a blue-eyed, laughing Canadian charter yacht skipper and racing sailor. Larry had begun building a cruising boat in his spare time. He cleverly lured me into his scheme.

"Stick with me, baby, and you'll go a long, long way."

That was Larry's parting promise at the end of our first day together. According to Larry's plan, if I decided to work alongside him, we'd set off within a year bound for Mexico. Then we'd spend three, possibly four months cruising around Baja California.

I made the leap, with enthusiasm.

Within three weeks, I'd quit my accounting job, moved into Larry's life (and his boatshed), and worked alongside him constructing the wooden craft he had chosen.

His time estimates, in both cases, were way off. It was three years before we set sail on our 24'4" cutter, *Seraffyn*. And the few months in Mexico? That expanded exponentially, as you will read in this book. But time was a gift, too; I found myself so amazed at the life I'd accidentally fallen into I had to have an outlet for the stories that began building in my head. That is when I discovered writing — an unexpected reward for my bold decision.

Writing is magical. You don't need any special equipment to do it. The words are free, just waiting there for you to grab as many as you like. You get them down on paper or on your computer, then move them around like the pieces of a gigantic puzzle. If you grab the right words, and move them into the right sequence, they can make someone smile, someone dream. They can even encourage someone to take a leap into the unknown. For me, my words helped finance our adventures and open unexpected doors, and each adventure gave me more stories to write.

My stories were about us and our event-filled sailing life. Fortunately, the boat Larry had chosen to build was not only a fine sailing vessel, but it looked romantic in photographs. It was small by most any standards and thus appeared to be within the budget of people with modest incomes. Because of our budgetary restrictions and desire to get out sailing as soon as the boat could be launched, we set sail with no engine, something that lent controversy to our story. Add to that our youth and the fact that in photographs we were fresh and pleasantly good-looking. The magazine editor who saw my first article stated, "I love what you've written. And even if the writing was lousy, even if I'd had to re-write most of your story, I know our readers would like to meet you."

The magazine series that ensued became the basis for our first book, *Cruising in Seraffyn*. Then Larry began writing too, highly practical how-to stories that complemented my narrative style. The income from writing supplemented the money we earned delivering other people's yachts, repairing rigging, restoring classic boats along our paths. Gradually, the three or four months a year we spent working in shipyards as we meandered eastward began to dwindle as the income from several more books grew. Eight years after we started voyaging, two years after I wrote my first article, writing covered most of the costs for our amazingly affordable life.

Neither of us had ever imagined or planned on circumnavigating, nor sailing onward year after year, when we built *Seraffyn.* But that four-month Mexican excursion turned into an eleven year, east-about circumnavigation of the world. It ended only because we both wanted a boat that could take us to more adventurous destinations and allow us to enjoy colder climates. Larry also was looking for an excuse to stay mostly in one place for a while. And that is when, as we spent three years building our next boat, my fascination with storytelling matured.

While we built 29'9" *Taleisin* (also timber, engine-free but this time with a lovely bathtub and oil cabin heater), 60 percent of my day was spent at a real desk from which flowed several more books. Three described *Seraffyn*'s further adventures. Two were on the highly practical aspects of offshore cruising, each written to answer readers' and seminar attendees' questions. I was highly motivated to write as this meant Larry could keep working full-time on our future home.

What a wonderful home she proved to be. And what fine adventures she added to our lives. In total, Larry and I voyaged together for 47 years and covered more than 200,000 miles, visited more than 70 countries, and met an amazing array of people.

All passages eventually come to an end. Larry's ended sooner than I expected. But mine has carried on.

As I sit here arranging and re-arranging words until they fall into a pattern that satisfies me, I am at anchor in an isolated cove thinking not only about the magic of writing, but the magic of finding something so worth writing about. I may not have had an acquaintance with the sea as a 20-year-old, but now 60 years later, it is my true home.

PASSAGES

Introduction

February 2024 – Hauraki Gulf, New Zealand

Reaching along at six knots. A white cresting wake rolling out astern. We are halfway from somewhere bound for nowhere as I calculate how much longer my fresh fruit and vegetables will last. I am content, unconcerned. That is, until the wake of a passing boat swishes against the hull and draws me slowly from my dream.

I try to recall the details. I am confused. What boat had I dreamed I was sailing on?

I don't open my eyes, hoping to recall some detail to give me a clue. I turn slightly in the bunk and a long arm reaches across my body and draws me against a lean, warm body. In my semi-somnolent state, this adds to my confusion. Now I slowly open my eyes. The misty blue interior surrounding me is unfamiliar, so unlike the mélange of highly varnished timbers I am expecting. A moment's reflection reminds me I have woken in this same cabin several hundred mornings. The same man has been lying next to me each time.

David and I set off together in *Sahula* just a few months after we met. Now, seven years later, we've just completed another highly satisfying sailing voyage together, venturing across the Tasman Sea to explore the vast lagoons of New Caledonia and on to Vanuatu before returning to New Zealand to settle in again. Last night, after a brisk sail south to rendezvous with city friends, we'd anchored near Motuihi Island rather than heading into the hustle of Auckland harbour after dark.

It isn't until I climb out of the bunk and venture on deck that I begin to sense the depth of that dream, its tentacles reaching out to grip me still. This is the first time I've been at anchor here on *Sahula*, a few hundred meters off the long sandy beach fronting this park-like island. It is the exact same anchorage Larry and I chose the first time we ventured into Auckland on *Taleisin* more than three decades ago. Ashore, absolutely nothing appears to have changed. The same cannot be said of my life — nor me.

PASSAGES

Part One
Underway

PASSAGES

1

If this had been my first

May 2018 - Fiji, on board Sahula

"If this had been my first offshore passage, I might never have gone to sea again," I stated as the two of us waited for our dinner to be served. My hair still dripped from the long, hot shower I had taken as soon as we came ashore at the unassuming Royal Suva Yacht Club. I took a sip of frosty sparkling wine and chuckled. "I couldn't imagine a worse re-introduction to voyaging."

The weather window that had looked almost perfect for our passage north from New Zealand towards Fiji closed soon after we set sail. Instead of the predicted moderate reaching winds hurrying us northward until we reached the tradewinds, we had two days of cold, gusty 25- to 30-knot following winds with a wicked cross sea. This was followed by complete calms, then 35- to 40-knot headwinds that forced us to heave to[1] for 20 hours and abandon our plans of stopping for a few days at Minerva Reef. And then, more calms. I was grateful that we were now securely anchored in Suva's safe-feeling tropical lagoon after an 11-day passage that included a serious accident just ten hours after we cleared the headlands of New Zealand's Bay of Islands.

I had only recently signed on as full-time crew on *Sahula*. David Haigh had anchored his 40-foot steel cutter near my home at Kawau Island

---

1 Heaving to - Getting a vessel to lie quietly, facing the seas. Used as a storm tactic or to stop the vessel's forward motion to wait for daylight, effect repairs or give the crew rest. After you heave to, you are laying hove to. See Storm Tactics Handbook, https://www.paracay.com/storm-tactics-handbook-3rd-edition/

New Zealand, several months before this voyage began. En route to completing the last leg of a ten-year circumnavigation, David planned to do a serious refit in New Zealand before closing his circle by sailing back to his hometown of Townsville in Queensland, Australia. Meeting me derailed his plans. As our friendship deepened, I spent six weeks on *Sahula*, helping David achieve one more of his goals, visiting the beautiful fiords at the far southern reaches of this long, narrow country. Even so, I would not say I was completely familiar with his boat, a boat that is far different than those I had voyaged on for the previous 47 years of my life. Not only is *Sahula* much bigger, but she has a generously powered diesel engine, electric anchor windlass, electronic navigation gear, systems that I had not contended with other than when, on occasion, Larry and I had delivered other people's boats. So, I was slowly, probably too slowly learning my way around these systems. Furthermore, I had not felt the restlessness of the Tasman Sea for more than six years.

David and me on board Sahula *as we head for Fiji.*

On the evening of the "event" we put two reefs in the mainsail, set the staysail, then rolled in the yankee.[2] *Sahula* was on a broad reach, moving at seven knots with 25 knots of wind. Despite the sloppy sea conditions, the

---

2   Yankee – a high-cut jib that doesn't overlap the mast and is used on the forestay of any sailing vessel.

windvane self-steering gear was holding her on a relatively steady course.

It was fully dark by the time David insisted on standing the first three-hour watch. So, I went below, spread out the bedding on the leeward settee, turned off all the interior lights, then climbed between the sheets.

Moments later a dish began rattling in the galley. I climbed out of the bunk. Aided by the bit of light coming from the cockpit, I began searching out the offender. *Sahula* lurched as she tried to surf off a particularly steep wave. I grabbed for a handhold. My hand instinctively reached for the post I had used during 23 years of voyaging with Larry on *Taleisin*. Of course, it wasn't there. In fact, there wasn't a handhold in reach, not for someone only 4'10" tall sailing on a boat outfitted for a six-foot-plus, long-limbed singlehander.

I flew out of the galley, hit the corner of the chart table and crumpled to the floor. As I struggled to breathe, the pain in my side was excruciating. In the dim light emanating from the chart plotter in the cockpit, I could see a swath of blood streaking down the front of the chart table. I screamed for David. He rushed down the companionway ladder, flicked on the chart table light. He looked down to see he was standing in a pool of blood. Fortunately, the light immediately revealed that the cut, a gash across the back of my hand, looked far worse than it actually was. What did concern me as I lay as still as possible on the cabin sole, wedged between the chart table and the navigator seat, was the pain running down my side and chest with each breath I took. My immediate assessment was: *I have really screwed up some muscles.*

David didn't hesitate. "First we have to stop this bleeding, then we are turning back!"

"Grab a wad of paper towels — that will slow down the bleeding. Let's just heave to and sort this all out," I insisted, trying to hide my embarrassment at having been so clumsy and also trying to hide the pain that came with each breath, each lurch of the boat. "Be a lot easier to bandage this up once we do."

It took only a few minutes for David to furl the staysail, disengage the windvane, then tighten in the reefed mainsail. *Sahula* rounded smartly into the wind, began to slow right down and was soon lying far more comfortably.

Once my hand wound was held together with Steri-Strips from the ship's medical kit, and the bleeding controlled by a taped-on wad of bandages, David helped me climb back onto the leeward settee bunk. The Tramadol pills started to kick in and I began breathing with slightly less discomfort. That is when I became very determined we should carry on. "We'll have a far easier time continuing towards Fiji than trying to fight back against this wind," I insisted. "You told me *Sahula* hates going to windward! Besides, winter's closing in. If we turn back now, we might not get another break for quite a while." I think I was trying to convince myself as much as David, but my reasoning seemed sound. "Let's stay hove to until daylight and make the decision then."

I could see how conflicted David felt as I downplayed any concerns. "Give me a night's rest and I'll be fine. Worst case, you have to take care of feeding us for a few days. I'll figure out how to get on deck and stand watches. You've had years of practice doing this solo, so what's different?" I couldn't have gotten off the cabin sole without his help. I could not have climbed into the bunk. And as I lay there padded against the movement of the boat by an extra duvet, I couldn't hold back my tears.

David took my tears as a sign of pain, but they had more to do with my extremely bruised ego plus my frustration. I had made an absolute beginner's mistake, forgetting years of "one hand for the ship, one hand for yourself" practice, belying my so-called "experienced sailor" image. I was afraid that by heading back to Opua, I would be giving up — in effect, *quitting*. Even worse, I might be ruining a relationship that was gradually growing, fed by our mutual love of voyaging and David's respect for my skills as a sailor.

By morning, with the help of a combination of painkillers, and with David assisting, I slowly rose from the bunk and climbed the five steps of the companionway ladder. That helped convince him I could stand (sit) watches so there was no good reason to turn back. Once we were underway again, I realized that was about all I could do: sit for three hours at a time during the night to spot any threatening squalls or shipping, and check that the windvane self-steering gear kept us on course.

By the time we arrived in Fiji, the pain had subsided enough that aspirin with codeine let me breathe without much discomfort. David saw to all the boat-handling chores and, though I went out of my way not to touch my left side or lift my left arm more than a few inches, I could do a bit of the cooking and climb the companionway without assistance.

Now, feeling clean and sated from the tasty dinner we'd savored on the Royal Suva Yacht Club verandah, all I wanted to do was head back to the boat. I was eager for a good, long sleep on a steady platform. David, on the other hand, wanted to get me to the local hospital.

"All that will do is confirm I haven't broken anything," I argued.

Just then a tropical shower marched across the club grounds. "Please, David — I'd really like to get back to the boat," I said. "If we wait until morning there will probably be a more senior doctor at the hospital."

"Okay, one more night won't change anything, but did you bring a rain jacket ashore?" he asked. (It must be added here that David, who has done a lot of mountaineering, always — and I mean *always* — carries a backpack that seems to have not only a rain jacket but an impressive, lightweight array of other survival gear in it.) He looked at my blank face and added, "No problem, I'll run out to the boat and bring you one."

Two or three minutes after David left me standing under the shelter of the verandah, a roar of wind sent deck chairs skittering across the lawn of the club. The dozen people who had been drinking at the outdoor bar rushed to shelter under the main building's thatched roof. I joined them to see the mast lights of a super yacht lying at a strange angle.

"Boy did she drag fast — that first gust must have been 50 knots or more," the bartender said.

Just then David reappeared, struggling against the storm force gusts. "Lin, you'll just have to get wet," he said. "I don't want to get out to the boat and then try to get back ashore in this. But I want to get out there — wind is from the worst possible direction. Sea will definitely build up. Don't want *Sahula* to drag anchor."

I grabbed my shower bag and towel and moved as quickly as I could. Even inside the protective breakwater of the club, the 8-foot inflatable dinghy was pitching and bobbing wildly. I nursed my sore side as I climbed in, gingerly.

Once I was thoroughly drenched by the relatively warm rain, I got caught up in the drama of the scene. Palm trees bent and whipped, halyards clanged as we coursed down the length of the yacht club marina. But the minute we cleared the sheltering breakwater all I felt was disbelief. Three-foot waves swept across the mile-wide lagoon. I couldn't locate *Sahula*'s exceptionally bright masthead light. "She's probably hidden by that ship," David yelled over the screeching wind as we surfed down another wave. The propeller of the 4-horsepower outboard roared, then settled momentarily into a more natural sound as it bit into un-aerated water, only to roar again as we surfed off the crest of the next wave.

We cleared the ship. David yelled, "There's her light. Something's wrong!"

As each gust of wind hit, I could see *Sahula* rock to leeward to lie over at a 15- or 20-degree angle, waves breaking against her windward side, her masthead scribing a wide arc as each gust eased off.

"She's aground," David yelled as we came along her leeward side. "Do you think you can get on board?"

I do not remember getting on board. I do not remember feeling any pain. Adrenalin had kicked in as I climbed out of that bucking dinghy and scrambled up the steeply canted deck, shielding my face from the heavy spray and slashing rain. David leapt out of the dinghy — literally *leapt* — and rushed forward.

"The anchor, it's gone! So is all the chain!" he shouted. "The line securing it to the boat has snapped. Get on the radio and call Pan Pan."

I didn't hesitate. I climbed into the cockpit, down the companionway and, forgetting my reluctance to use radios (and my inexperience), switched on the VHF "Pan Pan Pan. This is the vessel *Sahula*. We are aground."

I tried to keep a calm, steady voice as I began shivering from the cold and the emotional drama of the situation hit me. As soon as I took my finger off the send button, I started stripping off my wet clothes.

Almost immediately, an anxious sounding woman's voice rang clear. "We're aground too. Are you on the red steel boat? If so, you got hit by that big blue ship. So did all five of us." Now I flicked on the cabin light and looked around me. Though I'd left nothing loose on the counters when we went ashore, the cabin sole was now littered with broken dishes. At least a dozen bowls and plates — some plastic, some Corelle, some ceramic — had been flung from lockers, which had never before opened accidentally, even during the rougher seas we'd encountered. Shockingly, even some of the heavy plastic bowls had shattered. This alone proved *Sahula* had taken a very sharp blow.

"Harbor master's office," blared the radio. "Where are you located? How do we identify you?"

I described our location, the extra bright masthead light, the spreader lights I had just turned on.

"We are sending our harbor tug over to help you," a calm voice stated. "Have someone on deck to guide us in."

I pulled on foul weather gear over a nude, but now dry, body then went to join David on deck. The ragged end of the 16-millimeter chain snubbing line was hanging over the bow; the snubbing hook, the chain and anchor were gone *Sahula*'s brand-new wooden bulwark rail was smashed and broken along one side. Her bow pulpit had pretzel-like bends in it, the oversized stainless bow roller was bent and her stern pulpit had been ripped loose. Scraps of rust and blue paint littered the deck. Ahead of us, maybe 200 yards away, lay the 200-foot-long, 300-ton culprit, the derelict-looking ferry that had been on a big mooring about 300 yards downwind of us when we'd come in to anchor several hours earlier. The wind at that time had been from the northeast. The ship now lay beam on to the southerly wind, obviously aground, just as we were.

We saw the lights of the harbor tug approaching. David called, "You stick to the radio, I'll get ready to toss them a towline."

The rain had dropped to a misty drizzle; the wind was now a more manageable 30 knots. Despite the tropical temperatures, I was shivering with cold. I had also become very aware of the aching pain in my chest and arm. But I was reluctant to go below as I watched the lights of the tug getting closer.

Just as it was nearing, the tug slowly turned away. I hurried down the companionway as I heard the radio spring to life. "Sorry, we can't get to you. Too little water," said the tug skipper. "Are you on rock or on sand?"

I heard no hard grinding noises, no hard bangs as *Sahula* lifted slightly then heeled over again each time a wave passed under us. I was relatively new to radio communications, but said simply, "Sand."

"You will have to wait until morning. Then we can get a smaller work boat into you," the tug master replied. "Right now, we have three big work barges loose. Have to get those before they hit the rocks or another boat." Then he added, "Tide is rising. Maybe gain another six or seven inches in the next hour. You might ride a little easier when it does."

I relayed his news to David.

"I can feel her bumping a bit on each wave right now; she feels like she's almost on even keel when that happens," he said. "Get the engine started and we'll try to move her into deeper water. Have to do it in reverse, too close to that ship to try going forward."

Despite the darkness of midnight, and the misty rain that limited our visibility, *Sahula*'s spreader lights clearly illuminated the deck and waters around us. Now David rushed below and came back on deck with the most powerful flashlight we carried, then used it to help scour the water all around our stern to be sure there were no floating ropes or weed behind us. When he gave the signal, I put the throttle in reverse.

"Give her a real burst of power on the next swell!" he yelled over the noise of gusting wind, rattling halyards and thumping engine.

Nothing happened.

"Keep doing that, each time she lifts!" David called.

"Nothing's happening!" I yelled back.

"Doesn't matter. Just keep hitting her hard on each swell. Give her full throttle."

Using my good arm, I kept pumping the throttle, letting the engine scream at far higher revs than I'd ever seen David use as the boat straightened up each time a wave passed under us, then easing back when she lay over again. I am not sure if it was rain or tears that wet my face when I sensed *Sahula* had moved just a few inches astern. I kept watching the shore lights that I could make out just astern of the grounded ship.

Suddenly I saw one more light creep into view at the ship's stern.

Minutes later it was definite: We were moving. We were gaining a foot at a time as the engine growled and *Sahula* thumped on the bottom, then heeled to leeward each time she came down off another wind-blasted wave. Soon she was standing completely upright between each surging wave, and minutes later she was making steady progress and David urged me to push the throttle back even more.

"Get ready to put her into forward when I give the word," he called as he clung onto the stern pulpit. David swept the water astern of us with his high-powered torch and continued to keep an eye out for any floating lines that might threaten *Sahula*'s propeller. "The minutes you put her in forward, give her lots of throttle and turn her into the wind as quickly as you can, or we'll hit that grounded yacht."

Only seconds after we made the turn, I saw the depth sounder reach two meters, then three meters. The cold that was seeping into my sore, wet, tired body was forgotten as I concentrated on avoiding the other yachts, plus three huge work barges and two work boats that had blown loose during the original storm. Visibility was impaired by the blowing rain but every vessel in the anchorage had put on deck lights, including the anchored fishing boats, which helped considerably.

Strangely, as I circled around the fishing boats to give David time to hook up another anchor and rode, I found myself thinking about how well the two of us, despite the tense situation, had been working together. Though David is a strong-willed person who had been sailing mostly on his own for more than a decade, he had been listening to the suggestions I had made. He appeared fully trusting of my judgement as I worked to keep us clear of the other boats and chose a new spot to anchor.

It was after midnight when we finally set one of the spare anchors. Minutes later, the wind began to abate, the rain cleared, stars appeared. As we warmed ourselves with cups of hot soup, I radioed the harbor master to say thank you and inform him we were afloat and safely anchored.

Several other people on board the dozen yachts in the anchorage had been listening in over the past few hours and were eager to talk. Thus, we soon had a more complete picture of how *Sahula* came to be aground. "The minute the first squall blew in, that ship broke free of its mooring," said the owner of *Second Wind*, one of the grounded yachts we'd passed as we made our way clear of the shallow water. "You were the first boat it hit. Ship hit your bow, then kept dragging and soon you were laying against its side, grinding up and down. Then the ship dragged you down until it hit two of us," Gordon Gregg from *Ms Murphy* told us. "We were much closer to its stern, so we managed to motor clear. Unfortunately, our anchor got tangled with the boat next to us." It was a complicated situation. Gordon continued, "By the time both of us were able to cast off our anchor chains, both my boat and *Second Wind* ended up aground. Then the ship shoved you into a big catamaran. You hit right on her bows. Crew on the cat cast off their anchor rode and finally got clear when the ship went aground. Then they ran aground too. We saw your boat drift clear and then you were aground."

"Guess that explains the damage on both sides of the boat," David said. "But sure glad the anchor chain paid out and both the snubber and the chain retaining line broke. If the anchor had held, she might have been rolled right under that ship and sunk."

"Let's talk about it in the morning," was all I could say as I downed two Tramadol tablets, then climbed between the sheets. "She's afloat, that's all that matters."

But of course, neither of us could sleep as we lamented the fractured bulwark rail, a rail that had just been built six weeks before. Then there was the mess in the main cabin, the mangled bow pulpit, stern rail and stanchions that had to be fixed before we could sail much farther.

I convinced David to climb out of the bunk and get me a sleeping pill to add to my medical cocktail.

"Some diver is going to be harvesting anchors and chains in the morning," I said when he crawled back into the bunk. "Wonder how much it will cost to ransom ours. And how are we going to find someone who can fix stainless steel here. This is going to soak up all our cruising time!"

"The staff at the yacht club will know someone who can help fix things," David replied. "And I'm sure the shipping company will cover the cost of finding the anchor and the repairs."

"Sure, they will," I mumbled sarcastically as I drifted off to sleep.

2

Coming to know the man

2018 - Suva, Fiji. on board Sahula

"Right about there, go for it," I yell. I doubt they can hear me as they maneuver their workboat a hundred feet from where I sit. But my hand signals can't be mistaken. The wetsuited Fijian diver shoves an anchor overboard. The helmsman backs down to set it. I watch impatiently as the diver pulls on his fins, shoulders his air tank, then flips backwards into the murky, storm-stirred water.

I'd found David's note lying on the chart table soon after I had climbed gingerly out of the big double bunk that morning. *Gone ashore to see if we can find a workberth in the marina, find a diver to get the ground tackle back.*

I'd climbed out into the cockpit intending to have a quick look around before making a start on the pile of wet clothes and broken dishes that cluttered the galley and saloon floor. But I'd made the mistake of sitting down. Now, the discomfort from my bruised ribs made me reluctant to move. A gentle morning breeze ruffled the glistening turquoise water. Ashore, palm trees barely moved. A line of white breakers off in the distance showed where the fringing reef protected us from the open ocean. If I ignored the mess below decks, and overlooked the disarray on deck, the previous night's events could have been consigned to an over-active imagination.

Soon after I sat down, I noticed a rough-looking workboat leave the marina entrance. It headed past the grounded tattered and rusting hulk of *Princess Civa*, the interisland ferry that had caused such mayhem the previous night. I watched as the workboat headed directly for the two yachts that lay grounded almost side by side, about 300 yards north of *Sahula*. I saw lots of gesturing between the diver and yacht crews. Then the workboat headed closer to *Sahula* and began circling, obviously trying to decide where to start searching for the anchors and chains lost from the five yachts.

Princess Civa was refloated two days after the event and towed to a secure mooring.

My mind went into overdrive. Surprisingly, for someone who had voyaged without electronic navigation devices for 47 years of my life, I immediately thought of the chart plotter we'd turned off only after *Sahula* was securely anchored the previous day.

When the workboat crew was close enough to notice me, I got out on deck and motioned them alongside. "According to my computations, our anchor should be just 50 or 60 meters in that direction," I said. "Could be easy to spot the chain, it's got lots of fresh orange paint on it. The other yachts were anchored just to the west of us." The diver climbed on board and studied the screen, then asked me to point to keep him headed in the right direction.

I held my breath when I saw the diver's head pop up.

Nothing.

He dove again and seemed to stay down for a long time. Then I saw him clamber on board the workboat, trailing a piece of line. Seconds later I watched as he and his helper pulled up *Sahula*'s 44-pound Bruce anchor followed by her distinctive, orange-marked chain. A few minutes later they were alongside and carefully handing our ground tackle onto the foredeck.

That done, they set off to begin another search, lining themselves up with *Sahula* and my pointing arm. "Yes," I yelled. "That's about where

Ms Murphy anchored. As soon as I saw them bring up the next anchor, I reluctantly abandoned my cockpit viewing spot and climbed below.

David arrived not long after the diver and his crew had moved towards the area where the third set of ground tackle lay.

"Found the dive shop," he called as he secured the dinghy astern. "They said they'd send a diver out to help find our gear soon."

I smiled. I loved being able to say, "Take a look at the foredeck."

"That is fast work," he called. "Wonderful." It was good news all around. David had found a space to tie inside the marina. "We can go as soon as I can get the chain stored away," he said. "Really lucky as there is only one space left and we can just squeeze in between two of the local boats. But need to get moving before the tide drops. Won't be enough water at the entrance two hours from now. Man is coming down from the air conditioning factory in three hours to make a start on our pulpit. Seems they do all the stainless-steel railing work around here. Really busy, but lucky for us they have the exact right tubing we need."

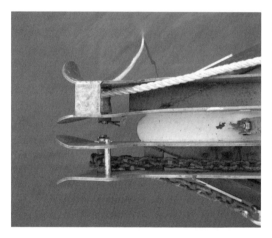

The ¼-inch-thick stainless-steel ear of Sahula's *bow roller was badly distorted during the* Princess Civa *incident. Both the bow pulpit and the stern pulpit were badly distorted and needed replacing.*

I was smiling as we motored *Sahula* carefully past the grounded *Princess Civa*, through the scattering of overseas yachts and derelict looking fish boats then into the neglected-looking, marina area. I grew ever more optimistic as I learned that David had successfully filled every minute of his two hours ashore. "Manager of the club was great. With her help I got in touch with the vice commodore. He's going to come down and meet with us. Wants to help negotiate with the company that owns that ferry. Doesn't want Suva to get a bad reputation." David stood on the side deck, enthusiastically reciting his good news while pointing out the clearest path through the boats around us. "Soon as we secure our lines, we must get in touch with the other crews who need to be in on the meeting. I've already had a phone conversation with the vice commodore of the club and he suggested getting together two hours from now. Only thing I haven't found is a carpenter to fix the rail, but I've got a lead on that." He set to work hanging fenders on each side of the boat, then added, "And there is a good hospital here in town with a clinic. You don't need an appointment. While I meet with the vice commodore, you can go and see a doctor."

Though David and I had been an "item" for almost six months, our time together had been about sailing, traveling, getting to know each other. Now I was seeing something new, the people organizer. I was impressed and became ever more so as the week unfolded.

David secured *Sahula* stern to a mooring ball, bow tied to a partially sunken walkway which led onto the steep bank surrounding the marina while I sat in the companionway feeling relatively useless. Even before the last line was secured, people began streaming onboard. It was almost as if a movie director had yelled, "Action!" The stainless-steel rail builder climbed on board to begin measuring and planning the repair work. Johnny, the very large Fijian who helped do small carpentry jobs around the club, had arrived to look at the shattered bulwark rail. The owners of the other four boats which had been damaged had all motored their dinghies alongside and were ready to join David and the vice commodore for their meeting on shore, and I was being helped off the boat.

I slid very gingerly under the bow pulpit and down onto a box Johnny had provided so I could more easily reach the walkway. "I'm fine, just need to take it easy for a few days," I protested as David marched me to the front of the club and hailed a taxi. "Take her directly to the hospital," he instructed the driver. "Lin, it might be a waste of time, but I won't feel good until you get checked out."

"What about clearing customs — immigration people who came on board yesterday said we had to go to their offices for our cruising permits," I countered.

"I am sure they already know we aren't going anywhere soon. Get yourself checked out today. Customs can wait until tomorrow," David said.

An intense meeting was underway when I arrived back at the club a few hours later. I tried not to cause an interruption as it became clear some of the owners from damaged yachts approached the situation with resigned acceptance while others were openly angry. David controlled the meeting, quietly but firmly. "Everyone needs to write up a rough assessment of their damages and repair costs for tomorrow afternoon's meeting. Try to get them to me by noon. Best not to overload the meeting so I suggest Gordon, who owns *Ms Murphy*, and I represent all of us." The vice commodore nodded his head in agreement, then added, "I've already been in contact with the harbor master. He'll join us and bring the ship's owners."

David turned to where I had been quietly watching. "Did you see a doctor, did you get X-rays? Did he give you anything to help with the pain?"

"Doctor yes, X-ray yes, pain no. Says the pills we have on board are just right. But he gave me a bag of balloons," I answered as I handed him the large X-ray envelope.

"Balloons — you must be kidding. Was he a pediatrician?"

"Nope, an orthopedic surgeon. I got lucky. He was on call because the national soccer team is playing here later today."

"Why balloons?"

"Seems I have pleurisy. Take a look at the X-rays."

It was heartwarming to watch David's face change as I pointed out the five broken ribs, the eight fractures that were the source of my discomfort. Tears sprang to his eyes. Then he rushed to find me a padded chair. "What are they going to do about it? Shouldn't you be in hospital? How dangerous is this?"

"After you buy me some lunch you can meet Dr. Taloga and hear for yourself. Seems the hospital just got a brand-new MRI machine and I am scheduled to be one of its first victims in just under two hours. Soon as it's done Dr. Taloga will meet with us, just in case there is something else wrong," I explained. "But he already said I am healing well. Lucky we weren't near a hospital when this happened. They would have operated and put a plate in to hold the ribs from shifting. But since you helped me stay mostly still, looks like I'm healing perfectly. And," I said proudly, "he thinks I am really tough. Says his soccer players would have been completely out of action for three or four weeks and drugged to the eyeballs if they had the same fractures."

"And the balloons, a consolation prize?" David asked.

"Nope, exercise to make me breathe deep. Blow a few of them up three times a day."

As I think back to my reaction when the accident happened, I am convinced the first-aid course Larry and I had taken when we were building *Taleisin* had once again helped me tremendously. Called *Where There is No Doctor*, three emergency room doctors and three nurses had spent 35 hours over a four-day period reinforcing what they called the basics: check for breathing, stop the bleeding, get the patient comfortable and lying still. Then one of three things will happen: the patient will naturally get better, the patient's condition won't change, or their condition will get worse. Only if it gets worse do you need to push the panic button and call for immediate outside help. I'd since tried to take a refresher advanced first aid course every five or six years. The skills have been useful, mostly to help other sailors and occasionally people in very isolated villages. Through the years Larry and I sailed together the only serious injuries we'd had when we were at sea had been a broken toe and an abscessed tooth. David, during his ten years of voyaging, had not once needed to use anything more than a few Band-Aids from his onboard medical kit until I made the foolish mistake that led to breaking my ribs.

It was late the next afternoon when I finally finished our clearance into Fiji. Back on board *Sahula*, I set to work preparing a platter of fragrant fresh tropical fruit from the open-air markets near the customs office. With the surgeon's assurance that I couldn't cause more problems by being somewhat active, and with a well-stocked selection of painkillers, I felt eager to be doing anything I could to make life more enjoyable as David worked to clean up the aftermath of our *Princess Civa* incident.

I did follow David's admonishment to "take things easy." I did hire Peni, a local youngster whose mother had a stall in the produce market, to walk along with me and carry my shopping bag. This not only saved me discomfort but improved the price and quality of my provisions as Peni bargained with the local stall holders on my behalf. He insisted on escorting me as I searched out the customs office. Then Peni demanded a fixed (lower) price for my taxi ride back to the yacht club. When I turned to give him some money for his help, he would only accept F$2.00 (About 90 cents US.) So, while David was on his mission as representative of the five crews, I had restocked our fresh food supply and now had a three-month cruising permit in hand.

Three things made our medical and collision repair situation far easier to handle. Not only does every Fijian seem to meet you with a smile and say "Bula, bula!" meaning "Hello, hello!" but most also have a relatively good understanding of English. This was an enormous help as we discussed the repairs we needed, the costs involved and searched out replacements for broken gear. Third, by paying a relatively small amount online, we were able to use our New Zealand mobile phone plans, which worked everywhere on the main island.

"You would have loved that meeting," David said exuberantly as he climbed back on board *Sahula* later that afternoon. "The owner of *Princess Civa* already looked concerned when the port captain said, 'we don't want to hurt our reputation among visiting yachtsmen, they support lots of businesses around here.' Then the port safety officer said, 'and if you don't pay up, your ferry won't get a health and safety certificate. No cert, no passengers.' Poor ship owner went white and said they would *definitely* pay up. Went even whiter when Gordon and I showed him the estimates — $45,000 Fijian dollars' worth of damages among the five boats."

Despite David's very positive description of the meeting, I tried to prepare both of us for a disappointment. The odds were against us. We were relatively wealthy-appearing foreigners in a country with limited resources and we also had a limited time before we had to set sail again. "The guys doing the welding were here a few hours ago with their supervisor," I said. "He figures all the work will cost about F$5,000[1]. The anchor retrieval cost us just F$200 plus two boxes of chocolate chip cookies." I was adding up the numbers quickly in my head as I was talking. Even if fixing up the woodwork costs another $1,000, with the marina charges it would be less than what the excess or deductible would be if we had collision coverage instead of just third-party insurance. "Even if we don't get paid, it might dent our budget, but it isn't going to change our cruising plans."

———————

"The most useless thing on a cruising yacht is a calendar." I read that somewhere and I couldn't agree more. And from all the years I cruised with Larry, I can count only a handful of times when we had to schedule our sailing around specific dates, other than those imposed by changing seasons. David had expressed the same philosophy about cruising, and indeed in his general way of living. "Why do we need a plan, let's just let things flow," he'd often said as we came to know each other. Thus, when we set sail together from New Zealand the closest we had to a plan was to get to Australia before the start of cyclone season. Fiji offered a cruising season full of islands and reefs to explore. Vanuatu beckoned with its string of volcanic islands, its variety of cultures.

But now we faced the delay caused by the *Princess Civa* collision. And there were other factors creating new pressures, pressures I had never before had to consider. Even if David believed in the no-calendar policy, in principle, unlike Larry and I who had no children, he had a close relationship with

———————

1   One Fijian dollar approximately US$ .40 US, AUS$ .75

his three daughters and arranged visits with them as often as possible. Also, from his years as an environmental lawyer and senior university law lecturer, he had a large circle of friends with whom he kept in close touch. Several of them arranged to meet up with him at various times while he wandered.

Within 24 hours of our arrival in Suva, the reality of this major difference thrust its way into our lives.

Just before we set sail from Opua, David had written to friends and family in Australia saying he was headed back to his hometown of Townsville via Fiji and Vanuatu after 11 years of wandering. When we connected to the Suva Yacht Club internet on the night of our arrival, emails from each of his daughters were waiting. "We're all flying to Townsville to celebrate Mom's 70th the last week of August," Annalise, his Hong Kong-based daughter, wrote. "The three of us will be waiting on the marina breakwater at 3 pm on the 24th of August. We want to watch the *Red Tin Can* finally come home." David's other daughters lived in Sydney and Melbourne. During his cruising years, each of his daughters had joined him in various countries and he had flown back to Australia to catch up with them and friends three times in the past. But it had been more than three years since he'd been with all three at the same time in person. This was a truly fortuitous chance for David.

It was more than a bit daunting for me, anticipating meeting his three daughters, an ex-wife, his brother and sister-in-law and probably a big group of his friends, all at the same time. On the other hand, though it shortened the time we had to explore among the islands along the way, at that time it seemed to fit easily into our sailing plans. We'd have four or five weeks wandering around the Fijian islands, a month or so to experience some of Vanuatu.

Then came the *Princess Civa* collision, and the ensuing repairs to eat into our schedule.

A few days after the bow pulpit and the stern rails had been taken off the boat David excitedly shared another email he had just received, this time from his friend, Gwen Amankwah-Toa. "I'm flying home to Vanuatu for my niece's wedding," she wrote. "My whole family will be coming to Vila from Santo, my home island. Let's meet there on June 24th." David described his 30-year long friendship with Gwen and her family. "You'll love her. Our kids grew up together." For me, this invitation seemed a fortunate chance to have an insider's look at Vanuatu. Almost as important, it would be an opportunity to glean more of an insight into this man who came from a far different background than me.

Unfortunately, Gwen's date gave us less than two weeks to complete the repairs on *Sahula* and sail 700 miles westward. "Remember, Fiji is only an eight- or ten-day sail from New Zealand. If we don't see it now, we can always come back later," David said as he dug out the charts for Vanuatu that evening.

"That's not what's worrying me," I answered. "Vanuatu has always been on my list of places I wanted to explore. And to see it with someone who speaks the local language, knows the customs? That is really special." Then I listed my concerns about getting the repair work finished and collecting the money from the shipping company in time. "Then there is the new controller for the wind generator. It has to come from New Zealand and there is no guarantee how long that will take," I reminded him.

"Let's just take things one at a time," David said. "I know the ship's owner wants to pay for our damages. He's already been in touch with the folks who are building the pulpit. The welder overheard him asking the supervisor to do the work at 'local' rates. And, if we don't get away in time to meet up with Gwen it won't be the end of the world."

Though he did seem sincere about his acceptance that we might not be able to meet up with Gwen, it was clear that missing the Townsville meeting with his daughters would be a major disappointment.

Despite my misgivings, the stainless-steel fabrication and the welding work on *Sahula*'s rails was done to high professional standards within a week. As the two fabricators installed the last gleaming stanchion, their supervisor came by to ensure we were satisfied with the work. He brought a message from the club office — there were two packages waiting for us in the club offices. Better yet, the resident electrician was available the next day to help David install the second replacement controller his almost new, but so far, not terribly successful, wind generator had required.

The bulwark rail repair was another matter. Johnny had built a fully successful handhold for the galley. But both his attempts to bend on a new section of timber failed. We realized, even if he did find a way to fasten the strake in place, the results would not be great. Johnny just didn't have the appropriate tools, or materials, for the job. "It's something to do when we get to Australia," David decided. "I'm fine with paying for that myself. Look at how much better the new pulpit looks. The old one was pretty battered even before the collision. Let's just get him to make some sort of band-aid to hold the bulwark in place right now."

With the potential rendezvous with Gwen looming over us I couldn't have agreed more. Johnny's look of relief when I suggested this was reward enough for the rough-looking patch I'd have to look at for the next few months. "Consider it a badge of honor," David said. "Good story behind it, too."

The owners of the four other yachts which had been involved in the *Princess Civa* incident had each reacted in different ways after David reported the results of his meeting with the officials and ship's owner. One had rudely suggested we were all wasting our time. "I wouldn't trust one word of any official. I wouldn't trust the work anyone here did," he said. "I'll get my insurance company to fix the boat when I sail back to civilization. I've already located a surveyor to send them a report."

Two of the other yacht owners declared they didn't trust the quality of workmanship that might be available in Suva. "I prefer getting the work done where they know yachts and the conditions are nicer," R said. "I plan to enjoy some cruising and diving, then sail up to Vuda, where they have a proper yacht marina. Friends say it's a fun, social place," he explained. "When the cruising season is over, I'll get the boat hauled out and leave her in their storage yard. They can refinish the topsides and bulwark while I fly home. That way I don't miss out on any cruising time."

J, whose boat had sustained a lot of scratches and damaged gelcoat, echoed these sentiments.

Ms Murphy, the steel, 36-foot van de Stadt sloop sailed by Gordon Gregg, had sustained the lightest damage of the fleet. With his anchor and chain back on board, his bow roller fitting reconstructed, new bushings on his rudder and the tip of the blades of his propellor straightened, he had invoices totaling F$750.[2]

The morning after our new pulpit was installed, David asked, "Lin, do you mind going to collect the money from the shipping company? Gordon is ready to go with you. Then I can work with the electrician when he shows up this morning,"

"I'm ready to set sail on Monday, with or without the money," Gordon explained as we walked through the commercial port district not far from the yacht club marina. "Be nice to get paid but I am ready to get out and do some exploring."

A mixture of non-descript, almost new commercial buildings with first-world style signage lay side by side with dilapidated corroding corrugated iron

---

2   Read Gordon's account of being hit by *Princess Civa* in Appendix I.

sheds, each with crudely hand painted signs which seemed more in keeping with the rough paths and potholed streets that surrounded them. And as we progressed a few blocks farther into the port precinct, the buildings became even more run down and appeared less inhabited. The only way we found our destination was by finally encountering a taxi driver who pointed to the side of a tilting wooden structure built over an old slipway.

Dozens of boards were missing from the sides of the building. A large fishing trawler was being worked on right next to the rickety stairway we were told took us to the shipping company office. Not one sign, not even on the door at the top, indicated we'd reached our destination. But the handsome young Fijian woman at the desk that blocked the entrance to an otherwise bare room spoke clear, concise English twinged with an Australian accent. Within minutes she'd summoned the man I now confronted. Gordon and I were escorted into his office, offered tea, cold drinks and assured, "Our company will pay you. But . . . " The but? "The government owes us many thousands of dollars and said they are paying us today. Right now, we have enough money in the bank to cover one of your claims, but tomorrow we will have enough for both."

Twice he took our invoices and disappeared for almost 30 minutes each time, only to return shaking his head and suggesting we come back the next day.

"I'll just have to stay here all day until I get paid," I explained. Composing my most concerned expression and using my most worried tones, I continued, "My boyfriend will be very angry if I don't come home with the money."

"You can come back tomorrow. I promise I can write both of you checks then and there will be money in the bank to cover it," the hassled looking general manager of the shipping company countered. "Besides, it is almost lunch time and we usually close for a few hours so our workers can have their meal."

"Nope, I'll just stay here. Maybe one of your staff can bring me something to eat," I said. "Can't leave until I have the money."

The concerned look on the manager's face echoed the look on Gordon's.

But I watched as he mulled over my comments, my demeanor and decided I was serious about sitting there all day. The general manager left and didn't return for close to an hour.

Gordon quietly asked me, "Do you really plan to stay all afternoon? Not sure that will accomplish much. They clearly don't have any intention of paying. Take a look around — maybe they just don't have any money."

"I've brought along a good book," I replied. "My ribs are giving me a lot less discomfort, but I still spend half the day sitting down on board and doing very little. So why not do it here?"

There was a big smile on the general manager's face when he returned. He handed Gordon a check. Then he turned to me and said, "We definitely will have the money for you when you come back tomorrow. I spoke with the government bank and they said they have sent it on."

"No problem, I'll have Gordon bring back my sleeping bag so I can stay right here until I have the money. My boyfriend told me not to come home without it."

Again, the manager disappeared. Almost an hour later he was back. He reluctantly handed me a check, saying, "If you get to the bank tomorrow, they should have the money."

Back on board that evening, the two of us were enjoying our evening ritual of sundowners. David laughed as I related my threat of camping in the shipping offices all night if necessary. "I think you would have done it!"

"I was planning on sending Gordon back here to get a sleeping bag and some food if nothing happened," I answered. "I knew that would shake them up." My threat had apparently worked as the manager had left his office and was away for almost two hours. When he returned and handed me a check, he explained he had to go halfway across town to get the second signature because it was over their one signature limit. Now I told David, "That convinced me the manager had done the best he could. I still doubt that check will ever work. Banks were closed by the time I got it. So we'll know tomorrow."

I had been mulling our options ever since I'd returned. I said, "I think we should forget about the money and just plan on sailing as soon as we can. Don't want to miss either our Vanuatu rendezvous or the one your daughters are planning."

"Sure would be good to have the money. Let's not write it off immediately," David countered. "You start getting provisions on board. I'll keep working at getting the electrics right. The German guy off the big ketch is giving me a hand and really seems to know his stuff. Another day or two could be handy. If we get away before the end of next week, we might not arrive in Vanuatu the same day as Gwen, but she did say she's staying for at least two weeks."

I was the first person in line at the bank the next afternoon. No luck, though the teller did say government payments often took an extra day or two to clear. On Monday morning, I was at the bank soon after it opened. No luck. This time I headed back over to the shipping company office. There was no sign of the so-called general manager. The office was almost deserted. But Ana, the receptionist, actually turned her computer screen around and showed me more than a dozen emails between the company and the government payment office. "We really are owed a lot of money and none of us who work here have been paid for more than three weeks," Ana explained. "Why don't you leave me your phone number. The minute I know the money has reached the bank I'll send you a message."

I left shaking my head. Just our luck to be downwind of a ship owned by a company that appeared to be on the verge of bankruptcy. I located Peni at his mother's stall in the marketplace. Together we gathered up several bags of fresh food. And this time he rode in the taxi to help me get the bags down to *Sahula*.

My phone buzzed a minute after Peni left. David had just hauled the last bag of provisions out of the cockpit and into the galley. I had just climbed carefully down the companionway to start packing things away. I grabbed the phone and swiped the answer button. "Money in the bank. - Ana," read the message on my screen.

"Come on, let's go cash that check," David said as he grabbed his ever-present backpack.

I was not as quick on my feet. "Let me rest a few minutes," I said. " I have to get these groceries in the fridge, have some lunch . . . "

"Nope, never know how many other people are rushing to collect that money . . . " He was already out the companionway.

Even the teller at the bank seemed pleased as she handed us a brown paper bag filled with crumpled, heavily used notes. "I hope you continue to enjoy your stay here in my country," she said.

I was reluctant to tell her we were leaving the next morning. For, despite missing out on exploring any of Fiji beyond the boundaries of the capital city, despite missing a chance to experience the small, isolated villages and local customs other cruisers had raved about, I felt we'd had an interesting, if different, insight into Fijian culture. We'd seen firsthand the difficulties of being a small, relatively poor, multi-racial island nation caught up in the financial problems of an ever-changing world. I loved the mad mix of colors, cultures and costumes that made the markets and streets an ever-changing visual delight. Though it should have been frustrating, I even enjoyed the challenge of shopping where finding hair clips meant a search through the local hardware store and locating wiring for the single-sideband radio led to a dig through a bin in the hairdresser's shop. Best of all I liked the warmth and curiosity of the Fijians we'd met so far, something I would not have expected in the "big city."

"Where can I find the fairest money exchanger?" I asked the bank teller.

"Where do you go when you leave Fiji?" she asked.

"Vanuatu."

"Then don't change the money now," she replied. "My brother works in Vanuatu, and he says they accept Fijian dollars at a far better rate than you can get here."

Within 30 hours of our check clearing, all of the electrical work had been finished, we'd stored all the tools and organized the interior of the boat, reprovisioned and gotten our customs clearance documents. We'd even found time for one last long shower and dinner at the Suva Yacht Club, shared farewell drinks with the vice commodore and were ready to set sail.

The sun had just broken the horizon when we cleared the pass that led us away from Suva. With the yankee set, the double-reefed mainsail full and pulling, *Sahula* headed towards Vanuatu at almost seven knots, driven by fresh southeast tradewinds.

"You sure handled things well ever since your accident. A bit more of an adventure than you signed up for, wasn't it?" David joked as he tossed the last mooring lines into the lazarette, then turned to engage the self-steering windvane he had named Valerie. "Wonder what's next for us?"

Nine days after the storm, we were able to set sail towards Vanuatu.

I moved away from the wheel to relax into the forward corner of the cockpit. As I did so, I realized the discomfort caused by my rib fractures had faded to just an occasional twinge. Even better, I realized, despite more than four decades of voyaging, I was excited to be heading off to sea, excited to be headed towards a place I'd never been before.

David stood on the afterdeck for a few minutes, watching to be sure Valerie was in full control. Then he came forward to settle into his favorite position: seated on the cockpit coaming, back against the bimini support, long legs folded comfortably onto the cockpit bench, long arms ready to reach out and move the wheel if need be, a contented, almost dreamy smile on his face.

As the tradewinds sent *Sahula* scudding westward, I watched David almost instinctively reach out and give the wheel a slight tweak, then tighten up the retaining lines that held it in position. He was in his element, at home, confident.

Once we arrived in Vanuatu, we found a quiet anchorage not far from Vila.

It can't be easy for him, I thought. Inviting someone with my temperament, my sailing background and history (some might call it baggage) into his life. Even before our recent trials I'd often paused to think about how we had moved so seamlessly into this partnership. The past few weeks had shown me new and heartwarming facets of his personality. I thought of the way he'd accepted my judgement and cared for me (and *Sahula*) after I broke my ribs at sea, how he considered and usually accepted every suggestion I'd made as we sailed onward from New Zealand. During the wild, stormy night in Suva, he had shown no hint of egotism, looking to me for suggestions, and trusting me to maneuver *Sahula* to safety after her encounter with *Princess Civa* while he worked sorting ground tackle so we could re-anchor. I enjoyed recalling his quiet determination and diplomatic management of the people situation as he worked with the port officials, other yacht owners, then tradesmen to effect *Sahula*'s repairs. Then there was his utter lack of frustration when it came to being flexible about changes to our plans.

Yes, I was beginning to know this man. And it was time I accepted the obvious: we were bound to have many more interesting adventures together. This acceptance set me thinking about the passages, both literal and emotional, that brought David and *Sahula* into my life.

3

When you've reached the goal

March 2002 - near Cape Horn, on board Taleisin

"Hey, Lin, wake up!" I hear Larry's voice over my storm-tossed dream. "You wanted this chance, come and grab it."

It takes my body and mind several moments to coordinate sensory information before I realize the dream I'd been having wasn't far off the mark. Larry and I really *were* trying to bash our way past Cape Horn and into the Pacific. But now, instead of the body-jarring crash and lurch of a hard-driven sailboat fighting to gain weathering against storm-force southwesterly winds of the Screaming 50s, I barely feel any movement at all. Instead of dark of night and howl of wind, I hear rambunctious terns and see streams of glorious sunlight pouring through the open hatch. Had I dreamed the snow flurries, and frequent squalls?

Was I really here?

I can look back at a dozen moments in my life when a decision, an event — accidental or intended — changed the whole direction of my life. There was the day I gave up trying to get into the school of engineering and dropped out of university. This was followed a few years later, when I decided to buy a sailing dinghy because I wanted to learn to sail. That was the year of threes: after three weeks I had thrown caution to the wind and, after only three dates, ran off with Larry to help him build his boat and sail full-time. Then there was the time I took up the challenge an editor tossed at me after I wrote a nasty letter about an article in his magazine. He sent a telegram saying simply, "Prove it." That led to my very first article. In retrospect I can easily see how my life had been marked by moments like those.

But only one time was I fully aware the decision I was asked to make was one that would mark a turning point in my life. This was the big one: Cape Horn.

If I agreed to sail against the prevailing winds around Cape Horn, a goal that had up until that time been only Larry's dream, I realized — whether we succeeded or failed — nothing would ever be quite the same.

How right I was.

That was perhaps our biggest adventure: Larry and me and our tidy *Taleisin* off on what I now call our Cape Horn Caper. Now, looking back, I know it is also the place to start the story of how I came to be sailing on a big red steel cutter with a retired Australian environmental lawyer and activist, tramper, and mountain climber.

At the sound of Larry's voice, I climb clear of the thick sleeping bag and grab my jeans, then add two sweaters over the thermal inners I'd slept in.

All around me are signs of hard sailing. Every device we'd installed to keep gear securely inside lockers and under floorboards is fastened. Sponges sprout around the edges of dishes and spice jars, a sure sign Larry has been in, to quiet rattles as I slept. On the cabin sole, forward next to the stove and out of the path of traffic, a half-dozen stray items have joined the basket of fruit and cheese — things I kept handy to snack on because it had been too rough to cook.

"Were you serious about flying the nylon drifter at the Horn?" Larry calls. "You've got your chance. This light air can't last long."

I don't waste a second. I'm out the companionway, gloves between my teeth, watch cap only half on as Larry pulls the drifter bag from the lazarette. He laughs as I spin in a circle and almost miss the most significant landmark of our lives together. Then, he reaches out to hug me while he stretches his arm out towards the north. "There she is, Cape Horn to starboard."

I am awestruck, afraid to say a word, afraid because I don't want to jinx the 8-knot southeasterly breeze that belies the legends surrounding this southernmost cape, where winds normally blow at force eight to twelve 24 percent of the year, where 78 percent of all winds reported come from the westerly quadrant. Then I grab the great big blue and white lightweight nylon sail and wordlessly, using the familiar routines of 37 years of sailing together, Larry and I get it flying.

I search out our cameras plus a one-pound bag of confetti I've snuck on board. Windvane set, we frolic and throw bright colored bits of paper into the air, then watch them drift slowly downwind towards the sparkling, sun-lit cliffs eight miles to the north. We snap photos. I say, "Now we have truly flown our nylon sail as we sailed west below each of the great southern capes of the world. Time to get it down, before we blow it out."

"Why take it down?" Larry counters. "Barometer is steady, it's keeping us moving. We need every bit of speed we can get to beat this east-going current."

In spite of the near-freezing temperatures on deck I can't stay below as, for the next ten hours, *Taleisin* moves serenely westward over a wind-rippled sea above the graveyard of thousands of far less fortunate sailors. I throw chunks of bread to the albatross that glide around us and laugh at their clumsy landings, their forwardness as they paddle right up to *Taleisin*'s side and look into the cockpit for more tidbits. Their massive, hooked beaks, their elegant long wings bring to mind what I once read, how each bird carries the soul of a Cape Horn sailor whose body lies beneath these icy waters.

I wonder what those professional seamen would have made of the fears that accompanied me for the past two years, the fear I still had as the southerly breeze freshens and we douse our drifter and set the working jib and staysail to leave the Horn astern and charge into the Pacific.

I now realize Larry always planned to someday "double the Horn."[1] In 1977 when we were in Malta, preparing 5-ton engine-free *Seraffyn* for the rougher weather of the Red Sea, Larry said, "Next boat we build, no cockpit to fill with seas. Then we could take it anywhere, even round the Horn." I should have linked the clues, but it was almost four years before the next one popped up. We were building *Seraffyn*'s bigger sister, *Taleisin*, and I was helping Larry line up his long drill so the 17th and 18th keel bolts went straight and true through the bronze floors, teak keel timber and lead. "Yes, I want those two extra bolts," he said when I questioned this departure from the construction plans. "You can call it overbuilding. I call it insurance to make her strong enough for anything, even Cape Horn."

After 3 ½ years of boatbuilding to finish *Taleisin*, then 15,000 miles of

---

1   To sail east to west against the prevailing winds from 50 degrees South in the Atlantic to 50 degrees South in the Pacific has traditionally been called "doubling the Horn".

engine-free Pacific voyaging, Larry convinced me to sail south of Tasmania, ostensibly as the logical route to Western Australia. Though the winds here are almost always from the west and often gale force or stronger, with careful weather planning and patience we found February gave us breezes light enough to fly our nylon drifter past Maatsuyker Island, and I ignored the next clue. "Do you realize we are only 700 miles north of the latitude of Cape Horn?" Larry said as we passed westward into the Indian Ocean.

Cape Leeuwin, The Cape of Storms, Cape of Good Hope. Over the next years we sailed past each, encountering stormy weather to reach them but nylon drifter weather as each cape lay on our beam. When we turned north towards Europe, after 12 years of voyaging on *Taleisin*, I relaxed. I hadn't heard Cape Horn mentioned in three years. Then in Norway Larry came back from chatting with a local sailor who had been hoarding charts of Patagonia. "He gave them to me. Fun to look at. Might be an interesting way to go home. Done Panama, not terribly fond of the tropics," Larry commented nonchalantly.

"Sure," I snapped. "Go find yourself another crew and do it. Panama is fine with me."

A year later he came across a copy of John Kretschmer's book, *Cape Horn to Starboard*. "John did it in a 32-foot Contessa, only half the weight of *Taleisin*," Larry told me. "Kretschmer says he didn't have a lot of sailing experience. We have an advantage there. John says he got lucky with the weather. We could, too. Let's give it a try."

As we explored the East Coast of the US from Maine to Virginia for three seasons, I talked of the allure of sailing to Trinidad for the wonderful carnival celebrations and diving in the San Blas Islands off Panama, hoping to nudge him into more rational plans.

Then, after listening to yet another one of Larry's musings about the allure of Cape Horn, I finally blurted out, "Can't we do something the easy way for once?"

"Why should we start now?"

"Larry, at my age, I've got nothing to prove."

"Lin at your age, you've got nothing to lose," he retorted without a second's hesitation.

My attitude was swayed the following year, in a conversation with another woman sailor, a woman whom I deeply respected.

We'd left *Taleisin* afloat, securely settled in a boathouse in the Chesapeake Bay and flown to our home base in New Zealand. It was during this yearlong break from cruising that Haven and Monica Collins (née McCants) came to stay at our island cottage for the weekend and help celebrate my 57th birthday. A well-known sail designer and racing skipper, Monica had been watch captain on the first all-woman team to do a major ocean race, the Transpac in 1980, and later, the only woman on the 80' *Challenger* in the Round the World race. Now, instead of keeping our plans to myself, I asked if she might consider crewing with Larry if he really wanted to go ahead with his Cape Horn caper. "Cut the crap," Monica said. "You've got a great boat, you've got lots of experience. Don't be a wimp. You can do it."

Monica was young enough to be my daughter, but her energy and assured attitude was contagious. I knew I *had* to give it a try.

———————

"Larry, I'll back you up on three conditions." I said late one night. "First, we take it on as a serious expedition. We go over every single inch of this boat and upgrade everything we can think of. We don't leave one item unfinished on the work list. Second, we don't tell anyone we're trying to do it. That way, if we change our minds, I won't feel pressured by the specter of explaining away our 'failure'. Finally, if it is just too hard, if I begin to feel we are risking the boat, we turn and run for the Falklands and on to Africa. I'd love to go back there again."

His warm hug and firm assurances didn't overcome my inner knowledge that I, with my over-active imagination (read: *fear*) and lack of real physical strength, was the weak link in his plan and, if I asked him to turn and run I would always feel, in Monica's words, I'd wimped out.

Together we studied pilot charts for the South Atlantic, consulted the British Admiralties tome, *Ocean Passages for the World*. We searched out old sailing ship routing tomes like A *Sailing Directory for the Ethiopic or South Atlantic Ocean 1883, ninth edition by Alexander George Findlay FRGS with addenda to 1899* [https://archive.org/details/asailingdirecto00findgoog/page/n6/mode/1up] to determine our schedule. Two periods showed slightly more favorable winds, March and April or July and August. During the former, the pilot charts showed 20 to 24-percent chance of force seven to force 12 westerly winds (right on the nose) once we reached 50-degree south latitude, but storms near Cape Horn tended to be of shorter duration than in other months. In July and August there tended to be more storms with winds above gale force 23 to 26 percent of the time and lasting longer, but almost 15 percent of all winds came from the south or southeast, which would give us a slightly better chance of fair winds. The long dark nights, plus the below freezing temperatures of the southern winter, left us little choice. We had to be approaching Cape Horn by March.

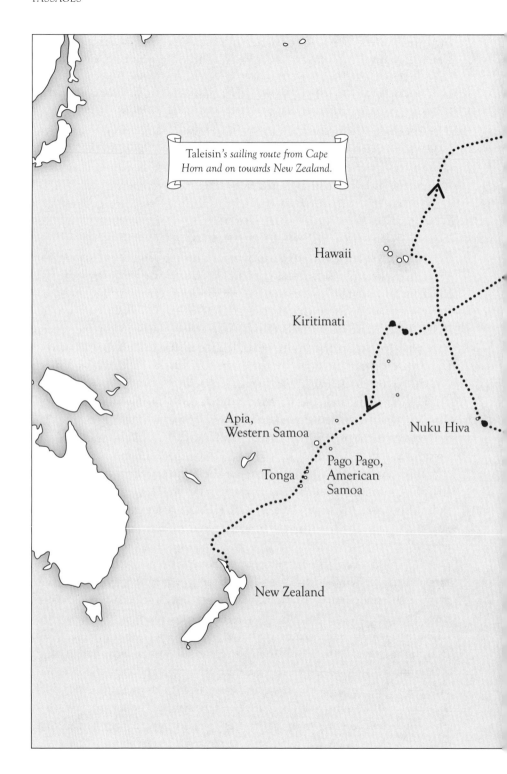

Taleisin's *sailing route from Cape Horn and on towards New Zealand.*

Hawaii

Kiritimati

Apia,
Western Samoa

Tonga

Pago Pago,
American
Samoa

Nuku Hiva

New Zealand

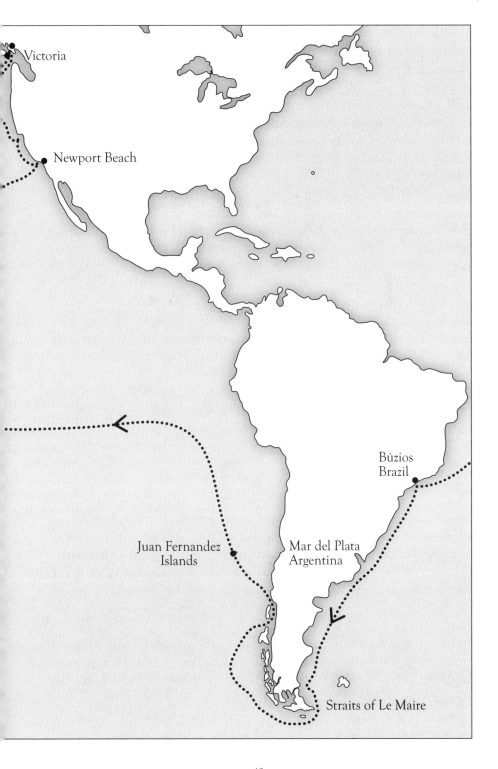

Victoria

Newport Beach

Búzios
Brazil

Juan Fernandez
Islands

Mar del Plata
Argentina

Straits of Le Maire

The Straits of Le Maire presented the first major hurdle. "The tidal streams create a rough cross-breaking sea which is impassable by boats and even dangerous to vessels of considerable size," read the dour British Admiralty pilot book. The Atlantic tide book showed a neap tide with only a 4-meter rise and fall for Tierra del Fuego between February 19 and 22 instead of the 11 meters of spring tides. That date became the central focus of our life as we prepared *Taleisin* to sail 8,000 miles from Virginia, across the Atlantic via Bermuda, then on to the Azores to rejoin the classic sailing ship route south and avoid hurricanes and headwinds to arrive at Mar del Plata, Argentina, our final provisioning port before the big one.

We wanted to save every spare day we could for final preparations. For the first time in 35 years of voyaging we had spent more time at sea than in port, stopping only at four carefully chosen re-provisioning ports for four days each. We arrived with six weeks left to reinforce our sails, anti-foul the bottom and inspect every inch of the boat from masthead to rudder pintles. We watched as the Argentinean economy collapsed around us and saw our warm Latin friends lose their hard-earned savings, then their jobs, and finally, their hope. The currency kept devaluing until we found we were provisioning for one-third the cost we had anticipated. We blessed the simplicity of our engineless boat since the devaluation also meant shops had few imported goods and even the customs offices closed down, so obtaining replacement parts for engines, electronics, or complicated sailing gear within a limited time became nearly impossible.

Our persistence paid off.

On February 21, 2002, after eight months of sailing through the calms of the Azorean High, the Sahara dust-laden northeast trades, the squally confusion of the Intertropical Convergence zone, the storm-tossed waters off Santa Catarina in southern Brazil, past the black cigar-shaped clouds of the Uruguayan Pamperos, then between the Antarctic-generated storms of the Roaring 40s, *Taleisin* and her well-rested crew lay hove to in a 30-knot northwesterly at 54°29"S, 64°46"W, surrounded by thousands of black-backed albatross, only ten miles north of the *Estrecho de Le Maire*. Rays of sunshine highlighted the hard-edged cumulus clouds, and the barometer began climbing from its low of 976 millibars as we waited to follow the instructions of the Admiralty pilot book. "In order to avoid the race and a foul tidal stream, vessels should arrive . . . at the beginning of the south going stream, one hour after high water at Bahía Buen Suceso."

The amazing vista of spiky, cloud-draped mountains on Staten Island to port, weather-worn, round hills of Tierra del Fuego's Three Brothers to starboard, brought back the words of Galileo Ferraresi, an Italian sailing instructor and noted mountain climber we'd met in the Azores when he and his partner, Marina, were homeward bound after two seasons of charter work in Antarctica and southern Chile. "Cape Horn is the Mount Everest of sailing," he'd told us. "Other mountains are technically more difficult to ascend. What is hard about Everest is getting to the final base camp with all your supplies and yourself in good condition, so you have the stamina not only for the actual assault on the summit but enough left over to safely descend once you've made it there."

With Cape Horn only 120 miles to the southwest, I felt we'd made base camp. Looking back, I realize the favorable wind made me say it, but once said, I was committed. "Larry, we'll sail through the straits on tomorrow's tide then I'm willing to spend as much time as we need getting around the cape," I said. "Let's give it three or four tries and if we don't do it now, we'll work into the Beagle Channel and lay up there and try it again in mid-winter. But I am f . . . g going to get this boat around that f . . . g point one way or another." I meant it. I'd fully committed myself to Larry's caper. Even when we got shoved back out of the Strait of Le Maire for the second time by a screaming southerly that turned the world white around us, my determination held. Even when, during the dark of night, tidal currents shoved us 12 miles off course in less than three hours and nearly put us on the rocks, I discounted that as part of the struggle that I'd agreed to. It took two-and-a-half days and three frontal systems to bash our way past the overfalls and currents of the straits. We spent the next three days getting our master's degree in working a small boat to windward in extreme conditions as we tried to make the next 90 miles against two knots of current. Three times we watched the barometer drop from 1025 mb to less than 980 mb, once going as low as 970 mb. Screaming southwesterly hailstorms would blow for two hours to become zephyr-like northerlies for an hour, then swing to a steady 45-knot southerly for the next hour or two. I apologized for laughing at Larry's purchase of the tiny scrap of bright orange Dacron I called our toysail, as that 40-square-foot flat-cut sail teamed with our triple-reefed main to keep *Taleisin* driving at five knots into square twenty-foot seas. I learned to let the sheet fly just as Larry reached the staysail stay to douse even that tiny sail for the worst of the squalls that screamed in at regular intervals.

Strangely, we both came to enjoy the battle, feeling close to those men of years past who'd had to fight these same conditions on ships far less weatherly, less handy, than ours. We worked to buoy each other's spirits with jokes, a hug, a food treat. Then on the sixth day I used our solar-charged, handheld VHF radio to ask for a weather forecast from a 250-foot Argentinean fishing vessel I could see just a few miles north of us. Its Norwegian captain quizzed me carefully, "Are you feeling good about your boat? Do you have enough food? Hope so, because these winds will grow stronger for another five days at least."

Less than an hour later, I was fully decked out in foul weather gear, three layers of warm clothes and gloves, assisting the windvane as *Taleisin* struggled to gain weathering in 35 knots of wind. Larry opened the hatch to hand me a hot cup of chocolate. Then he pushed the pram hood forward to take a look to windward, and a wave slapped against the hull. A heavy shower of saltwater drenched him and his last set of dry, warm clothes. That afternoon we ran out of propane. We hove to while Larry assessed the situation.

"Valve on the new tank is leaking," he said.

Though we had an extra tank to back up the two that normally provided six to eight weeks of cooking, we were depending on the oven to back up our kerosene cabin heater. An hour later, when the clouds lifted and Isla Nueva at the entrance to the Beagle Channel showed clearly 20 miles north of us, we both agreed. Not only were we concerned that we could run short of heat, we were being crowded by bags of now-wet clothes. With Cape Horn temptingly close, only 40 miles to the south, we eased sheets to turn and reach towards the shelter of the Beagle.

Attempt number one was behind us.

The confines of the canal, with rocks, reefs, thick kelp beds and few fully protected anchorages, plus screaming williwaws interspersed with drifting calms, was more intimidating, more dangerous, and more challenging than the open waters we'd left. The history-soaked wilds of southern Argentina, the magnificence of Estancia Harberton made it worthwhile. There, we were befriended by Natalie Goodall and members of the Bridges family, whose forebears had built this ranch. Three weeks later, in the tiny Chilean military outpost at Puerto Williams, we reveled in the company of a small band of intrepid sailors who, like us, were bound from the Atlantic Ocean to the Pacific. These encounters made our month-long, propane-forced diversion one of the highlights of our cruising life.

Each day we checked for weather information, waiting for a break between closely packed low-pressure systems. Then, on March 11,, 2002, bundled up like a teddy bear against the near-freezing temperatures and 50-knot southerly wind, I walked into the Capitan del Puerto's office at Puerto Williams to see a weather FAX printout. A potential three- or four-

Though it was early autumn, the temperatures we encountered in the Canal Beagle were near freezing.

day high-pressure gap had formed between this storm and the next two lows bunched together 800 miles to the west. If, during the next few hours, we could arrange port clearance, buy final provisions and sail out through the Beagle Channel and back to our inbound track, 90 miles in total, we'd find southeast winds to round the Horn.

"Got to go tomorrow at first light," Larry said as we computed the tides.

"In fact, I'd like to leave at 0400 before the tide turns."

"This storm isn't going to ease off before tomorrow night," I said.

"Wind will be on the beam for the first 40 miles. After that, islands will be only 15 miles upwind until we get south of the cape – they'll break the seas down. If we wait, we'll have to fight headwinds all the way down. Might be too light to beat the east-going current. It was over two knots the last time."

A full gale drove snow flurries and hailstones across our deck as the ten survivors from the previous night's farewell party, including the crew from the well-known sail training yacht, 65-foot *Alaska Eagle*, helped us cast off our lines and wished us a fine farewell.

To save wear and tear on the mainsail, once the winds topped 30 knots, we used the storm trysail to beat to windward.

Never have we set sail in such unfavorable feeling conditions. Never have I been more impressed with Larry's determination and stamina. For 16 hours he hand-steered *Taleisin* through rock-strewn channels, urging her through short steep seas as squalls swept down through mountain gullies, short-tacking right to the edges of kelp beds, calling down to me, "How close can we go, any rocks in this kelp? Can I take this lift?" He drove with all the intensity of his days as a racing skipper while I plotted our position and handed up hot drinks and baked potatoes to warm his hands. Every hour or so I'd come on deck to helm while he went below to warm up and relieve himself. "Boy do I envy your plumbing," he joked when he came back after searching through four layers of clothes to reach his. "At least you don't have to grab yourself with icy cold hands!"

By dark we had sailed clear of the brutal wave-swept rocks and desolate islands of Nassau Bay. When I'd come below for my second off-watch, winds had dropped to 30 knots and Cape Horn lay less than 15 miles to windward. Despite the weather predictions, I hadn't really believed we'd have light, fair winds for our rounding. Then Larry woke me.

March 13th 2002, 1600, Cape Horn aft of the starboard beam, I wrote in our log.

It had taken years for Larry to infuse me with his dream. Now I'd felt the fever and the wonders of reaching that dream. As we sailed gently past this sleeping monster and into the Pacific, I also felt a tremendous sense of relief. Though we had a thousand miles of potentially storm-tossed seas ahead, from now on I'd wake each and every morning of my life knowing I no longer *had to* sail around Cape Horn.

Our fair winds continued as we cleared the last islands of Tierra del Fuego and sailed into the Pacific Ocean.

Part Two
The Long Way Home

On board Taleisin

4
After the Horn

April 2002 - Chilean Patagonia

"We did it! We are out of the Screaming 50s!" I yell. "Come on down. Open the champagne. Steak's going into the grill."

It has taken us almost six days and 520 miles of sailing from the moment we passed south of Cape Horn to reach this point. Days full of shifting winds, shifting moods. Even though we've had light to moderate winds from the south or southeast each of those days, even though I have wanted to head due north to get out of the freezing cold as soon as possible, Larry has determinedly kept us heading west-northwest out into the Pacific Ocean.

Each time I've suggested easing sheets and turning due north, each time I've complained about the damp, or the low temperatures that have given me a serious case of chilblains, Larry reminds me, "We agreed we wouldn't turn north until we have at least 150 miles between us and Patagonia." He's right. When I agreed to take this route from the Atlantic to the Pacific almost a year before, we studied the charts showing the rock-bound, hostile shores of Patagonia. Then we studied the South Pacific pilot charts. The pilot charts indicated a 70 percent chance of strong westerlies in this area and a 22 percent chance they would reach storm force. Getting well to windward, having what the old-time sailors called a safe offing, made sense.

It had taken us three days to gain that offing before we finally changed course to head directly north. Since making that turn the wind has remained fickle but fair. Now the seas undulate with a long, low, westerly swell but don't hinder our progress. Each day grows noticeably warmer.

Today we've been moving along sedately, wing and wing, nylon drifter held in place to starboard by the spinnaker pole, jib held to port by its sheet, which we have led to the end of the vanged out boom, mainsail down and nestled in the lazy jacks. Chilblains on the mend, I've spent a few hours out on deck wearing only three layers of clothes. After three days of overcast weather, there are some breaks in the clouds. Larry is finally able to get two sextant sights to confirm our position. At 1500 he marks our computed position on the chart.

I glance over his shoulder. The closest islands of Patagonia and the rock-strewn entrance to the Gulf of Trinidad lie more than 160 miles east of us. Even better, we have only ten miles to go before we've officially "doubled the Horn" and reached the southern limit of the Roaring 40s. I have an extra reason to be excited as the pilot charts show the percentage of days with gale force winds drops dramatically, to less than a 12 percent chance, once we sail clear of the Screaming 50s.

I climb out into the frigid air of the cockpit half a dozen times over the next three hours to check the taffrail log and calculate how far we've traveled. As each mile ticks off, I feel ever more ready to celebrate. I dig out a bottle of French champagne from under the locked floorboards, one I've secretly stashed there, and reach into the deepest depths of the bilge where I've stored a frozen sirloin roast. The seawater outside the boat, chilled by the northern reaches of the Cape Horn current, has kept the bilges cold enough that the roast is still solidly frozen when I saw off two generous slices.[1]

At sea, Larry usually enjoys two glasses of wine with his dinner, then climbs right into the pilot berth for the first off watch of the night. That way he falls instantly to sleep and three hours later has slept off any possible effects of the wine. Normally I don't drink at sea and thus take the first watch. But tonight, I can't resist. Now that we are well on our way towards ever better weather patterns, my fears seem a thing of the past. I totally relax and guzzle far more than my share of the champagne.

My mood is infectious. Larry laughs as I become sillier and sillier. Then the ship's bell chimes six times. "Okay, it's after 7," Larry says. "Time for one of us to turn in, and tonight you need to climb into that bunk more than I do. Besides, wind is freshening so I want to take some sail off."

---

1   In most instances, all the fresh food that required refrigeration would have been stored in our well-insulated ice chest. This time, I'd depended on the cold current to let me carry extra fresh provisions. When we set sail from Puerto Williams, we wanted to be sure we could stay at sea for up to two months, if required, to reach our goal of rounding the Horn and sailing into the Pacific Ocean. So, I'd stored a plastic container full of frozen meat just forward of the sump in the bilge.

I agree, and once I have wriggled my way into the sleeping bag and arranged three pillows between me and the hull, I watch as Larry puts his feet into his tall seaboots. His foul weather pants are ready to go, bunched around the tops of the seaboots in what he calls his "fireman's position." Before he's even pulled them up, and added his heavy foul weather jacket, I am asleep.

———————•———————

I didn't hear him lower the drifter or stow the spinnaker pole. I didn't hear him take down the working jib, then put two reefs in the mainsail. Three hours after celebrating leaving the Screaming 50s, I woke to the sound of water surging past the hull. "Wind's up a bit," Larry said as I climbed out of the bunk. "But she is moving wonderfully."

Yes she is, I whispered to myself after I pulled on two more layers of warm gear and my foulies to climb out into the cockpit. But I could sense the swells were building; the skudding clouds were moving fast above us. Though I hated to wake Larry, an hour later I shook him lightly and said, "Wind's headed us a lot. I'm going to tack and get her sailing offshore again." I climbed out on deck, released the self-steering gear, then tacked and sheeted in the staysail. Close-hauled, *Taleisin* began to buck and throw spray. I waited only a few minutes before deciding to take down the staysail and sheet in the mainsail to get her to heave to.

"Might have hove to a bit early," I said as I climbed below into the relative warmth of the cabin.

"Never too early," Larry answered. "You did well. But I think I'll go up and drop the mainsail, put up the trysail just in case the wind increases. Then let's get a good night's sleep and see what daylight brings."

I marked our position on the chart, warmed up water in the kettle and when he came below, poured him a mug of hot instant soup.

"Not a bad place to get some heavier winds," I commented as I climbed into the pilot berth and snuggled into the sleeping bag. According to the position I'd marked on the chart, we had sailed clear of the area where the South Pacific Drift or Cape Horn Current splits to form the Peruvian Current — one branch bending southward towards Drake Passage, the other turning northward, leaving the area where we lay free of currents. I hoped that meant if this wind increased even more, we wouldn't be threatened by steep overfalls that can happen when wind opposes current. We were also well clear of the continental shelf — another plus, I reminded myself. Technically, the deeper water meant the seas should be less confused here if this wind grew stronger.

Three hours later, Larry woke me from a very restless sleep. I dragged the spare sleeping bag from the windward pilot berth and used it like a blanket, then lay down on the leeward settee. "No need for you to go out on deck," he said just before he drifted off to sleep. "Everything is well snugged down. But look out the companionway every half hour or so and make sure the lashings on the tiller aren't loosening off."

Within minutes of climbing into the pilot berth, Larry was snoring. I lay on the settee feeling the boat lifting to the growing seas, listening to the hum of the rig as the wind increased until I knew it was well above gale force. *Taleisin* lay well, rising to each oncoming sea, only occasionally being thumped by a bit of heavy foam that splattered across the decks. Compared to her motion when we had been charging forward, she lay comfortably. But comfort is a relative term. As the wind gusted above 50 knots, she laid at an almost constant heel so I could stay on the settee without a lee cloth. And if I held on very firmly when I got up every half hour or so to check things, I could move around safely. But I did have to unwrap myself half a dozen extra times to stuff sponges between pots in the galley or wine bottles in the bilge to quiet them down. And I did have to jam a towel into the bookshelf above the chart table to keep things from shifting as the boat rose to the top of each swell, heeled an extra eight or ten degrees, then seemed to straighten and swoop down the backside.

Just before dawn, Larry insisted I change places and climb into the warm sleeping bag in the leeward pilot berth. I woke almost five hours later. The wind still howled, *Taleisin* still lay hove to. Larry was no longer in the cabin. I climbed out of the bunk and carefully opened the retaining lock on the companionway hatch. "Larry, are you okay?" I screamed, hoping to be heard above the blasting wind.

"Okay? Hell yes I'm okay! This is amazing. Get on your gear and get out here, you little mole!" he yelled. Larry had settled himself on the windward deck, back against the cabin sides, feet against the bulwark. "Bring out the cameras — wrap them in plastic bags. I want to get some photos of these waves. They are amazing."

I gathered up our Hi8 video camera and wrapped it inside two plastic bags, then grabbed the waterproof still camera, pulled on all my gear and carefully climbed clear of the companionway. Larry handed me the spare safety line he'd rigged from a strong point on the cabin top and I secured it around my waist, then crawled out onto the deck to sit next to him.

In the light of day, the waves that marched towards us were truly awe-inspiring. *Taleisin* lay about 50 degrees off the wind, heeling almost 15 degrees despite the small size of her bright orange trysail. The wind seemed to increase as she rose up the face of each of the towering seas, until at the top I could feel the full power of the storm — but only for a few seconds as we slid down the back of the sea. Up and up she seemed to rise. At the peak of each rise I could look for hundreds of yards around and see spume being blown off the breaking crests that marched towards us. At the bottom of each trough all I could see was the next towering wave before *Taleisin* began to rise again.

Larry reveled in watching the approaching seas and the slick Taleisin *created as she lay hove to.*

Just as we slid to the bottom of one particularly deep feeling trough, a momentary bit of low morning sun broke through the heavy clouds. The top of the crest to windward turned translucent, turquoise deepening slowly to indigo as *Taleisin* began her steady ascent. It is a sight I can visualize to this day. But the other thing that really impressed itself in my mind was how these towering graybeards didn't have breaking crests stretching the whole length of the wave like you see on a shore break. Instead, hundred-foot lengths of cresting water topped parts of each wave while, between these crests, there was no white water, just blown spume creating an almost lace curtain effect down the face of the sea. And, as Larry pointed out, the slick *Taleisin* was making as she was shoved to leeward by the shrieking wind could be seen trailing to windward hundreds of feet, and there, the water was almost smooth. I watched in amazement as the crest of a wave broke just a dozen feet ahead of our bow, but when it hit *Taleisin*'s slick, it turned to foam and only a bit of spray came flying towards where I quickly sheltered the video camera under my jacket. Yes, she was laying wonderfully under the trysail.

Yes, it was amazing and yes, within minutes I didn't want to be watching one second more. I wanted to climb back into the relative calm of my cocoon of a cabin where I could try to ignore all this sound and fury.

Larry, on the other hand, seemed thrilled by the whole scene. He sat on deck watching for most of the day, only coming below to warm up, or to grab a handful of the trail mix or the peanut butter and jam sandwiches I cobbled together. The change in his mood from that of the previous few days was stunning.

I'd been surprised by the hours-long bouts of depression that had begun plaguing him in the days after we'd rounded the Horn. Though one of the real strengths of our relationship had always been our ability to communicate, for the first time ever I couldn't seem to get him to open up. I attributed it to tiredness and tried to get him to spend extra time in the bunk, so I knew he'd had sufficient sleep. I knew he wasn't ill as he was fully attentive to the boat's needs, stood his watches carefully, changed sails without hesitation. But he wasn't the content man I usually saw. Watching him now, I finally found a clue to work with. I didn't bring the subject up until, almost 30 hours after we'd first hove to, the wind began to ease and settle back into the southwest.[2]

By noon, we were able to set the mainsail with two reefs in it plus the full staysail and could have been more comfortable heading due north. But when Larry was able to get the second sight he needed to confirm our position, I agreed wholeheartedly with his suggestion we head directly offshore as we'd been driven 35 miles closer to the lee shore of Patagonia during the hours we'd lain hove to. We both wanted to regain our 150-mile safety margin.

We settled *Taleisin* onto a close reach and, without any preamble, Larry said, "You know, Lin, I've dreamed of sailing against the wind around Cape Horn since I was a kid. Until this blow, until I got a chance to see true graybeards, it all seemed anticlimactic. And sitting out there seeing how the boat we built handled it all, watching the slick *Taleisin* made as it sapped the energy out of those crests, that is what I needed."

---

2   Shore stations recorded the winds in this blow at 50 with sustained gusts to 60 knots.

At dusk we once again had our safe offing. Larry went on deck and changed course almost 20 degrees. Then he eased the sheets and *Taleisin* was off on a very fast beam reach, the taffrail log spinning furiously, spray flying across the foredeck, the motion settled enough so I felt comfortable making up Larry's favorite offshore dinner, corned beef hash topped with eggs and fresh tomato chunks. As the clock chimed for 1900 hours, he climbed into the pilot berth and arranged the three pillows to wedge himself into a comfortable position. "Come here a minute," he asked. He took my hand and held it against his cheek. "Thanks to you, I can now say I have done everything I ever wanted to do in life and more." And with that he seemed to fall instantly asleep.

This time, Larry slept soundly through his full three-hour off watch. I hummed happily as I came below just before 2200 hours to wake him. I'd been out on deck, fully decked out in foul weather gear but only three layers of warm clothes and seen patches of clear sky, a smattering of stars. The boat was moving swiftly and the taffrail showing we were making seven knots.

My elation was to be short-lived.

I clambered into the still warm bunk. Larry kitted up and climbed into the cockpit then yelled, "Looks like a true Granddaddy squall headed our way. I'm dropping the sails." I was barely out of the bunk when the wind shifted suddenly from the southwest to the northwest and, within minutes, increased to gale force.

Once again *Taleisin* lay hove to on the offshore tack, storm trysail holding her steady. "You already had your Cape Horn storm — did you need another?" I jokingly asked as I prepared to get back into the bunk.

But Larry wasn't in a joking mood. "Wind's a lot more squally than the last time. I'm going to get the para-anchor out just in case. Have it ready here on the cabin sole," he said as he reached behind the companionway to where we kept the para-anchor and other storm gear when we headed off to sea.

"Just in case what?" I asked.

"In case the seas change at all. In case the boat starts reaching out of her slick or doesn't hold her head up. Or, we start taking any green water on board. That happens, I'm going to set it. I'll need your help so try to get some sleep."

I tried, and then I actually did doze off. The clock showed three hours had passed when suddenly I was awakened by the whole boat vibrating. Then the rigging began to screech. I have never heard sounds like this before, sounds made by what we later learned were winds sustained above 75 knots with gusts to 90 knots. "I've got to get that cover off the windvane, it's going to shake the self-steering gear to bits," Larry yelled as he climbed the companionway ladder.[3]

"The parachute — do we need the parachute?" I screamed as he crawled through the companionway and started to pull the companionway hatch shut.

I didn't hear his answer. I got out our big torch to light the cockpit as he determinedly secured his safety line then crawled aft to where I could see the whole windvane shaking and vibrating in the howling wind. Spray mixed with heavy rain blew horizontally across the cockpit, at times almost obscuring Larry though he was only six feet away from me. I clung tightly to the handles alongside the companionway ladder, my foul weather jacketed head and upper body sticking through the narrowest possible opening of the hatch while I tried to direct the beam of the light to illuminate the vane. Larry reached the boom gallows frame at the aft end of the cockpit. Once he had pulled himself up into a standing position, I watched him secure yet another line around himself. Then he carefully released his grip on the frame and used both hands as he reached up to release the three ties that secured the Dacron vane cover. I held my breath as he stepped onto the taffrail then raised himself onto the tip of his toes to reach the highest tie. The minute the cover was stripped off the vane frame, the screeching metallic sounds stopped. But as *Taleisin* reached the crest of each huge sea, the gusting wind still made the boat vibrate.

Larry crawled back to where I waited and yelled above the fury of the wind and pounding rain, "Grab this cover. She's got too much sail on. I'm going to tie a reef in the trysail. Give me that flashlight and get back below. Nothing you can do out here."

"The parachute — do we need the parachute?" I yelled again.

"Don't see what good it will do. She seems to be laying okay. Not taking any heavy water on board. Close the hatch — no need to get the whole inside of the boat wet."

It was almost an hour before Larry came below again. I'd been lying there, listening to the sound of the storm, the rattle of the trysail as it was pulled down, the grinding of the winch as the reefed trysail was raised again. The shrieking of the rigging never diminished, but once Larry had reduced the size of the trysail, *Taleisin* no longer vibrated, no longer heeled nearly as far at the tops of the waves. The feeling of apprehension I'd had slowly ebbed until it became a sort of dull acceptance. *Not much more we*

---

3   We did not carry any wind measuring instruments on board *Seraffyn* or *Taleisin*, relying on sea state to guestimate wind strengths. Wind strengths mentioned here are those reported by shore stations or two boats that had been within 75 miles of us at the time of these two storms.

can do but wait it out, I recall thinking. I had been able to boil up a kettle of water and handed Larry a mug of hot chocolate and a handful of his favorite caramel candies when he came below.

"Can't believe how clumsy I was. Broke the damn windvane frame when I was taking off that cover," Larry grumbled as he pulled a broken length of wood from the jacket of his foul weather jacket. "Won't be hard to fix when we get somewhere calm."

"Clumsy? No, you weren't — you were a downright hero." I replied. "I can't believe you could even move around out there in this wind, let alone climb up and untie knots."

"There you go, the perpetual cheerleader," he replied. "But more important, you called me crazy a few months ago when I wanted to put a reef in that trysail. Well, that reef is paying its way now. Absolutely wild out there." Although obviously tired, Larry was wired, almost euphoric and completely uninterested in trying to sleep as he sat in the port watch seat right next to the companionway and braced himself against the surge and heave of the boat. It took me almost an hour to convince him to climb into the more comfortable leeward pilot berth. "Even if you don't sleep, be a good idea to get some rest in case things get worse," I said, sure he needed some rest. I climbed into the windward berth and secured the lee cloth to ensure I couldn't be tossed out.

I couldn't sleep. Thinking back, I don't remember feeling scared, just resigned and eventually bored as my body moved back and forth against the motion of the boat, while the howl of the wind became almost natural and the time ticked slowly away.

The very first glimmers of morning began to light the cabin. Nothing seemed to have changed outside. The wind still howled, the boat still heeled almost 30 degrees at the top of each crest. Time after time sheets of heavy spray swished across the deck to thud against the cabin side. I'd almost become used to the sound, the motion — then suddenly, the boat seemed to levitate, almost as if she was suspended in mid-air. Then she fell and appeared to keep falling. She landed with a crashing jolt I was sure must have fractured her planking. I could hear the sound of a heavy wave washing right across the decks. A shower of saltwater hit my face, water forced beneath the thick gasketing of the firmly bolted down skylight hatch. Larry and I almost collided as we leapt from our berths.

"Grab the bilge pump handle," Larry yelled as he knelt down on the cabin sole and began twisting the lock that held down the floorboards over the sump of the bilge. I tried to reach past him for the handle when he looked up and, in a voice filled with amazement, said, "Not a drop of water. She's tight." Then he turned to me. "Are you okay?"

"Are we okay?" I whispered, tears streaming down my face. I tried to hide them as Larry knelt on the floor securing the locks. But he finished quickly and turned to see me bracing myself on the settee. He soon had his arm around me.

"Relax, she's riding just fine now," he said. "Look at the compass. Her heading is just like it has been most of the night."

I leaned against him and watched the telltale compass as it swayed and tilted in its holder on the table stanchion. *Taleisin* continued to fall away from the wind about eight or ten degrees, then come back up to lay close-hauled. The wind continued to howl, the seas to swish and rumble. Our motion was just as it had been before the great thump. The intermittent dollops of spray swished across the decks as before to expend their energy against the side of the cabin, then flow down the deck.

As the hours ticked slowly by, the storm began to ease, the wind to back. Larry went out on deck every 30 minutes or so and had a long look around. Each time he urged me to come out to feel the force of the wind, to see the amazing height of the waves, the way the boat was riding, the albatross soaring. But I had no desire to do anything more than lie in the bunk and ignore the outside world.

Nineteen hours after we'd hove to, the wind dropped to gale force and backed to the west. The towering waves were still marching towards us, but now the caps weren't overhanging, just crumbling masses of foam. I finally went out to join Larry as he took the reef out of the trysail and set the ridiculously small storm staysail we'd bought for this voyage. It might have looked small, but that bright orange, 40-square-foot sail, along with the 90 feet of trysail, soon had *Taleisin* reaching along at five knots.

The motion was much steadier now. By dinner time I was able to fry up some eggs, bacon and tomatoes for dinner. For the first time since the latest storm began, I looked into the shelf behind the chart table for a real glass (we'd been using coffee mugs during the blow). Five of the six glasses stored there had been sheared in half.

When Larry came below I showed him. "Look at this. Must have happened when she fell off that wave."

Larry finished removing his foulies, sat down on the settee and opened the special padded box where we kept eight long-stemmed wine glasses. Though the bowl of each glass was fully intact, the stems had been snapped cleanly by their holders.

"Must have been the shock of that fall," Larry said.

Over the next days we found other signs of the forces that had been exerted on the boat. Most of the dust jackets on books stored in the shelves of the forward cabin were stuck to the underside of the deck, though the books themselves had dropped right back into place. And the following spring when we dried out *Taleisin* against the seawall in Puerto Montt we saw the only structural damage she'd suffered.

Taleisin's rudder has 7/16-inch diameter pre-stretched Dacron preventers (rudder stops) on each side, to keep the rudder from slamming over against the stern and shearing off the pintles. The force of the skid, ending in what felt like a free-fall of a dozen feet, had stretched these just enough to allow the rudder to slam an extra degree or two, enough to fracture a small portion of *Taleisin's* solid teak stern post (the large timber which supports the transom and rudder.) Repairs to fix the 7-inch crack along the edge of the stern post took only part of a day — but resoundingly proved the worth of these two simple pieces of low stretch line.

For the next four days we continued north, cautiously increasing the sail *Taleisin* carried as the force of the squalls lessened and the temperature grew ever warmer. My log entries recorded the mandatory cryptic notes about course, windspeed and direction, distance covered, plus a bit about the sail changes we made. But mostly they are long notes about our moods, our discussions as we covered the last 500 miles towards the entrance to the Gulf of Corcovado, which would mark the end of our Cape Horn adventure.

"Now I've done it," was one of Larry's comments. "Just have to sail this boat safely to Canada so my friends and family can see it. Then we can go home to New Zealand, and I'll feel like a complete winner."

As I read that now it brings to mind a conversation the two of us had soon after we met. I'd asked Larry why he'd given up competitive racing and a potentially lucrative career in that profession and decided to go cruising instead. He told me fun stories about being paid to help other skippers get their boats across the finish line in first place. I'd had the privilege of being with him while he was being paid to improve the performance of a handsome racing yacht by its wealthy owner. I'd heard him turn down other similar offers. But Larry's answer always stuck in my mind. "Lin, no matter how good you are as a racing sailor there is always someone younger, bolder, more clever waiting to push you aside," he'd said, after pondering my question for a few minutes. "So sooner or later you end up a loser. But cruising? If you don't put any boats on the rocks, the older you are, the more respect you gain."

I don't remember thinking about his youthful comment as we reached towards the Golfo de Corcovado at the northern edges of the Roaring 40s. What I do remember is lying awake the night before our landfall feeling a slight sense of apprehension. By talking about getting 'home to New Zealand', was Larry trying to tell me he was tired of voyaging and ready to settle back into a life on shore? I didn't ask him and prayed that wasn't the case because this voyage had whetted my appetite for other, more adventuresome future cruising destinations. Yes, weathering the challenges we'd faced as we doubled the Horn had not only made me feel like a winner but also laid to rest the very last apprehensions I felt about my own sea-keeping abilities.

5

The Afterglow

2002 - approaching Puerto Montt, Chile

"No bottom at eight fathoms," I call to Larry.

He makes no reply. His stance doesn't change. We are shrouded in an impenetrable fog.

Visibility is limited to the length of the boat. I can see Larry is listening intently for clues that will let us know how close we are to shore. But the only sound is the whisper of water burbling past *Taleisin*'s stem as she slices slowly through the smooth gray sea.

I wait four or five minutes, then slowly coil the leadline until the four-pound sounding weight is hanging just off the deck. I reach outboard and begin swinging the lead in an arch alongside the boat. When it has gained momentum, I release the coil of line. The lead plops into the water 15 feet ahead of us and sinks quickly. When it is hanging straight up and down, right alongside where I stand, I again call, "Still no bottom."

Then I hear the bark of a dog, not very far away. Larry hears it too. "Take another sounding now, a slightly deeper one."

This time I let out 10 fathoms of line. The lead finds bottom. "Why don't we anchor right here?" I suggest.

Larry looks down at the chart, lying on the cockpit sole in its clear waterproof sheath. "Chart shows the bottom rises gradually all along this island," he says. "Ten fathoms puts us at about a quarter mile from shore. Let's go until we're in five fathoms. Less likely boats will be moving past us if we are that bit closer to land."

Almost a week has slipped away since we sailed out of the stormy South

Pacific through the Golfo de Guapo and into Golfo de Corcovado. Here, under the shadow of the stunning volcanos and peaks of the Andes, we've encountered surprisingly light winds and calm waters. Our experiences in these relatively lonely waters at the very north end of Chilean Patagonia encapsulate both the challenges and joys of our systems-free sailing life.

The distinctive cone of the Corcovado volcano to the right.

Our engine-free status had unexpectedly caused a stir when we presented our departure forms, passports and ship's papers to the officer at the front desk of the Chilean naval office at Puerto Williams. This small outpost nestles under the towering craggy peaks of Isla Navarino on the southern shore of the Canal Beagle, just 60 miles due north of Cape Horn. The official shook his head and handed our papers back. I understand quite a bit of Spanish, Larry very little. Thus, he was in the dark at the somewhat rapid flurry of words between the official and me. I turned to Larry and explained, "He says it is impossible to sail in these waters without an engine." I didn't tell him the official had also decreed that until we fixed our engine, he could not allow us to leave port. Over the next minutes I tried to be patient and calm as I explained we didn't actually have an engine but did have a long history of voyaging. I offered to provide proof of our abilities. Nothing moved him until I said, "I realize this is too serious for you to handle without approval from someone more senior. May I please speak with your superior?"

Minutes later we were escorted into the elegantly appointed office of the commandant himself. He spoke some English and was bemused by the situation. "My assistant is not completely wrong. These waters are dangerous even with a big engine. But you got here safely so I will give you permission to continue onward. The only thing you must do is stay inside the canals where we have some chance of coming to your assistance should you get into trouble."

"It is much safer for us to be out in the open ocean. No williwaws, no rocks," Larry replied. "The canals are really dangerous."

I could see that the commandant was not swayed by Larry's words. It was only when I unabashedly turned on a torrent of tears and told a lie, did I sense the tide turning. "We have made a promise to a magazine that we will sail right around Cape Horn. That way they can say we have achieved a record, sailing the smallest boat to sail around all the great southern capes against the prevailing winds, and engine-free. They won't pay us unless we are successful."[1]

He left his office to return with a handful of tissues, then departed again.

Larry and I sat in silence, listening to the sound of several different phone conversations through the walls of the office. Then I heard someone leave the building. It was almost an hour before the commandant returned.

"I have been down to look at your boat," he said. "I will give you permission to do as you wish, but ... " His conditions were simple: We were to contact any ship or manned lighthouse we passed and provide our position and request the information be forwarded to him. "And remember," the commandant said as he handed us our signed *zarpe*[2], "you said the longest time it would take for you to get to Puerto Montt is 30 days. If you don't arrive by then, I lose my job."

We did exactly as the commandant asked, using our handheld VHF, powered by a flexible solar panel we acquired just for this passage, to chat with the lighthouse keeper at Isla Hornos, again with the officers on the two ships we passed soon after clearing the Drake Passage, and finally, the lighthouse keeper at the entrance to the Golfo de Corcovado. The officialdom problem caused by our lack of an engine had been a negative

---

1   We had not told anyone — not family, nor friends, nor magazine editors — that we intended to sail outside around Cape Horn from the Atlantic to the Pacific. In fact we'd said our destination was Argentina, to learn to tango. But once we had successfully completed our Cape Horn journey and shared this fact, several magazines offered very generous sums for the story, enough to provide us six months of work-free cruising.
2   *zarpe* - port clearance papers, required when clearing customs and immigration at the next port of entry

at the time, but once inside the gulf, it had a silver lining. The challenging part of our voyage had taken 21 days. Now we had just 150 miles of sailing to reach Puerto Montt. That gave us nine days before we were required to fulfill the promise we'd made. And with the very limited range of our handheld VHF, no one would be trying to contact us.[3] Our charts showed a potential anchorage just a few miles to the west of our course, far from the only village in this remote corner of Chile. The winds inside the gulf had dropped off to eight knots. I knew as evening approached they would drop even lower. I said, "Larry, we're not in any hurry. We aren't going to get very far tonight anyway. Let's work our way into this little cul-de-sac and have a few days just to ourselves."

Two days later, as we reached slowly clear of the rock-bound cove, I realized how important that pause had been. Though we'd been at sea for almost three weeks, though we had been through two powerful storms, the last few days of the passage had been relatively benign. We both felt well rested, the boat was tidy inside and out. So it was not that we needed a break. Instead, we had needed a chance to privately celebrate the passage that was, in many ways, a culmination of four decades of preparation.

We replayed each stage of our Cape Horn adventure, then segued off into other adventures we'd shared during the previous four decades together.

"I wonder if we'd have kept cruising all these years if we'd had an engine?" I'd asked Larry.

"Doubt it," he replied immediately. "Keeps the challenge level up. I need that. I still get a buzz out of working in and out of tight spots."

I'd laughed as I recalled his quick answer to those who questioned our choice: "Cheap thrills!" But in many ways, it wasn't the easier maintenance, the lack of breakdowns or the fact that we were never stuck in an out-of-the-way port waiting for parts to arrive that made us revel in our simplistic mode of cruising. It was the constant feeling of adventure, the warmth of working as a team. Each time we hauled up our anchor or untied our dock lines we had to have a plan. Each time the plan worked, we looked to each other with a shared sense of accomplishment. Like addicted bridge players, each time we felt we could have done better we endlessly replayed our moves and figured out how we could have handled the situation more gracefully.

The winds stayed light as we drifted north using the big nylon drifter we called "Big Blue" and the bright red nylon staysail nicknamed "The Red Baron." The windvane self-steering, despite the light winds, kept us

---

3   Any yacht sailing inside the Patagonian canals is required to provide a detailed itinerary listing each port or anchorage and the expected dates of arrival and departure.

right on track, freeing us from a task that would otherwise have become burdensome. Occasionally, we sailed past fishermen working out of small wooden boats and exchanged a few words. Once we dipped our Canadian flag to a passing naval patrol boat. But mostly we were on our own, enjoying pleasantly warm, almost cloudless days, and stunning views. To the east the snow-covered volcanic cones of the Corcovado and Yantales stood out boldly from the dramatic line of the Andes. To the west the indented, rocky coastline and off-lying islands of Isla Chiloe presented constantly changing vista and plenty of landmarks to provide us bearings to mark our position. At night there were times when the water around us was completely still. Then the reflection of the Milky Way made me feel like we were suspended among the stars. Though we covered less than 30 or 40 miles each day, neither of us felt like being anywhere else.

This changed abruptly when, after four days, we reached the northern end of Isla Chiloe, where the cold waters of the Pacific Ocean surge through the Canal Chacao. The temperature took a dramatic drop. The waters around us became rippled by occasional current-driven overfalls. Then the fog rolled in, silently, suddenly. To add to our discomfort, the fog seemed to amplify the thump, thump, thump of motors. We'd seen a few fishing boats working not far from us, just before we lost visibility. Now we could only guess where they were and sound the airhorn we carried to help them avoid us. I went below and checked the chart. "Only sensible thing to do is work into the shallows of Isla Tabón," I suggested. "It's only a few miles north of us. Hopefully the fog will clear."

We were particularly fortunate in that Tabón, which marks the entrance to Reloncaví Sound, wherein lies Puerto Montt, is one of the few sand-fringed islands in all of Chilean Patagonia. Once anchored, we slept soundly together that night, though conditioned by our weeks at sea, I woke every three hours. Twice I went on deck. The second time I was encouraged to see the flash of the lighthouse at the far end of the island glowing through the fog. It definitely had not been visible the last time I checked.

By morning, visibility had returned. So had my desire to reach Puerto Montt and complete this voyage.

"Sure wish this wind would fill a bit," I complained as Larry finished stowing the anchor and I sheeted in the drifter. "I'm desperate for some fresh tomatoes, ice cream, a meal out. And our mail. Bet we have a pile of it waiting for us. It's been two months since we had any. And might even have some emails. That would be like magic."

"Relax. We'll get there soon enough. Only 20 miles to go," Larry commented as he went down below to warm up a cup of coffee.

Only the day before I'd been completely content to drift along. Other than the need for someone to be out in the cockpit keeping a watch during the dark of night, life on board had felt little different than it might have on a lazy weekend in a house on shore. I'd done a bit of locker sorting, some mending, baked a loaf of fresh bread. Larry had made up a new leather protector to go around the Highfield lever on the staysail stay. Together we'd continued discussing ideas for the video we planned to make using some of the footage we'd shot over the past weeks. By the time we'd anchored the night before, my notepad was filled with notes and script ideas. But now, with the hills of Puerto Montt in sight, it was as if a switch had been thrown. I felt like a caged lion, prowling the deck looking for signs of real wind, not this fickle breeze that kept us moving at a frustrating 1½ or two knots.

The anchorages and port area of Puerto Montt are protected from the southerly winds and swells by a steep-sided offshore island. The channel between the two is narrow. The tidal range can be as much as 25 feet, the current as strong as six knots as it surges through the narrows. I consulted the tide tables a dozen times. "If we get to the channel by 1700, we'll still have at least an hour or two of tide with us," I told Larry after checking the tide tables one more time. "That should give us enough daylight to sail the last two miles, then work into the marina."

"Relax," he said yet again. "We'll get there when we get there."

My visions of being secured alongside a pontoon for the night disappeared along with the breeze soon after we actually sailed into the channel, just as I could discern there were a few other sailing boats in the small marina on the far side of the town.

"You go down and start making us something for dinner," Larry suggested. "I'll get out the oar and scull us over to this shallow spot. If I get moving, we can be anchored before the tide turns against us."

It was dark by the time we were securely anchored a half-mile short of the marina, the boat settled for the night and the anchor lamp lit. Strangely, the restlessness I'd felt all day disappeared. "I spotted *Sina's* spars," I commented, referring to the New Zealand cruising boat we'd last seen in Puerto Williams. "Can't wait to hear about Noel and Litara's trip through the rest of the Canal Beagle. I'll get up early tomorrow and use our last apples to bake up a cake for them."

Before I climbed into bed, I went out on deck to listen to the sounds of the town, the hum of cars, the occasional bursts of music, dogs barking in the distance. I reflected on the moods induced by sailing as we did, with no engine to turn to when the winds died off. At times it tested our patience, at times it added almost breath-catching thrills to our sailing lives. It built our sense of being a team, kept our skills growing and gave us a closer connection to the conditions around us. And a distinct positive — though we had just completed a very challenging voyage, the worklist had only two items on it: Check stitching on the third reef clew of the main, fix lower strut on the windvane frame.

Larry climbed out of the cabin and walked over to where I leaned against the boom gallows. He put his arm around me and stood quietly for a few moments. "You thinking what I am?" he asked. He didn't give me time to answer before continuing, "Now we're actually within a few feet of our goal, I'm reluctant to finish. Doubt I'll ever feel this satisfied again."

His comment caught me slightly off guard.

"Not exactly my thoughts," I quietly replied. "I was thinking how nice it is to have one last night with just the two of us before we jump into the rush and complications of shore life."

PASSAGES

6

The Perfect Passage

2003 -approaching the Marquesas Islands, Polynesia

"What was your favorite destination?"

I struggle whenever I try to answer this question.

I have so many favorites. Baja California's Sea of Cortez and its magnificent rugged mountains and stark black beaches set against turquoise tropical waters; Finland, with its amazing music festivals and hundreds of tiny offshore islands; Tonga, where we planned to stop for a week and left three months later — only because cyclone season threatened; South Africa, where we kitted out a second-hand 4WD pick-up truck and spent seven months getting to know the !Kung people in the Kalahari desert; New Caledonia, with its hundreds of islands and reefs where fun-loving locals put on a seafood feast to celebrate my 79th birthday. Those are just the first that come to mind.

But ask me about my favorite passage. I don't hesitate. Two stand out above all the rest. Both found us at sea for weeks at a time, both followed the classic routes perfected by the captains of square-rigged sailing ships that once plied these seas. Both were preceded by extremely difficult passages. Each was distinctly different.

Several years before our Cape Horn caper, we'd voyaged from Cape Town, South Africa, to Rio de Janeiro. With our normally relaxed attitude towards calendars and destinations, an interesting and eventful year slipped by as we enjoyed the delights of Rio — bicycling with local folks along the famous Ipanema and Copacabana beaches, being introduced to Brazilian-style cruising as part of a local sailing fleet amidst the islands (and wonderful seafood) of Ilha Grande 100 miles south of Rio, exploring the rainforests of the highlands with our new friends. It was here, during quiet days in more isolated anchorages, that we wrote the first edition of *Storm Tactics Handbook*. Just when we'd been told we wouldn't be allowed to renew our Brazilian visas for a third time, we received two invitations we couldn't resist.

After a four-year hiatus, the French authorities were preparing to host the second Festival of the Sea, a massive gathering of wooden sailing boats and tall ships at Brest, in the northwest corner of France. And only ten days later, there was to be another wooden boat festival and regatta in Douarnenez, an afternoon's sail south of Brest. We'd heard wonderful reports from friends who had taken part in the previous festival, where more than 2,000 wooden vessels turned up. We didn't hesitate. "If we plan it right, we can spend this winter sailing north, and reach the west coast of Ireland in time for summer," I said as I prepared to write back to the festival committee.

Taleisin *can carry up to six months' worth of provisions, including 140 bottles of wine in the bilges.*

Larry added, "Then we can head to Falmouth, England, for next winter. Our friends there will help us find a good place to give *Taleisin* a thorough cosmetic refit before we hit the festivals. Want her to look as good as the local boats."

Out came the pilot charts for the South Atlantic and North Atlantic, along with our favorite routing manual, *Ocean Passages for the World*[1]. Using the sailing ship section, we planned our route, laying closehauled for 250 miles on the port tack out of Rio, sailing in a southeasterly direction to get beyond the strongest flow of the southbound current, before tacking north with a chance of clearing the bulge of northern Brazil to lay Isla Fernando de Noronha. From there the pilot charts indicated we'd find more favorable winds to head for the narrowest part of the ITCZ then on to the Azores, and finally to Dingle, Ireland.

The first leg of that voyage would not be on anyone's favorites list, though it did prove *Taleisin* could go to windward. Almost constantly heeled to nearly 20 degrees in 20 to 25 knots of wind, the bulwark often awash, decks lashed with spray, two-and-a-half days of sailing directly away from our goal, then 12 days on the northbound portion of our track. I'd often used the phrase, "working to windward". And this passage truly was hard work. Thinking out each move as I worked to come up with simple but nutritious meals despite the motion and dwindling fresh provisions, struggling to keep the cabin in some sort of order. I came to hate damp foul weather gear; we tried to dry it out by draping it over every bulkhead near the companionway. The windvane self-steering gear did an amazing job of working the boat to windward and freed us from having to sit in the wet cockpit holding a tiller hour after hour. But the need to tend to the sails and check the horizon for shipping every ten or fifteen minutes, day and night, meant climbing into that heavy, stiff foul weather gear that never seemed to dry out.

After 1,600 miles, when we eased sheets for the last two-mile reach into the lee of Fernando de Noronha, I weighed eight pounds less, pounds removed by three weeks of steadying my body against the constant motion. We'd planned to top up our provisions here — but the shelves in the two island shops were almost bare. Fortunately, the local supply ship was due from mainland Brazil five days after our arrival.

The day after the frenzy of "ship day" we set sail again, two large baskets filled with a variety of fresh fruit and two more with vegetables. Each basket was securely lashed down in the forward cabin. Our well insulated ice chest held 120 pounds of rock-hard ice produced by the local fish plant, plus a

---

1   *Ocean Passages for the World* is a British Admiralty publication. For more than a century it has been updated on a ten yearly basis with information provided by ships officers on both sail and engine powered vessels.

generous variety of meats and cheese that I knew would last at least two weeks. This time our sheets were well eased on a delightful beam reach with the northeast trades rushing us towards the equator.

Three days later, after Larry had taken a noon sight and finished his calculations, I plotted the updated position on our passage chart. It showed we were within a few miles of the ITCZ, the band of fickle winds and weather that lies between the southeast tradewinds of the South Atlantic and the northeast tradewinds of the North Atlantic.

"We'll sail out of this nice wind soon," I commented. "Sure hope we don't have to spend days working through squally, fluky winds."

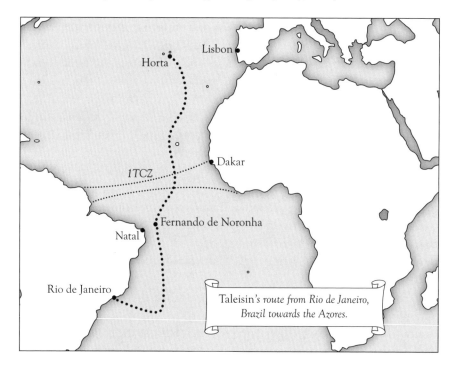

Taleisin's *route from Rio de Janeiro, Brazil towards the Azores.*

"Relax, Lin, the ITCZ position shown on the pilot charts for this time of year is just an approximation," said Larry, "Weather patterns change." He picked up the book he'd been reading before he went out to take his sights.

And, over the next few hours nothing did seem to change. We romped northward at a steady six knots. But by morning the wind gradually began to ease, and a band of clouds rolled towards us out of the north. "Get out the rain catcher. Looks like a good fall coming our way. Might as well fill up our tanks," Larry called down from the cockpit. "And throw me my foul weather jacket — I'll stay up here and tend things."

Instead of the gusting winds that precede a normal tropical squall line, our breeze dropped off to nothing. A solid wall of rain seemed to march slowly over us, rain so intense that I could barely see Larry though he was only six feet away from me. I hastily put up the companionway cover to keep the cabin dry.

The rain pelted down in a biblical-like deluge and lasted more than an hour. At some point, I couldn't resist joining Larry on deck as we filled every spare water jug, every container I could find. Then, I lathered up my hair and laughed as the soapy bubbles seemed to wash away even before I'd finished spreading the shampoo.

Then, the rain moved off at the same stately speed as it had arrived, to leave us sitting motionless in a flat, sun-soaked sea.

Within a few minutes, the water to the east began to darken. A light breeze filled in. We hesitated for only a few minutes, then worked together to set the big nylon drifter and get us moving. A few hours later we added the nylon staysail to grab an extra half-knot of speed. And onward we sailed: flat sea, breeze between five and seven knots, day after day after day.

Our noon-to-noon runs were rarely over 80 or 90 miles, never below 60. The deck was so steady, we used our stemware for the evening glass of wine. A pod of seven dolphins found us soon after we crossed the ITCZ and stayed with us for two weeks. Much of the day they hid under the shade of *Taleisin*'s hull, only to dart off after a feed of flying fish or to leisurely swim over to investigate what might be lurking under a bit of flotsam. At night I spent hours sitting on the side deck watching them, mesmerized by the bioluminescence trails that slid off their bodies as we moved ever northward, together.

Time seemed to flow with gentle ease, the days filled with excellent books and easy conversation. We finished a few onboard projects such as sewing up a new windvane cover, touching up some sunburned varnish spots. I even hand-sewed a new top for myself using fabric I'd bought on a whim when we were exploring southern Africa. We found time to work on the outline for a book, and I filled notebook after notebook with first drafts for future articles.[2] Sometimes we took the quarter berth cushions out into the cockpit where they formed a perfect double bunk. And there, in the shade of the cockpit awning, we lazed together as the windvane kept *Taleisin* meandering along.

The same flotsam that attracted our pod of dolphins added a special

2   When we reached Falmouth later that year, the outline became the basis for *Cost Conscious Cruiser*.

flavor to the days we spent drifting north. We frequently changed course when we saw a flock of birds on the horizon. Inevitably the circling birds marked the spot where a floating log or patch of sargassum weed provided shade and shelter for an inverse pyramid of sea life: algae and small crabs clinging to the flotsam, then a school of tiny fish nibbling at the algae, then larger predators which we could see ever-increasing in size as we looked deeper into crystalline waters.

The saloon table has removable fiddles.
The table also has an adjustable tilting mechanism to accommodate us when we are heeled.

As we passed the two-thirds mark of our leisurely passage northward, a relatively large flock of birds drew our attention to something that reflected the sunlight far ahead of us. As we got closer, I got out the binoculars. "Looks like a fishing beacon of some sort," I told Larry.

"Let's sail over and check it out." Larry unclutched the windvane and took hold of the tiller. "Be worth retrieving it. When we reach Faial in the Azores, might find a fisherman who could use it."

For the last several days of our dream passage, the 10-foot-long pole, with its radar reflector at one end and a large floatation canister at the other, lay lashed to the bulwark rail as the winds very slowly increased and drew farther forward until *Taleisin* lay on a beam reach. The day before we spotted the towering volcanic cone of Pico, we replaced our nylon headsails with the Dacron working sails to a breeze that now kept us moving onward at close to hull speed, even while the decks stayed dry and steady.

Though this was before internet access was possible on board, and we did not carry an SSB or ham radio, we did not worry about the lack of weather forecasts as we made this passage. Outside the cyclone season, between Fernando de Noronha and the area south of the Azores, winds above Force 7 were almost unheard of. It was only during the final approaches to Horta that there was any risk of stronger winds. And even there, according to our pilot chart, the risk of winds over 32 knots was approximately one percent.

Our arrival in Horta was just as memorable as the passage that preceded it. The easy sailing meant nothing had been added to the worklist. We'd had plenty of water for refreshing hot showers. The boat was tidy, other than a relatively big and constantly expanding bag of laundry stuffed in the lazarette. So, unlike the end of some other passages, we weren't overly eager to reach shore. The only things I really looked forward to doing when we did reach Horta included finding some ice cream, having a night off from cooking and once again exploring the island we'd visited and enjoyed many years before.

Soon after *Taleisin* was secured alongside the stone quay in front of the customs office, Larry began chatting with a man on a small fishing trawler which lay astern of us. "You get your paperwork finished," the fisherman told us in heavily accented English. "Then I'll take you to the tavern and get you a big jug of good wine in exchange for that fishing marker."

The six-litre jug of hearty red local wine was accompanied by a long leisurely lunch shared by all of Carlo's fishing crew. Together they planned who we'd ride with the next day for a christening party on the far side of the island. By the time we staggered back to the boat late that evening, I had filled a page in my ever-present notebook with the names of our new friends, their phone numbers and the plans they had for our stay.

Larry reached over and wrapped his arms around me when I climbed into the forward bunk to join him. "Be hard to top this one," he whispered.

"It was magic," I murmured, but he'd already drifted off to sleep.

After reaching the Azores, we explored from the Irish isles to the Baltic Sea; we circled Britain, Scotland and the Outer Hebrides; we crossed the Atlantic three times and voyaged south to round Cape Horn. Some of the passages were pleasant, some were difficult or boring, some tested our abilities and *Taleisin*'s strength. Each of these passages was rewarding in its own way but none equaled the magic of that meander from Fernando de Noronha to the Azores. None, that is, until seven years passed and we'd battled our way around Cape Horn and into the Pacific, then north past Patagonia to Puerto Montt, Chile.

It was on the voyage north from Puerto Montt to British Columbia, Canada, that we experienced the second, almost magical "perfect passage."

By mid-March 2003, a year after we had sailed into Puerto Montt, the winter storms had spent their fury, and the days began to lengthen.[3] We had almost 10,000 miles of sailing between us and our northern summer goal. Though we could have cut this down to just 7,600 miles by sailing non-stop directly to Victoria, British Columbia, neither of us was attracted to the idea of spending almost three months at sea. Thus, we planned a longer and potentially easier route, with three stops along the way to let us reprovision, top up our water tanks and spend some time around other people.

From previous experience, I knew the shops we'd visit during those stops were on relatively isolated islands and might have very limited supply choices. Thus, I'd spent almost two weeks scouring the markets of Puerto Montt for long-lasting provisions that would add variety to our at-sea meals. I was sick of shopping by the time we finally untied our dock lines and headed towards the Canal Chacao, the northernmost pass leading out of the Patagonian islands and into the South Pacific.

Robinson Crusoe Island, a rugged Chilean outpost, lay 600 miles ahead of us and 250 miles offshore of mainland Chile. For seven days we worked northward, clear of the Roaring 40s towards the first stop on this passage. *Worked* is the operative word. Changeable winds, choppy seas, occasional calms followed by squally nights.

Unfortunately, the anchorage at San Juan Bautista, the only village on Robinson Crusoe Island, is both deep and exposed to a ceaseless swell. Anchor down in 70 feet of water, we steadied *Taleisin* by setting our flopper-

---

3 We spent two months recording the audio for our Storm Tactics video program on board *Taleisin* in Puerto Montt, getting to know the local area, and many of the local sailors. We then rented a storage room from the yacht club and removed all of our sails and upholstery from the boat and covered all her varnish work before flying to our adopted homeland, New Zealand. We had come to realize it would be far easier to work with an English-speaking video editor and have the convenience of my home office as we finalized this project. Once we returned to Chile ten months later, it took about three weeks to put everything back on board and de-winterize the boat before we could set sail again.

stopper and a riding sail. But the sound of breaking surf on the rocks just 300 meters away from us often woke me during the night. In spite of the discomfort, we spent a week here for the same reason we'd spent a week at Fernando de Noronha off Brazil, several years before. The three local shops were completely out of fresh vegetables and meat. And the supply ship was due to arrive in five days. "Might be a sign of good luck," I wrote in my logbook. "When this happened on our way north from Brazil to the Azores, we had a great passage."

There was another similarity between the Azorean passage and this one. In each case, our planned route followed the ones favored by the sailing ship captains of old. Each was significantly longer than the rhumbline course would have been. During our passage from Rio to the Azores, the extra distance had been about 750 miles. In this case, though a straight line between Robinson Crusoe Island and Hiva Oa in the Marquesas covers just 3,600 nautical miles, it goes right through the center of the South Pacific high, an area known for its almost complete lack of wind. Our planned route, heading almost due north to skirt the high-pressure area and find the southeast tradewinds before arching westward on a course that kept us south of another area of calm surrounding the Galápagos Islands before turning directly towards our goal, added an extra 600 miles to the voyage. There the similarity ended.

Seven years previously, *Taleisin* had bounded north away from Fernando de Noronha towards the Azores, running wing and wing on brisk tradewinds, then spent three weeks meandering along in light drifting winds. But this time we sailed gently away from Juan Fernández Archipelago with our drifter set on a reach. We then gradually eased our way into the long passage as each day the wind slowly built and added another eight or ten miles to each noon-to-noon mileage total. Eighty miles a day soon became 90, then 110 as each one saw us shedding another layer of winterlike clothing. By the middle of our second week at sea, we were running in fresh trades, comfortably knocking off runs of 150 or 160 miles each day, and I spent the days completely nude, sheltered from the sun by the cockpit cover we rigged.

This gradual increase in wind strength let us ease gently into the rhythm of being at sea. At first the seas were almost smooth, the decks steady as we regained our sea legs. Then, by our second week out, the seas, driven by 25 knot tradewinds, grew to five meters in height. But my body had adjusted to the motion so moving around the boat felt natural and comfortable. *Taleisin's* decks stayed dry as she surged down the face of each wave, foam spreading in a wide roaring V astern of her. Then she climbed the next wave without hesitation.

Within three days of leaving Robinson Crusoe Island, we'd both fallen into the rhythm of watches, and sleep came easily. Larry would climb into the leeward pilot berth at 1900 hours. Then, in an at-sea routine we'd come to enjoy, I'd sit on the settee next to his bunk and read aloud, sharing a chapter of a book we'd selected together just for this special few moments each day.[4] Then I'd give Larry a hug, pull the curtain across the front of the pilot berth and climb out into the cockpit to scan the horizon for ships lights, and check the set of our sails. By the time I'd done my on-deck check, I'd hear Larry's gentle snoring. I'd head back into the cabin, get out my steno pad and set the wristwatch alarm to remind myself to climb on deck for a look around every 12 minutes. My first three-hour watch usually saw several pages filled with writing. During my second watch, I'd spend a few minutes doing leg exercises to make up for all the sitting I was doing. Then I'd indulge in another of the novels or history books we'd gathered for this passage.

Larry usually let me sleep as long as my body demanded each morning. He'd make his own simple breakfast. When I awoke, after sometimes sleeping four, even five, hours, I'd usually find him on deck, sextant in hand, taking the morning sight. With the few hours remaining before it was time for his noon sight, we'd both do small jobs the boat needed to keep things running smoothly.

My favorite photograph of Larry was taken as *Taleisin* rushed across the South Pacific headed for the Marquesas Islands. On his previous watch, Larry had noticed the lashings on three of the upper mast slides were beginning to fray. Rather than try to take the mainsail off to repair them, we left the working jib winged out on the spinnaker pole, then set the staysail on its small whisker pole opposite the jib to keep the sail plan balanced. Once the boat was again rushing along, Larry pulled the mainsail down into the lazy jacks, then climbed onto the boom and set to work sewing up new lashings. All the time *Taleisin* kept moving at almost seven knots, surging down the faces of the seas, Larry riding the boom as if he was on a galloping horse.

Our afternoons saw Larry taking a two-hour snooze after lunch to top up his ration of sleep to equal eight hours. What little time there was left before the evening routine of dinner and settling the boat for the night was filled to over-flowing with reminiscences of the adventures we'd shared, the schemes for the future.

I laugh when I hear people say *"Live in the moment."* As our noon

---

4   We usually chose a book of short stories or essays to share for this bedtime routine. On this passage my favorite was — First You Have to Learn to Row a Little Boat by Richard Bode

position marks marched steadily across the chart towards Hiva Oa, and the baskets of fresh provisions emptied, I can't remember once wishing to be anywhere else but where we were: together, on a fine boat with a fine wind on an exceptionally fine passage.

Just after lunch, 31 days after setting sail from Robinson Crusoe Island, Larry spotted the distinctive peaks of Hiva Oa just breaking clear of the clouds ahead. I joined him on deck. "I'm ready for a dinner out," I said happily.

"I'll bet you're tired of cooking," Larry answered. "But I'm more interested in sleeping right through the night together. Just hope Atuona is tenable with these big seas rolling right into the cliffs around it."

I rushed below to dig out the detail chart of the anchorages on Hiva Oa. I could see why Larry was concerned. The long headland of Teaehoa Point, only a few miles past the entrance to Atuona Bay, projected out right into the path of these seas. I'd seen the backwash from a point like this cause a very uncomfortable surge in other similarly situated harbors. Atuona only had a small breakwater. It only extended part way across the inlet to stop this surge entering the anchorage. "It's got to be okay," I optimistically called out to him. "This is the only port of clearance at this end of the Marquesas Islands. This is the only place island freighters can offload their cargo."

"Lin, I'm not sailing into a place that will feel like a trap. If it isn't good, we'll just sail overnight and get to Taioha'e Bay on Nuka Hiva. We can clear in there," he replied as we drew closer to the land. "We know the anchorage there is safe, even if it has a bit of swell running into it."

Each mile closer to Atuona lowered my excitement a notch. As we sailed nearer to the island, the rising seabed was noticeable in how quickly the swell began to increase. And when we came abeam of the eastern end of the island, I could see waves crashing against the cliffs, throwing spume towering into the air. But still my hopes of a meal ashore kept me urging Larry to take a closer look. He sensed my disappointment and continued onward until we could actually see the spars of a dozen yachts over the small breakwater.

"Get the binoculars," Larry suggested. "See how they're laying."

As soon as I lifted the binoculars to my eyes, my spirits flagged. Even though we were still more than a mile offshore, I could see the masts describing 20- and 30-degree arcs, prancing and dancing about like excited ponies. My dream of something fresh to eat, and a break from the constant motion, evaporated.

"Okay, let's tighten up the sheets and head for Nuka Hiva," I conceded as I helped trim the sails to beat clear of the point and continue westward.

I was radiating disappointment when I climbed below and examined the wilted-looking cabbage. This would be dinner; I'd almost thrown it overboard when we spotted land.

A few minutes later, after setting the windvane to steer us on our new course, Larry came below too, and began scouring the Marquesas detail charts. "Take a look at this anchorage. It should offer us a calm night's sleep," he said. "It's just beyond the pass and really easy to get into. If we're lucky we might be able to reach it before dark."

I agreed it was worth a try, as I set aside the idea of cooking dinner for the moment and went on deck to help keep the boat moving at top speed directly towards the setting sun.

The moment we rounded the northern tip of Tahuata, and reached into its lee, the seas dropped off, and so did the wind. We still had two miles to go, two miles almost directly to windward. The sun dropped below the horizon, and dark came crashing down — and with it my thoughts of a night at anchor.

"Lin, I could see four or five boats at anchor in that cove," Larry said. "It's worth taking a chance they'll soon light their riding lights, and those lights will guide us in."

I was a bit skeptical as we usually avoided entering new anchorages after dark, but realized the stars were outlining the pinnacle-like peak mentioned on the chart. That would give us something we could get bearings on to keep us clear of the rocky arms of the cove.

Then, minutes later, the first anchor light flashed on. Larry began taking short tacks directly towards that beacon. I stood on the foredeck shining our biggest flashlight to illuminate the rocks on each side of the cove. All was quiet except for the whisper of the water slipping past *Taleisin*'s stem as she worked to windward, moving at about three knots in five or six knots of breeze, plus the murmur of restless water against the rocky shores. Shortly before we came abeam of the first anchored boat, I took a sounding.

"About 50 feet," I called back to Larry.

"Okay, that's good enough, let go the anchor," he called.

I went forward, backed off the clutch on the windlass, and gave the anchor a push. It splashed into the water. As the chain rattled out, I heard applause. When the rattling stopped, a cheer rang out across the water. "Congratulations!" someone yelled.

"For what?" I yelled back into the night.

"For completing your second circumnavigation," the unknown caller replied. "We'll row over in a minute; got something you probably need."

Robyn and Mark Rogin came alongside in their tender and handed us a delicious looking array of fresh vegetables: two tomatoes, a cucumber, a green pepper. "We've followed your adventures in the magazines as we outfitted *Mintaka*, then sailed her down here from Puget sound," Robyn explained. "Must have been 20 years since we read about you sailing down to the Marquesas after you launched *Taleisin*. Then a few months back someone showed us a copy of a magazine with a story about you making it around the Horn and safely into the Pacific. So that means you've closed the loop."

Neither Larry nor I had even considered that our arrival in the Marquesas tied the knot of another meandering circumnavigation, one which had begun more than 17 years before and covered more than 65,000 miles.

A short while later, when I set a fresh salad and an omelette on the cockpit table, Larry opened a bottle of Chilean sparkling wine. "What a passage. And what a fun greeting," he said. "Glad Atuona looked like such a lousy anchorage — this is so much better."

I nodded in agreement. The soft feel of a tropical night, the occasional sound of laughter from one of the other boats anchored inshore of us, the broad band of the Milky Way overhead: this was a fine way to end a perfect passage, and an eventful and eminently satisfying circuit of the world.

.

7

Crossroads

2003 - Nuka Hiva

We'd spent almost a month in Taioha'e Bay on Nuka Hiva during our previous voyage through the Marquesas Islands. We'd sailed in and out several times during our stay, to explore nearby anchorages. We knew the anchorage area was quite generous and free of dangers. Our relatively up-to-date chart showed little had changed in the intervening 20-plus years. Thus, we hadn't been concerned when, on the 9th of May, after a leisurely 100-mile passage from Tahuata, we made our approach just at midnight.

We short-tacked into the long, relatively narrow bay, each with a large flashlight at hand to illuminate the rocks when we got close to either shore. Soon after we entered the bay I commented to Larry, "Lot more lights than I remember. Village must have grown." But as we neared the anchorage I realized, though there might have been a few extra lights on in the village, the majority were anchor lights. A fleet of yachts — a large one, and a distinct change since our previous visit.

"Nope, not worth it," I said as I swung the flashlight beam across the mass of anchored boats. "Too hard to figure out where to anchor without fouling someone's ground tackle. Let's get out of here and come back when it's light."

Larry didn't hesitate. He eased the jib sheet, then the mainsheet, while I pulled the tiller to windward. *Taleisin* turned to run gracefully down the length of Taioha'e Bay.

Towering volcanic plugs mark each side of the entrance to this stunning, almost fiord-like, inlet. We sailed between them and into clear water. Once we were a mile offshore, beyond any immediate dangers, I headed the boat into the wind. Larry lowered the jib and lashed it loosely in the jib net while I put two reefs in the mainsail. Soon we had *Taleisin* laying quietly hove to in the 10-knot breeze, sheltered from the heavy tradewind swells by Tikapo Point five miles to windward.

I suggested Larry take the first off watch. As soon as he climbed into the pilot berth, I settled in the cockpit with my reading light and my notepad.

Three hours later I woke Larry and handed him a page of calculations. "Despite the three nights we spent anchored at Tahuata," I excitedly told him, "that fast passage from Chile has put us 18 days ahead of schedule. We can spend some extra time here!"

For the first time in our voyaging lives, we had a schedule to keep (other than the one imposed by seasons). We had spent several months working in New Zealand to finish our Storm Tactics video. When we returned to Puerto Montt where *Taleisin* lay waiting for us after our Cape Horn adventure, it was the first of March. We both agreed we needed to recoup the costs and pay for the hard work we'd put into the video project. The best way to do this? Accept the invitation to be guest speakers and have *Taleisin* open to the public at two wooden boat festivals, one in Victoria, British Columbia, the other at Port Townsend, Washington, followed by a fundraiser at the Seattle in-the-water boat show for Footloose, the local organization for sailors with disabilities. Our calculations showed we had to sail about 9,600 miles to reach Victoria in time for the first of these festivals. If we could get *Taleisin* ready and set sail by the 15th of the month, we would have 140 days to cover that distance.

"Not too difficult," had been Larry's assessment at the time. "We should have the tradewinds helping us most of the way, could cover 150 miles a day. But based on the worst case, even if we only do 100 miles a day, that's 96 days of sailing. That would give us ten days at each of our three reprovisioning spots, and still leave us two weeks to clean up the boat, freshen the varnish work and generally get ready for the festivals when we reach Victoria."

I'd still been reluctant to make the commitment. But Larry reassured me. "Remember, if we do get delayed, we can leave *Taleisin* in Hawai'i and fly to Victoria. We've cleared that with the organizers."

Larry gave me a hug when he climbed out of the pilot berth to take over the watch. He glanced at the calculations I'd done as we lay hove to in the shadow of Nuka Hiva. "Maybe now you can relax a bit, you little worrywart," he replied. Then he added, "Come on out into the cockpit and have a few quiet minutes with me before you climb into the bunk. It is really beautiful out here. Besides, I know you – the minute we get anchored you'll have us all caught up in a social whirl."

When daylight came and we again short-tacked up the length of Taioha'e Bay, I was glad we'd spent the night hove to. More than three dozen yachts lay at anchor, some with stern anchors set to hold them head to the incoming swell, some swinging to just one anchor, most trailing dinghies on varying lengths of line, all rolling gently as each swell passed under them. In the dark, we'd have been extremely fortunate to find a clear spot among this fleet.

Twenty-seven years back, fewer than a dozen boats arrived during our month-long stay at this unique cruiser crossroads.

———

There are about a dozen ports in the world that could be called true cruisers crossroads, places where voyagers from all points of the globe arrive after crossing an ocean, then pause to reprovision before setting off again. These are places like Bermuda; Horta in the Azores; Gibraltar; Cocos Keeling Atolls; Cape Town, South Africa; Nouméa, New Caledonia – to name a few. But my favorite must be Taioha'e Bay in the Marquesas Islands.

Unlike most other cruisers crossroads, there are no marinas here; everyone lays at anchor. There is no large local fleet of yachts, so you are surrounded by sailors who have just crossed at least one ocean to reach this isolated spot. Onshore, instead of the hustle and bustle of a city, there is a small welcoming village. This is not a tourist destination; there are no hotels, only a few small guest houses so each non-Polynesian you meet on shore is probably a cruiser. This makes for easy interactions between all the different voyagers regardless of boat size, nationality, budget or cruising style.

Then there is the call of the drums. A highlight of each year in French Polynesia is the traditional dance competition, which takes place in the capital, Papeete. Dance groups from each island and atoll practice all year long then gather there in the first weeks of July for the final competition. Two or three times a week during our stay, as soon as dark fell across the bay, the sound of wooden drums pounding out the distinct rhythms of Polynesian dance music rang across the water. We'd row ashore to watch as youthful, athletic Polynesian men and women spent the next hours practicing their moves, the sensuous hip swaying Tamari'i , highly intricate fire dances, accompanied by the throb of hollowed hardwood drums being struck in intertwining rhythms. We mingled with the dancers' families who invited us to settle on the mats they'd spread on the village meeting area, right next to the rocky foreshore of the bay. I often brought ashore a big bowl of fresh popcorn to share with children and adults alike as drinking coconuts were passed around. The finer details of the dance routines were pointed out to us — including the tiny errors that could jeopardize their team's chance of winning.

Larry was right: between scouring the shops for interesting provisions to top up lockers depleted by our long voyage from Chile, sanding and applying a coat of varnish to the cabin sides, hatches, bowsprit and boomkin, checking the sails and lines for chafe, we did get to know the sailors around us. And we were soon caught up in a round of shared drinks, gatherings on our boat, their boat, on the beach, or joint forays to one of the small cafés on shore.

I am not the only one who feels it, this special rapport that exists among people who have taken time away from "normal" shore life to cross oceans in their own boat. The ease of forming deep, lasting friendships with other cruisers is what many other sailors have told me they missed most when they moved ashore. There are a lot of reasons these cruising friendships form so quickly.

You can forgo the normal "getting to know you" phase and feel an almost instant connection since conversations with fellow cruisers always starts from common ground. You don't have to explain why you have "run away," or what it feels like to be at sea, or how annoying it is to try to locate a replacement part in a foreign port. You don't need to take time to describe the pleasures that make up for the inconvenience of living in the limited confines of a small boat, or why you willingly put up with the discomfort of being at sea in exchange for the excitement of a new landfall. You don't feel like a name dropper or braggart when you talk about walking along the Malecón in Acapulco or climbing the steep track leading up the Rock of Gibraltar, meandering through the fiords of Norway or diving for crayfish off the islands of Panama.

Cruising gets you away from the normal distractions of life on shore. That means you can have leisure and the mental space to get to know someone new. I can't count the number of times during our cruising years that someone I hadn't met before happened to row by and pause for a chat, then came on board for the cup of coffee and a few hours later suggested we adjourn to their boat for lunch. There were times when we changed our cruising plans because of chance meetings like this and spent the next week, even a month, accompanying our new friends to a place they'd always wanted to visit, one that hadn't been on our radar.

Deep friendships often form within a day or two of meeting these kindred souls. Friendships that appear destined to last for just a few days as one or the other of you sail off to a new destination often last a lifetime.

Neither boat size nor style, nor cruising style, seem to matter. Though we sailed into Taioha'e Bay on one of the smallest boats, we forged warm friendships and spent several evenings with the crew of the largest boat there. We had moored next to Alan and Monica Gross, on board their Chuck Payne-designed 65-foot sloop *Evolution* and barely finished setting our stern anchor when I heard one of the children on board yelling, "Lexi, slow down." I looked over to see a flying mane of bright red hair disappear in a splash of salt water near the bow of *Evolution*. When no one on board *Evolution* seemed concerned, I relaxed as I watched four-year-old Alexi swim the length of the boat, then climb back on board again. Alan rowed over to explain, "She gets moving so fast, she forgets she is on a boat."

Alan and Monica were voyaging from Juneau, Alaska, with their four children. When their oldest turned 11, they decided to take a break from working as doctors and spend two years circling the edges of the Pacific Ocean. Not only did they want to show their children a different way of life, but Alan wanted the leisure to learn more about playing his violin. We spent ten days at anchor near each other. I loved waking in the morning to the sound of children's laughter. We came to call Lexi the Little Red Rocket, as she always ran, and never walked anywhere. The evenings when Alan rounded up any other sailor who played an instrument to join him in the cockpit were memorable. Language barriers seemed to fall away as half a dozen of us attempted to play our assortment of instruments in unison with each other (with some mixed results) and our partners added their voices to the chorus.

I particularly enjoyed getting to know some of the so-called Newbies we met at Taioha'e Bay, people who had just completed their first long ocean passage. In most cases, these sailors were exhilarated by the experience and eagerly looking forward to the next part of their voyage. Several talked about all the things they worried about before they left, worries that, once underway, proved to be unfounded or easy to handle.

"I was most worried about running out of food, especially if we got becalmed. I worried about the price of food in Polynesia. Other cruisers said it costs a fortune," said Ruth, who was sailing with her husband on a 34-foot sloop out of Seattle, Washington. "We did get becalmed, but only for a few days," Ruth said as we sat chatting together at the dinghy landing while I waited for Larry to row in and pick me up. "We did run out of our favorite treats, but I enjoyed the challenge of coming up with interesting meals from what was left," she continued. "I am having fun topping up our provisions with some of the French treats I am finding in the shops here.

Sure, they cost a bit more than I am used to paying, but we didn't spend anything while we were at sea so why not splurge a bit?"

On board the four dozen different cruising boats that sailed into Taioha'e Bay during our stay, there were a handful of people who had not enjoyed their first ocean passage or were uncomfortable about continuing onward. Boat problems, crew problems, the aloneness of being at sea, the sense of being cut off from family and friends, financial concerns, the remoteness of Taioha'e Bay, and lack of easy communications with the outside world seemed to exacerbate their problems.

A few days after our arrival, we were invited to a handsome and well-fitted-out older 37-foot sloop for sundowners. We'd only been on board a few minutes when Ben blurted out, "Do you two still deliver boats?"

"Haven't done any deliveries for a long time," Larry replied.

"Would you consider doing one now? I'm looking for someone to take this boat back to Los Angeles so I can sell it." Ben explained he had dreamed for years of sailing around the world. "My son and wife were really on board with the idea." After three years of preparing to go, selling their house and possessions, they set off for a five-year circumnavigation. Their son was 14. During the six months they spent doing sea-trials, then meandering south along the Baja California coast of Mexico, all seemed to be going well. They had very few boat problems, lived easily within their budget, enjoyed the sailing, the ports, the people. But the moment they set off on an actual ocean passage, crossing the 2,800 miles between Cabo San Lucas and Nuka Hiva, Ben began worrying. He worried so much he couldn't sleep. His concern? Everything from falling asleep on watch to hitting a container, to screwing up his navigation. He worried the mast was going to come down because he noticed a bit of chafe on the rigging, then there was the concern that someone on board might become sick or break a bone far from outside assistance.

"I hate it. The responsibility is overwhelming. I'm always tired, feeling grouchy," Ben told us. "It's not fair to my wife and son. This whole thing was a bad idea. I hate to be a quitter but it's time to cut my losses."

We listened as he shared his concerns. His wife and son interjected that they were actually enjoying most of their life afloat. But they agreed with Ben's description of his own behaviors and anxieties.

Ben's dilemma kept Larry and me from falling asleep that night. "Sure wish people didn't tell everyone they planned to sail around the world," Larry said. "Sort of traps them. Means if they decide to cut their voyage short, they feel like they failed."

From the very beginning of our voyaging life, Larry had warned me against telling people our long-range sailing plans. "Just tell them we're headed south for as long as it's fun," he'd suggested. "You might not like sailing once we actually get out there. We might just go down to Baja California and that's enough. Besides, if you don't tell anyone your long-range goals, no one will be concerned if we are delayed, or we change our plans. We'll never feel trapped by our own words, never feel like we failed." The story we'd listened to that evening made me even more appreciative we'd stuck to Larry's original plan all through our cruising life.

"I wonder if Ben realizes how successful he actually has been," I said as we kept turning over his problems long past midnight. "He got the money together to get the boat, broke away from his everyday shore life, kept his family enthused, spent six months exploring the shores of Mexico — and he got here, too." By the time we finally fell asleep we'd decided we should encourage Ben to try a different approach.

Larry found a quiet time to talk to Ben the next morning. "I think you should consider another option," he suggested. "Sail the boat to Papeete. You only need to spend a few nights at sea between here and there. At least you'll get a chance to explore a few of the Tuamotu atolls along the way, spend a bit of time enjoying French Polynesia. You'll be far more likely to find someone available to take your boat back from Papeete than from here."

Over the next several days as we got to know Ben, his wife and his son better, we slowly introduced the idea that by the time they'd meandered through the islands as far as Bora Bora, Ben's confidence, and his trust in his crew, might have grown to the extent that he would be comfortable sailing the boat north to Hawai'i , then on to California. "Save you a lot of money, especially as any yacht delivery team will charge a lot more right now because it's just a few weeks before the hurricane season officially starts in the waters between Hawai'i and the mainland," I mentioned. Ben's wife and son soon seemed to be echoing our words. Their encouragement lightened Ben's mood. By the time we began our preparations to head on to Hawai'i Ben had decided to continue on to Papeete and look for someone to deliver his boat from there.

A year later we learned Ben did sail his boat beyond Papeete, then on to Hawai'i and California. "You were right," he wrote. "Sailing through the islands was far less stressful. By the time I got to Bora Bora I felt I could handle sailing the boat back to California." He hadn't enjoyed or felt completely comfortable on the two longer passages, but he came to trust his crew. "Learned I am a coastal cruiser," Ben wrote a few years later. "Love it. So does the rest of the family." We laughed as we learned his idea of coastal cruising reached from the Gulf of Alaska to the Gulf of California.

I try not to be superstitious, but I wish I hadn't mentioned the risk of cyclones in the waters around Hawai'i because, a few days later those words came back to haunt me. As we began preparing to set sail from Nuka Hiva, I made the trek up to the local internet café each afternoon to check each of the four weather sites I had come to trust. Five days before our departure, the very first signs of a tropical depression in the Gulf of Mexico were showing on three of the weather sites I viewed. The next day, it had formed into a true tropical low and was approaching mainland Mexico. As it crossed Mexico and reached the waters of the Gulf of California it had deepened and now was causing storm force winds. Two days before we hoped to leave, Larry joined me at the internet café and looked over my shoulder as I pointed out how the tropical storm had weakened a bit as it crossed Baja California with winds only gusting to 45 knots.

"Maybe this is a warning," Larry said as we walked back to the dinghy landing. "As much as I want to spend time sailing around my old stomping grounds, and show my friends and family this boat, wonder if we are pushing our luck a bit. Maybe we should change our plans and sail home, then fly to Victoria."

I was a bit surprised by his words as I had always considered *Taleisin* to be my home. And we'd always called the small house and miniature boat yard we'd rescued in New Zealand our *home base*.

"What about our plans to explore the islands far to the north of Victoria and the fiords in the Gulf of Alaska?" I asked.

There was a long pause before he answered. "Sometimes wonder myself. But forget I said anything. If that storm has weakened more by tomorrow morning, let's stick to our plan. Really don't want to disappoint anyone."

Before we lifted our ground tackle to leave Taioha'e Bay I made a last foray to the internet café and learned the storm had dissipated as it reached the cooler waters of the California current. An area of gale force winds was the only sign there had been a disturbance and that was more than 1,000 miles east of our course to Hawai'i.

Warm wishes for a good passage had been shouted from a dozen boats as we set our sails and, at noon, skimmed down the bay. The winds were light and fair. Once we'd cleared the headland and set our course past Motu Iti, which lay about 30 miles to the west of Nuka Hiva, I set lunch out in the cockpit as Larry rigged our small sun awning.

"That was really enjoyable," I said to Larry as I shared out the salad I'd made. "So many fun folks, time flew."

"Only problem is," Larry answered, "we got completely caught up with all the other cruisers. We didn't have any time to spend getting involved with the local folks."

We had come to know some of the town folk by name as we enjoyed watching dance practice sessions. I'd formed a warm relationship with Monica, the owner of one of the shops who remembered me from our visit many years before. She would take a break from her work to come out to sit and chat with me on the steps in front of her shop when I stopped in. Then Monica almost always added a gift of fresh fruit from her own garden to my bag of groceries as I was leaving. But Larry was right. Our social calendar had been so full, I'd never thought to invite her to bring her family out to *Taleisin*. That would certainly have led to a deeper friendship and a chance to gain a better understanding of local life. Yes, cruising along the well-traveled tradewind routes, which is often called the "coconut highway," or the "milk run," had this one serious pitfall. It is so pleasurable to spend time with other cruisers, you can accidentally miss the chance to connect with the local people, as we did during this pause in Taioha'e Bay.

8
The Far Side of Cruising

June 2003 - Hilo. Hawai'i

Snaking rivulets of molten lava glow red, just an arm's-length away from my feet. I step gingerly along the solid black rock that not too long ago had been flowing lava. Because I'd been warned my shoes might suffer during this hike across the lava plain on Hawai'i's second highest volcano, I'd worn my oldest pair. The soles are thick, but still I feel the heat emanating from the volcano beneath us. The warmth is welcome. The road we'd taken to reach here left the tropical heat of Hilo, then climbed more than 7,000 feet. Now we are walking through the cold, damp clouds that crowd against the upper reaches of Mauna Loa, a huge volcanic peak that towers another 6,000 feet above us.

As we continue exploring this primordial scene, I realize volcanos are a recurrent theme on this voyage from Chile to Canada. The distinctive towering volcanos of Chile marked the beginning of this season's voyage. Their peaks had been visible for three days after we set sail from Puerto Montt. The volcano I am now standing on marks the middle of this voyage. And, waiting at the end of our northern dash, there is Mount Baker, the volcano that will guide us through the Strait of Juan de Fuca when we sail into Canada.

My thoughts drift from volcanos when Lynn Oakley, our host on this foray, asks about our passage from Nuka Hiva, in the Marquesas Islands, to Hilo on the southernmost Island of Hawai'i. I explain that it had been relatively easy. Both Larry and I had felt refreshed and relaxed when we set sail after our 10-day stay in Taioha'e Bay. There had been no sense of urgency because we had 78 days before we needed to be at Victoria and only 4,600 miles of sailing ahead of us.

Though we'd had highly changeable winds for three days as we sailed out of the South Pacific tradewinds, through the ITCZ and into the North Pacific tradewinds, the majority of the time we had fair winds and easy sailing. Only twice had the wind topped 20 knots for several hours.

The first time the wind was on the beam. I had been on watch as the wind began increasing. So, rather than interrupt Larry's sleep, I doused the small genoa we were carrying, hoisted the staysail, and then pulled the jiffy reefing lines to tuck one reef in the mainsail. With the gusts sometimes reaching 30 knots, *Taleisin* was in her element, clocking off more than seven knots, windvane steering perfectly.

Larry used a pennant to ensure the "toysail" (which was cut to work as a staysail) had a good sheeting angle when he used it on the forestay.

Unfortunately, a few days later when the wind blew up for a second time, *Taleisin* was sailing close-hauled. The wind slowly increased from 15 knots until it topped 25 knots. The rougher motion woke me from a sound sleep. I lay listening as Larry moved around on deck, reefing the mainsail. The boat steadied out a bit, and I dozed off, only to be awakened when I heard him fossicking in the sail locker under the cockpit.[1] A few minutes later I heard Larry making his way along the side deck and onto the foredeck. I lay in the pilot berth, unable to sleep until I heard him climb back into the cockpit.

I laughed when I awoke and clambered out on deck after my off watch. Larry had invented a new sail combination. Now the bright orange, 40-square foot "toysail" was flying from the headstay at the end of the bowsprit. He had insisted we have a sailmaker build this tiny storm staysail for our Cape Horn voyage. It had been used just three times during that passage. Then, it had disappeared from view, stowed away under all of *Taleisin*'s light-air sails.

"She didn't seem to keep driving in this lumpy sea," Larry explained. "I tried shaking out a reef in the mainsail. Just made her heel more. She definitely needed a bit more sail to keep her driving through these confused seas. So thought of the little toysail. It's doing the job. Working like a storm headsail, adding more drive without the heeling."

I laughed. "I often wondered when, or if, we'd ever use that sail again. Call me an accountant, but I thought we'd wasted our money on that one."

Larry gave me an "I told you so" look as he headed below.

The gentle glow of the kerosene lamp we kept burning when we were sailing at night illuminated the familiar scene of him shucking off his foul weather gear, his clothes, and then climbing into the still warm berth. He adjusted the pillows between his shoulder and the side of the boat and turned to sleep. A few minutes later he called out, "Feels like she's being lifted. Keep an eye on the compass, we might be able to ease off a bit. Try letting out the mainsail first when you do." Then he turned over and was soon asleep.

I sat there, marveling at Larry's ability to sense every change in the boat's motion and every variation in the wind, even when he was below decks. Though he seemed to sleep soundly whenever I was on watch, every once in a while, he'd wake momentarily and call out, "You might tighten in the

---

1   *Taleisin* has a flush deck from the aft end of the cabin to the transom instead of the more common sunken cockpit. Not only did it make the boat stronger, but it increased the space below decks and allowed us to install a sitztub under the companionway. I worried about this idea when it was first proposed, but came to really appreciate the wisdom of Larry's idea the longer I sailed on her.

mainsail just a bit," or "Jib probably could be eased a few inches." He was always right. Despite all the years we'd spent refining *Taleisin*'s rig and sailing gear, he kept trying new ideas: moving sail leads, changing the way lines ran, adjusting, readjusting. While I usually got the boat sailing nicely, then let the windvane do the work, Larry kept tweaking, checking, adjusting. And he did get a smidgen of extra speed out of *Taleisin*. Even more important, his attention to the rig and deck hardware, and the sails, meant we'd only once, in all our years of sailing together, had a gear failure at sea. And that was when one of our two spinnaker halyards chafed through because I had not checked to ensure it was led properly. I credited Larry's wonderful seat-of-the-pants awareness, his ongoing interest in refining the boat, to his early years of sailing. Until he set off in search of a boat he could take cruising, he had raced extensively on his own boats and those owned by people who hired him to help them win races. I also think his "tinkering" is what kept him so completely interested in voyaging onward.

Sixteen days out of Taioha'e Bay I was sure I'd spotted the peak of Mauna Loa just at sunset. But Larry didn't agree. "Just clouds, you couldn't see land from 90 miles away," he'd commented, "but we should pick up the lighthouse on the south end of Hawai'i before morning."

At 0200 I climbed out on deck. A flicker of light caught my eye. Odd color, I thought. Must be a ship. An hour later the same light had become distinctly orange and was joined by half a dozen more spots of light. "Must be lights from some small town," I said to myself as I went below for the binoculars. "Wonder why I can't pick up the lighthouse."

I climbed onto the cabin top to get a better view. Enhanced by the binoculars, the orange dots became a solid line against the black of the night. I gasped as I slowly comprehended the reality of this, the sight that had been like a message from the gods to the first Polynesians who risked everything to find these islands. Like them, my first verifiable sight of Hawai'i was lava forced from the center of the earth to flow in all-consuming glory down the sides of the volcano ahead of me. As I watched that fiery river grow ever closer, I felt a sense of connection to those first sailing-canoe-born voyagers and realized how, for them, with their limited supply of food and water, a timely landfall had been a matter of life and death.

I woke Larry just before dawn so he too could witness this fiery, primordial reminder of timelessness. Then I began listing the provisions we'd need for the last and final leg of this voyage.

———————•———————

Radio Bay was a wonderful surprise. A quiet backwater, tucked away in the southern corner of Hilo's commercial harbor. Nowhere could I see the high-rise resorts, the tourist crowds I had associated with these islands. Ashore there were no cafés visible, no tourist facilities, just a few low-slung utilitarian buildings inside a chain-link fence. Tropical trees swayed along one side of the bay, a few local children playing on the sand around them. Afloat, only a half-dozen local fishboats lay nestled between three anchored cruising boats. Another three cruising boats lay tied, stern-to, off the stone wall at the head of the tiny bay. We'd hoisted our yellow quarantine flag as, in the light winds, we maneuvered around the small harbor, jib down, staysail and mainsail helping us tack smartly while we decided where to lower our anchor.

"Make sure you leave a clear channel for the harbor tug," a woman on a cruising boat with a home port of Honolulu called over. "Tug's out now. But it will be back soon. Captain makes a real fuss if anyone anchors too close to the wharf over there."

We settled in a spot which would, we felt, keep *Taleisin* in line with the other anchored boats, then launched *Cheeky*, our eight-foot fiberglass tender, and rowed ashore. "Should we go back and stay on board until the customs and immigration folks come down to clear us?" I asked the official in the building marked, Port Authority. He laughed, "You'd be sitting there all week if you tried that. Don't get many foreign yachts dropping in here. In fact, don't get many yachts at all. " He then directed us to the commercial port offices, a ten-minute walk beyond the fenced area, where we could get all our paperwork done in one place.

A few hours later, Larry and I walked back to Radio Bay replete after clearing our paperwork, and then enjoying a meander into the rural feeling town center of Hilo, just a short distance from Radio Bay. We had indulged in a leisurely café lunch followed by a big bowl of tasty ice cream and a stop to pick up a prepaid access card for the cellphone Larry and I shared, plus fresh food for dinner and a bag of ice to chill down the bottle of white Chilean wine I planned to use that evening.

Just as we prepared to climb into *Cheeky*, a large tugboat rounded the end of the long, shed-covered commercial wharf that protects the northwestern side of Radio Bay. The wind had shifted a few degrees from when we first anchored. Now *Taleisin*'s stern was slightly closer to the wharf than any of the other anchored boats and the tug was headed right at her, horn blaring.

"Come on, quick, climb into the dinghy," Larry said in an agitated voice. "Not sure what's bothering him. Lots of room for him to clear us."

The tugboat stopped just feet from *Taleisin*, its horn blaring again.

I scraped the skin off my shin in my scramble into *Cheeky*. By now the crews on each of the three yachts secured along the stone wall were on deck watching. Their rude comments about the tugboat skipper turned to laughter when the loudspeaker on the tug roared out, "Larry Pardey, get your ass out of bed!"

"Must be someone you know," the lady on the yacht closest to us said as the tug backed slowly away from *Taleisin*, turned and slowly came towards where we were now rowing clear of the boats moored to the seawall.

They were right. We'd last seen its skipper, Rudy Kok, 18 years previously when we set sail from Bora Bora in French Polynesia.

"Can't invite you on board right now," Rudy called down from the bridge of the port authority tugboat us as we rowed alongside. "Just came in to change crew. I'll pick you up at the gate when I finish for the day and take you up to our house for dinner."

One of my favorite cruising traditions is that of keeping a guest book. Each time we have someone new on board, I wait until their visit is winding down and bring out my spiral bound, leather-covered book. Its pages are laid out to provide a space for our guest's name, their boat's name, contact information and comments.[2] If our guests are fellow sailors, even before they add their names, they invariably begin thumbing through to see if anyone they know has also been on board. For non-sailors, we explain, "This helps us remember folks by name, and more importantly, to recall their boat's name and where we last met when we run into them in another port."

As soon as we got back on board *Taleisin*, I got out our guest book to jog my memory and read the entry Rudy had written.

In their mid-20s Mary and Rudy bought the professionally built hull and deck of *Eleu*, a 31-foot Cape George cutter, and moved on board even before she was finished rather than "waste money on the renting and outfitting of a shoreside home." Over the next few years, as they worked finishing the boat and saving for their adventure, they began making sailing forays to the nearby islands. With the confidence built by three years of local cruising, they set off despite the boat not being fully completed and headed for French Polynesia with the funds and desire to cruise for a year before returning to Hawai'i, where both planned to work towards obtaining their captains licenses. We'd been impressed as we watched them working together, competently sailing *Eleu* through the reef passage into Moorea

---

2   Under traditional British yachting protocol, bringing out the guest book is a way to signal to your guests that it is time for the gathering to end. Thus, we learned the hard way, if you are enjoying someone's company, it is important to avoid bringing it out too soon.

and, without starting their engine, set their anchor not far from us. We rowed over to greet them, and ended up spending several days cruising in company, sharing forays ashore and often racing *Taleisin* against *Eleu* as we all explored the leeward islands of French Polynesia.

When we joined Rudy and Mary onshore our first evening in Radio Bay, we learned their year of cruising extended to almost 12 as they meandered around the islands of the Pacific before returning to settle on the big island of Hawai'i where Mary had grown up and had a large extended family. Now they both had interesting skippering jobs, a home on shore, and a safe place for *Eleu*. Mary, who has native Hawaiian ancestry, had also become involved in the campaign for indigenous rights. As they gave us an insight into the life they'd built since their return, their sense of accomplishment and contentment was obvious.

When we got back on board *Taleisin* after that first of what proved to be several interesting visits with Mary and Rudy, I thumbed through our guestbook. Our evening with Mary and Rudy had reminded me of another Hawaiian native we'd met as we voyaged on board *Taleisin*. I soon found her name, Lynn Oakley. This released a flood of memories of the times we'd spent with Lynn when Larry and I sailed into South Africa several years after we'd met Rudy and Mary.

We'd first encountered Lynn at a cruiser's Thanksgiving gathering on the lawn at the Richards Bay Yacht Club in South Africa. Situated 90 miles north of Durban, Richards Bay is the most popular port of entry for voyagers crossing the Indian Ocean. The majority arrive during November and, American or not, looked forward to this distinctly non-South African event. To make their foreign visitors feel welcome, the local yacht club members host a fine barbeque, which is supplemented by a wide variety of additions from each attendee. Amidst a colorful crew of characters hailing from ports all around the world, Lynn Oakley definitely stood out. Wearing a brightly colored muumuu (a loose fitting, ankle-length traditional Hawaiian dress) she also wore a crown of fresh flowers ringing a mass of gold hair which tumbled almost to her knees. A large handsome russet-colored Rhodesian ridgeback hound walked quietly alongside her. Lynn greeted each person she met with a warm "Aloha." She had sailed into Richards Bay a few years previously after crewing with her boyfriend from Hawai'i, through the South Pacific and on across the Indian Ocean. After two years of sailing together, their relationship foundered as they neared the African shores. Lynn, along with being professional crew on Hawaiian tourist fishing boats and charter catamarans previous to setting sail, had credentials and background as a museum curator. During the days she spent in Richards Bay after splitting with her boyfriend, she made friends among the local people. This led to an invitation to a dinner where she met several important black South African dignitaries. By good fortune, she was seated next to Mangosuthu Buthelezi, a Zulu Prince who founded the Inkatha Freedom Party, a group formed to counter the growing influence of the African National Congress as South Africa began moving towards the end of apartheid. The prince and Lynn quickly became friends when she offered to help edit a speech he intended to give at an important international meeting. Soon after, Lynn flew home to Hawai'i. Only a few days later, she received an invitation to return to South Africa to help upgrade a museum featuring Zulu history in the small town of Eshowe, a two-hour drive inland from Richards Bay. An airline ticket had been included with the invitation. Lynn jumped at the chance and after a stint as the prince's speech writer, spent three-and-a-half years on the intensely interesting but often politically fractious Zulu museum project, driving down to the coast to spend each Thanksgiving at the Richards Bay barbeque where we met her.

There seemed to be an immediate attraction between the three of us, one that developed into a close friendship and led to us, over the next year and a half, learning far more about the interplay of cultures in South Africa than we might otherwise have. Not only had we spent time with her in the cottage next to the museum, but Lynn had joined us on board *Taleisin* various other times. In the ways of wandering sailors, especially before easy internet access, we'd written to each other a few times after setting sail from Southern Africa, but gradually our communications had dropped off.

Now, I read her note in our guest book:: *My Mom's phone number. She'll know where I am.*

"Give her mom a call," Larry suggested.

I loaded my pre-paid card onto the cell phone I'd plugged into our simple solar charging system and dialed, wondering if, after almost ten years, the number would still be valid.

"Hello, I am trying to reach Lynn Oakley," I said when a woman answered my call.

"Lin!!! This is Lynn. I'd recognize your voice anywhere. Where are you?" said Lynn in the exuberant way I remembered so well. "I'm living here on Oahu. Give me a few days to sort things and I'll fly down and show you my favorite island."

Lynn Oakley arrived in Hilo four days before we were preparing to set sail for Canada. She too spoke warmly about the time she had spent cruising. "The sailing was great. But even better, it led me to Eshowe and one of most unusual experiences of my life." Lynn stayed on board *Taleisin* with us and we talked late into the night about our African experiences. We now learned more about the political chaos and tribal disputes which erupted around her when, three days before we set sail to leave South Africa, Nelson Mandela was elected as president of South Africa. Lynn had found her work in South Africa rewarding but at times far too tumultuous. She left a year after we did. And here in Hawai'i she had created a life that suited her well.

Now, with Lynn as a guide, we began seeing glimpses of "old Hawai'i." Together we explored the back roads of the island, stopped at tiny roadside booths to sample local delicacies, walked through sometimes strange but always beautiful landscapes, each time turning back before we came near the tourist beaches on the western side of the "Big Island."

In mid-June, all of Hawai'i celebrates the birthday of King Kamehameha who in 1810 united the native people of the islands of Hawai'i. The three of us sat on grass mats watching relays of local women dance the hula at a small park not far from where *Taleisin* lay at anchor. We were among the few non-Hawaiians who whiled away the afternoon enjoying the laid-back atmosphere, the traditional foods, traditional music, and dance. Unlike the throbbing rhythms of the French Polynesian dances, the hula of Hawai'i is far slower, and in many ways, more sensuous. Grass skirts gently swaying, arms and hands gracefully weaving through the air, bare midriffs and bare legs glistening with oil as the dancers' hips moved to the gentle rhythms of drums and ukeleles. We watched entranced as Lynn explained the stories being told by the hand movements of the vibrant young dancers. As the afternoon began drawing to a close and the evening light cast a warm glow across the park, several older women, obviously mothers or grandmothers of the dancers who had held the floor most of the day, climbed onto the small stage. As these older women began to dance, the chatter among the audience faded away. Even young children stopped playing to watch. Gradually the younger women stepped off the stage and turned to join the admiring crowd. Despite their billowing ankle length muu muus, their gray hair and aged faces, these women evoked the mystery, the sensuality of the hula in a way that entranced us all.

Our 17 days in Radio Bay had flown by, enjoyably filled by the excursions and gatherings suggested by our Hawaiian friends. It had also been relatively stress-free as we had arrived with only a few simple items on the boat to-do list. A few lines were showing signs of chafing, the shag carpet protectors on the end of one of *Taleisin*'s lower spreaders had been worn smooth and needed replacing. A few minutes' work each day had whittled the list down to just one last item. On the day of our departure we'd rowed ashore to spend the morning at the local internet café, then walked over to the supermarket and filled two shopping carts with fresh provisions. Before loading everything into the dinghy, we'd had a long hot shower in the shoreside facilities next to the dinghy landing. Back on board, I finished stowing away the provisions in preparation for our departure the next day. Meanwhile, Larry knocked off the last item on the worklist, splicing up a new control line for the windvane self-steering gear.

As the last rays of the sun began painting the clouds surrounding the slopes of Moana Lua in golden hues, I set a chilled bottle of Californian chablis and a small selection of nibbles out in the cockpit. "Lynn Oakley, the Koks, they seem to have been fully sated by their cruising time," I commented as I was climbing the companionway ladder. "They seem completely content with the life they've created here. They're a real contrast to the cruising friends we met up with in Puerto Montt."

"Yes, but the people we were with in Chile were truly addicted voyagers," Larry replied.

"Addicted voyagers," I replied as I stretched out next to him. "I guess that is what we are. Ever wonder what happens next?" I am not sure if he heard my question as he poured a glass of wine for each of us, then put his arm around my shoulder.

He pointed to the North Star, which had just become visible in the growing darkness. "Feels good to have that star to guide us again. Makes me feel like I'm in home waters," Larry said.

My question went unanswered that evening. But later, when we climbed into the big double forepeak bunk together, I lay awake thinking about the long discussions we'd had with the three other long-term cruising couples we'd come to know when we arrived in Puerto Montt after our foray around Cape Horn, the ones Larry had dubbed addicted voyagers.

By wonderful coincidence, as we had sculled into the small marina in the relatively isolated port at the head of the Patagonian canals, we had been greeted by two couples we'd met in other far-flung ports. We'd come to know Beth Leonard and Evans Starzinger on the US East Coast when they had just completed their first circumnavigation on their 38-foot Shannon cutter *Silk*. We'd later crossed paths in other ports on other oceans but were unaware they had spent the past several months exploring some of the more remote regions of Chilean Patagonia on their most recent boat, *Hawk*, a 47-foot van de Stadt-designed aluminum cutter which they'd commissioned as an "expedition boat" to let them explore more remote reaches of the world.

Through the years we'd been cruising, friends often told us about the second couple, Noel and Litara Barrett, who were well known in offshore cruising circles. Though we often were in the same oceans at the same times, we had never crossed paths with them until we sailed into Puerto Williams in the Canal Beagle after our first, failed attempt to round Cape Horn. The bond was almost immediate as we had much in common, even beyond our love of cruising. Noel, a native New Zealander and Litara, a Samoan of royal blood, had met when she was studying to be a nurse in his hometown. Together they built two different wooden boats and used them to take their children on extensive voyages, including a circumnavigation on the engine-free 38-foot cutter *Messina*. Now they were returning to New Zealand from a voyage with their daughter Sina on their handsome 53-foot Colin Mudie-designed cutter also named *Sina*. Their daughter had finished her undergraduate studies with honors and, when asked what she would like as a graduation gift, had answered, "I'd like to sail to Iceland and come home by way of Patagonia before I begin studying to be a doctor."

Noel Barrott, Litara and their daughter Sina.

The third couple, Becky and Evan Hoyt, we met for the first time on our arrival in Puerto Montt. The two of them had created a two-part life, cruising for several months at a time, then finding a safe place to leave their 45-foot, Finnish-built motorsailer, *Finnrose*, while Evan worked as captain on cruise liners for half of each year and Becky returned to her nursing career.

Together, the eight of us had long wine-fueled discussions during the few weeks all of us were secured at Puerto Montt.

"Where you been?"

"Where you headed?"

"Have you met . . . ?"

We shared our thoughts on favorite destinations, craziest adventures. But the topics we seemed to return to most frequently: When is enough *enough?* When will you decide to stop cruising, where will you settle, what will you do then?

I'm not sure which one of us said, "It's easy to return to shore life if you only cruise for six months or a year. If you stay out longer, it becomes an addiction." This comment released a flood of stories about cruising friends who'd moved ashore and found their relationships floundering, or restlessness made them regret the decision. The concern for aging parents, or the desire to be nearby when grandchildren came on the scene, or a need to be near assistance when age began to set in, were acknowledged in our discussions. All of us were a bit surprised when it was Larry who said, "There has to be a far side. Be a good idea to think about that."

In Puerto Montt I remember changing the subject by answering, "We'll be too old to change our ways by then. And now, as I tried to get to sleep here in Hilo, I recalled that, just as he had earlier this evening, Larry had seemed to ignore my comment.

"Come on, turn over and get some sleep," he said when the ship's bell rang four times to mark 2200 hours. "Good idea to start off well-rested tomorrow."

Before I turned over to nestle into his arms, I said, "I loved the primordial feel of walking across the lava plains on Moana Loa. Let's plan on sailing to Vanuatu after we've had our fill of the Pacific Northwest. I've read you can stand right on the edge of the volcano there and watch it erupting."

Just as I drifted off to sleep, I heard Larry whisper softly, "Will you ever feel enough is enough?"

9

Can you go home again?

2003 - North Pacific Ocean

Two distinct, and in many ways unique, weather phenomena affected our passage north from Hilo. We could have avoided the first by setting an alarm clock. I doubt timing would have had any influence at all on the second.

Unless there is a tide to consider, our normal procedure is to set an alarm for a half-hour before dawn when we are starting a passage. Then we hoist our anchor and leave right at daybreak. The winds are usually lighter than later in the day, and there is less boat traffic so tacking clear of the anchorage is easier. This early morning start also gives us the whole day to get well clear of the land and settle into a sea-going routine before nightfall.

Unfortunately, when it came time to set sail from Hilo for the last leg of our passage to Canada, Larry and I didn't stick to our normal procedure. Complacency, a feeling that there was no reason to rush as our goal was now only 2,500 miles away, the assumed consistency of the northeast tradewinds – these were just a few of the reasons we agreed to sleep in. And then, when we finally did wake up, we took our time getting ready for sea. It was midday before we winched *Cheeky* on board, secured her in her cabin top chocks, then lifted our anchor and hoisted the mainsail and working jib to reach clear of Radio Bay on a 10-knot offshore breeze.

I was quite surprised when, only a few minutes after we sailed clear of the protecting wharfs of Radio Bay and into the large open expanse of Hilo Harbor, our breeze dropped off almost completely. At first, I appreciated what I thought would be a short pause. It gave me a chance to head below and make up some sandwiches before we reached out from behind the two-mile-long breakwater and felt the rollicking tradewind seas.

Fifteen minutes later when I brought our lunch out into the cockpit our sails hung limp. "Must be the heat from the land. It's blocking the tradewinds," I said.

Larry's voice had a sharp edge when he answered, "You've got lots of theories, but none of them will get this boat moving. Put the sandwiches in a safe place. Help me set the drifter."

Two hours later, my positive mood had completely deteriorated. We'd added our bright red nylon overlapping staysail to assist the big blue nylon drifter. Larry tried every trick he knew to keep *Taleisin* creeping along in the fitful three- and four-knot puffs of wind. And still it had taken us more than an hour to work clear of the breakwater.

"Tradewinds must have taken the day off," I joked as we came out from behind the protection of the breakwater and encountered the six-foot swells that rolled under us and shook what little wind we had out of the sails. My joking didn't even bring a smile for Larry, and soon I wasn't in any mood for humor as the first signs of seasickness set in.

Though I had often been seasick in the early days of our cruising life, through the years I'd suffered less and less, to the point I hadn't kept anti-seasickness pills in the everyday medical kit for several years. This onset completely surprised me. I went below and managed to find some Stugeron pills in the big medical kit.[1] Then I'd laid down on the settee while Larry struggled to keep *Taleisin* moving. An hour and a half later, when we had managed to sail only two miles beyond the breakwater, and the seas hadn't moderated at all, Larry asked, "Want to turn back? Might have better luck tomorrow."

I crawled out on deck and lay in the cockpit, my head nestled in Larry's lap. For a few minutes I watched the puffy tradewind clouds above us. They were moving to the west at a brisk pace, just as they had been every day since we arrived here. The clouds were still being pressed against the volcanic peaks of the island, wisps streaming to leeward like a bride's veil caught in a howling wind. And as I lay there, between the snapping sounds made by our sails, I thought I could hear a wind blowing on our seaward side, not too far away from us. Add to this the roughness of the waves that kept my seasickness from abating, that too seemed to indicate there was wind close by. Otherwise, I thought, the waves would have smoothed out by now.

---

1   I have found Stugeron to be successful in controlling my seasickness. It is one of the few remedies that works when I feel ill, if I can keep it down. In my book, *The Care and Feeding of Sailing Crew*, there are several other suggestions to help prevent mal de mer.

After another trip to the leeward rail, I said to Larry, "No, let's keep moving. I am sure the wind will fill in by dark."

"How can you sound so confident?" he asked.

Despite the headache that plagued me, I explained my thought processes.

Through our years of sailing engine-free, I'd come to expect light or fickle winds on the leeward side of islands where most ports around the world, and all the better anchorages lay. But rarely had we sailed out of ports on the windward side of any island and never one with such a high mountain so close to the shoreline. Now I realized, as the huge mass of the volcanic slopes absorbed the ever-growing heat of the day, the wind was drawn uphill, leaving a void that, in this case, stretched several miles offshore.

"If you are right, means we should tighten in our sheets and head even farther offshore," Larry said as he winched in the headsails. Inch by inch we drew farther offshore. At the same time, the slopes of the volcano were beginning to cool off as evening approached and the sun slid behind the cloud shrouded peaks.

Within an hour Larry agreed. The sound I had been hearing was the whistle of tradewinds blowing just to seaward of us. He climbed onto the cabin top. "Lin, I can see a line of whitecaps to windward. We should have set that damned alarm clock."

I can still feel the sheer sense of exhilaration, the beauty of the moment when, six hours after we worked free of the anchorage, just as dark was falling, we broke through into the fresh tradewinds. Suddenly the big nylon head sails stopped flapping and sagging, the mainsail stilled and bellied out into the perfect curved shape envisioned by the sailmaker. *Taleisin* seemed to lift her skirts and dance along the wave tops and my seasickness disappeared almost instantly as she steadied onto a fast beam reach. What were probably the most frustrating hours of our engine-free sailing life were behind us and almost forgotten as we headed due north, clocking off a steady six-and-a-half knots.

Head south until the butter melts, then turn west. That is the common strategy suggested for sailors cruising from the west coast of California towards Hawai'i. To get back to the mainland from Hawai'i? Head north until the butter firms up, then turn east. The most recent pilot charts appeared to confirm this. In the year before we'd met, Larry had made this passage twice as first mate on the *Double Eagle*, an 85-foot Bahamian schooner. His story of sailing on a fast beam reach, headed north along the Hawaiian side of the Pacific High-Pressure zone, had helped lure me into his life. Once the *Double Eagle* was well beyond the top of the high, they had a few days of light winds, then a fast broad reach towards the west coast of the US mainland. I was looking forward to a straightforward, relatively easy passage that would give me time to work on the outlines and sort photos for the seminars we'd agreed to present over the coming months.

In the days before we left port, I had kept an eye on the current North Pacific weather patterns by scouring the online weather sites at the local internet café and checking the forecasts posted on the port authorities bulletin boards. But once we were a hundred miles from land, beyond the range of local broadcasts, our weather information was limited to what we could pick up on our portable, battery-operated Grundig multiband shortwave radio receiver, the barometer and hygrometer plus our onboard observations. We opted to sail without two-way communications, due not only to cost, but because neither of us had the patience to fiddle with tuning radios nor keeping schedules. We carried the Grundig receiver for entertainment when we were near shore and more important, to obtain the time ticks necessary to ensure our chronometer was accurate for our celestial navigation when we headed offshore.[2] Several international radio stations provided this on an hourly basis. Only one, WWV, the station run by the US National Institute of Standards and Technology, provides a constant time update, a loud beep marking each second and an automated voice announcing the exact time once a minute, 24 hours a day. Another special WWV feature for those sailing in the North Pacific or North Atlantic was the hourly 45- or 90-second weather information broadcast at eight minutes before the hour or eight minutes after the hour.[3] In that short time span a recorded message listed any gale or storm warnings, the location and diameter of any low. Most important for us on this voyage, they also listed the location of the center of the Pacific High.

When we left Hilo, the center of the high was just where our pilot charts indicated it normally lay in late June, halfway between us and the mainland and about 500 miles to the north of Hilo. But each day, as we worked to gain our northing, the high seemed to be rushing to stay north of us. By our tenth day at sea, the WWV forecasts stated the center of the high, instead of being at the same latitude as Central California, was almost at the latitude of Ketchikan, Alaska. Before I made lunch, Larry came in from taking a noon sight and set to work calculating our position on a plotting sheet. Then he sat down on the leeward settee and picked up a book. I took his place at the chart table and transferred the coordinates

2   Larry and I depended on celestial navigation for the total of our cruising life together.
3   This weather information broadcast was suspended in 2015 and replaced by atmospheric weather information (i.e. conditions such as sunspot activity, which can affect radio broadcasts.)

from the plotting sheet onto our passage chart where I kept track of our noon to noon runs and also the position of the Pacific high-pressure system.

As I saw the results I grumbled, "How are we supposed to go over the top of this damned high? I'm sure as hell not ready to sail into the Gulf of Alaska just to get to Victoria, not with the two storms WWV is reporting."

Larry abandoned the book he was engrossed in. "Come here and sit down," he said as he moved over to make room for me on the settee. Then he put his arm around me and added, "Of course it makes no sense to sail too far north. Let's keep reaching north for two or three days more. And if nothing changes, we'll try going under the high. Probably means we'll have to do some tacking, but it will keep us below the track of those storms."

Each day since we left Hawai'i, I had been recording the barometric pressure reading alongside our noon position. Each day it had risen as we headed almost due north, windvane steering, taffrail log spinning off five or six knots, and still it continued to rise. Three days after our discussion, on our thirteenth day of working northward, we were almost at the same latitude as the Columbia River, between Oregon and Washington State. Still the barometer reading had refused to drop. In fact, at 1035 mb, it was the highest I had ever seen it. The midday report from WWV stated the pressure was even a bit higher to the north of us. As agreed, we tacked and put *Taleisin* hard on the wind on a course towards the mainland in an attempt to sail under the high. Over the next days, *Taleisin*'s bowsprit pointed fifteen or twenty degrees below our rhumbline course no matter which tack we chose. The skies became grayer and grayer and so did the mood on board.

I usually treasured the time we spent at sea, far from the distractions of shore life. Once we have settled into our sea-going routine, there is plenty of time left over to become immersed in the conversations that helped Larry and me keep our lives on an even keel. These conversations ranged far and wide. During our first days at sea, we tended to replay the events that had filled the days in the port we had just left. But after a few days at sea, the conversations turned to our life in general; the writing plans I was considering, thoughts about a video Larry dreamed of creating, how our quite divergent backgrounds affected our political perceptions, our plans for our future, and how to resolve any problems we might see forming in our personal or increasingly public life.

For the first several days after we'd left Hilo, between sail changing, caring for the boat, and getting enough sleep, there seemed to be little time for these conversations. But even after we had settled into our sea-going routine, I noticed we were spending less time chatting than we usually did at sea, and more time hiding away in books. And then, unexpectedly, the morning after we tacked to sail under the high-pressure system, Larry completely disturbed my sense of equilibrium.

During all of our sailing life, our night watch routine rarely varied. Three hours on, three hours off, with me taking the first watch. This meant, nine hours after our watches started, Larry took the dawn watch. He usually let me continue sleeping as long as I liked which meant my morning sleep often stretched to five hours in the bunk. (Larry routinely took a mid-afternoon nap to ensure he got a full eight hours a day of sleep.) When Larry saw me beginning to rouse, he'd usually greet me with a perfectly brewed pot of tea and a small plate of cookies (my favorite is and always has been Pepperidge Farm soft-baked chocolate chip.) As I climbed out of the bunk, he would rewarm the pot of coffee he'd made from fresh ground beans at the start of his dawn watch, pour himself a cup full and join me on the settee. There, while I finished waking up, Larry often shared thoughts he had mulled over during his night watches.

This morning he'd said, "Lin, been thinking. With our Wooden Boat Festival commitments, we're not going to have much time to explore around the Gulf Islands before winter sets in. I know we are already planning to spend next summer sailing north to Desolation Sound. But there's so much good cruising beyond there, so many friends I want to catch up with. One season won't be near enough time." Then he dropped the bombshell. "I've been thinking, I'm tired of crossing oceans. Maybe it's time to stop and really explore around here, it would take a lifetime to see it all. Maybe we should put our place in New Zealand up for sale, then keep an eye out for a small piece of waterfront land we can afford in the Gulf Islands."

Larry didn't seem to notice my silence as I sat slowly sipping the tea he'd poured for me. Instead, he carried on reminiscing about the years he'd spent learning to sail then racing and playing in the waters surrounding Vancouver and Victoria. He began listing the friendships he was looking forward to rekindling, the places he wanted to revisit, the islands he'd never had a chance to explore.

As he rambled on, I felt a growing sense of unease. I made no comment, just listened quietly, waiting for a chance to change the subject. Fortunately, our ship's bell came to my rescue as it chimed five times.

"Time to take a sight," Larry said. When he returned below decks and finished working out his sextant reading, I was busy in the galley and our conversation was taken over by the practical matters of sailing. But his musing had loosened a torrent of conflicting emotions which slowly eroded the usual sense of serenity on board. Over the next several days, the skies became ever grayer, the sailing more frustrating as we could rarely lay directly towards our destination. Adding to the gray tone was my discomfort with Larry's idea.

Larry had never before spoken about settling in Canada. In fact, he had often expressed his dislike of the climate and short sailing season. Through the years we'd visited British Columbia to spend time with Larry's parents. Each visit ended in conflict. Only a few days after she first met me, Beryl, Larry's mother, had said, "If he hadn't become involved with you, he would have gotten over being a sailor, moved home, built a house close by me, and had children, like a normal son would." Over the intervening four decades, Beryl's attitude never seemed to waver. She seemed unable to be in my company without becoming angry, and Larry refused to visit if I wasn't welcome.

In direct contrast, Larry and I developed a truly pleasurable relationship with my parents, and they had joined us in various ports around the world and seemed to relish the excuse we gave them to travel to places they might not otherwise have gone. Larry's mother had expressed her jealousy when she learned of each of my parents' visits. And this had led to Larry and me trying yet again to forge some kind of bond with her and Frank, his father. Each attempt ended in disaster. And each time it led to sleepless nights while we mulled over what we could do to improve the situation and build some kind of workable relationship. The breaking point came a few years before our voyage towards Cape Horn. Frank had been hospitalized several years previously, after a massive stroke left him 90 percent paralyzed and unable to speak, though he did seem to be aware of the people around him. As requested, his father's doctor contacted Larry to inform him his father had only a few weeks to live. So once again, Larry flew to Canada to be with him once more while I stayed in a cottage we had rented for the winter in southern England. While Larry was at the hospital with his father, his mother had called me to firmly state, "'I've told Larry he has given you enough of his life, now it is time for him to divorce you and stay here to take care of me.' I couldn't believe she was serious, but on his return, a few days after his father passed on, Larry assured me she truly was. For three years after that Larry had refused to communicate with his mother and I had finally given up encouraging him to mend the situation.

A few days after we arrived in Hilo, when Beryl learned we were sailing towards Canada, she had contacted Larry to say, "My doctor says it is bad for my health to keep hating Lin. So please come and see me as soon as you two sail in. I promise we can all be family like we should be." I began to worry because now, Larry kept mentioning his desire to rekindle the close connection he remembered from the time before he left home to go sailing. I suspected Beryl was just being manipulative. I really worried Larry would once again be hurt if we spent time with his mother at her island home just north of Victoria.

It wasn't just the conflict with his mother that concerned me. There was the weather, with harsh snow-filled winters and month-long spells of gray drizzly days, plus the social conservatism of British Columbia which were in direct contrast to my Southern California upbringing.

Besides, we already had a home base, the cottage and miniature boat yard we'd stumbled upon when we voyaged to New Zealand for the first time. Like many people of our generation, we had been influenced by Henry David Thoreau's book, *Walden; or, Life in the Woods*. We'd often quoted Thoreau to explain our wandering ways; "Let not to get a living be thy trade, but thy sport. Enjoy the land but own it not." And to us, *Taleisin*, our own private turtle shell, truly suited our interpretation of Thoreau's philosophy. Thus, we had not been looking for a home, or a shoreside base, just a calm anchorage when, 20 years into our wandering life, we sailed out of a westerly gale and anchored in North Cove on Kawau Island, 100 miles south of New Zealand's Bay of Islands. We had already decided to rent a place on shore for the winter months near Auckland, about 30 miles south of Kawau, so we could finalize Larry's boatbuilding book. The project included creating over a hundred diagrams and setting up a dark room to reproduce clear copies of several hundred photographs.[4]

A few weeks after visiting North Cove, we happened to be with Robin Harris, a local boatbuilder and sailor who anchored near us. Larry surprised me by telling him, "I'd love to find a little place in North Cove where I could do some boatbuilding when we get too old to keep cruising."

Robin answered, "Not many Kiwis want waterfront places on hard-to-reach islands. Prices on Kawau are really low. I've heard there was a bach (Kiwi word for casual summer cottages) going for $25,000 ($12,500 US) in North Cove. I'm thinking of looking at it myself."

Less than two weeks later we learned Robin was right. Prices were rock bottom, not just for the property Robin had mentioned, but for several more in the same cove. Within a week of visiting the island with the local real-estate agent, we had broken Thoreau's cardinal rule. Instead of one of the $25,000 properties that Robin had mentioned, we'd bought what the agent called "the ultimate fixer upper," a very run-down boatshed, a dilapidated jetty and a roughly built one-bedroom cottage on a very steep, two-acre tree-

---

4   In pre-internet days, publishers required physical copies of photographs and diagrams.

covered plot with absolutely no flat land. The attraction: It would provide us our own place to keep our boat in one of the most protected anchorages in New Zealand and the property came complete with a business license for a boat repair facility. The house had stood abandoned for eight years on an island with no roads, no shops and only about 100 inhabitants spread thinly along three miles of coastline, five miles off the mainland. The jetty needed a complete rebuild and the foreshore was littered with the remains of seven steel barges. The owner was so eager to sell he lowered the price by 50 percent to meet what we had in the bank, the 40,000 US dollars we'd received when we sold Seraffyn[5].

"Lin, I know it's not the right timing," Larry told me. "We really don't need a home. But they aren't making any more waterfront property so we'll never have another chance like this. Besides, it seems a good idea to have a home base." He went on to describe how we could gather all of his boatbuilding tools in the same place: the ones he'd stored in my folks' garage just north of Los Angeles, and the big bandsaw and thickness planer we'd left with another boatbuilding friend in Corona, California. "On the other hand," Larry added, "we might not like owning a place like this. Could turn out to be a real handicap. But, even if we decide it is a bad decision, just cleaning up the place and fixing that jetty would mean we could sell it for a profit."

It was while we were making the final decision that Doug Schmuck, a good friend from Southern California, flew to New Zealand to visit us. To this day, Doug and I laugh together whenever he recounts Larry taking him for a tour of the place. Doug had commented about some of the challenges facing us if we did buy it, the tangle of fallen trees that blocked the path between the cottage and the jetty, the pile of old beer bottles next to the boatshed, the mass of rusting junk filling the shed itself. Larry put one arm around Doug's shoulder, spread his other arm out as if to encompass the whole property and said, "Yes, but just look at all the potential."

Right from the beginning, I was very much in tune with the whole idea, only feigning a show of reluctance at times to ensure we thought through all the potential work that lay ahead of us. And work there was. We'd spent much of the next five years, working five hours a day on money-earning projects, writing, repairing and refinishing classic boats, and the rest of the day working alongside each other renovating the property. As the old barges were impossible to move, we got permission to build a seawall to hide them and protect the foreshore against future storm erosion. To build that 750-foot-long, six-foot-high wall, I mixed 20 tons of cement one

---

5   The equivalent, adjusted for inflation to 2024, is about US$137,000.

(Top) When you look at this foreshore shot, you can see why the real estate agent called this property "the ultimate fixer-upper."

Larry used anchors and a chain come-along to straighten each of the pilings on the 250-foot-long jetty walkway.

(Top left) Holes for each of the pilings for the eventual 780 feet of seawall had to be dug out by hand. (Right) By the time the seawalls were finished, I had mixed 20 tons of cement in this wheelbarrow.

(Bottom) Sorceress, a Giles 47-foot cutter, was one of our favorite customers.

wheelbarrow load at a time while Larry dug 180 holes using a handheld boring tool to cut into the clay foreshore for each piling. The holes had to be five feet deep, so he only could dig five or six between each tide. Then came the boards he nailed up, one at a time to complete the wall. In total Larry moved 95 tons of timber, piece by piece. The work was physically hard and I was truly grateful we could only work on it for five or six hours at a time while the tide was out. The reward: We ended up with a substantial area of flat usable land next to the 12-by-33-foot boatshed.

This shed, which was a licensed boat repair shop, was one of the big attractions when we decided to become landowners. Friends who brought their boat in for a few repairs gave us this sign as a joke.

One of the better decisions we made was to avoid personalizing the cottage, and only make it livable and tidy so we felt comfortable using it. "When or if we decide to stop cruising and make this our home, we can rebuild it, but not now," I'd suggested. Larry had agreed wholeheartedly. "That way we won't worry if we decide to rent it out."

We didn't give up sailing to do this work. In fact we seemed to find even more pleasure than ever with *Taleisin*, breaking up the work by sailing off to Australia for six months, or taking month-long cruises amidst the local islands, or sailing to the city for four or five days at a time to take part in two-handed and classic boat racing, shop for building materials and groceries, then spend time with the ever growing group of Kiwi sailing friends we were meeting.

I think both of us became restless at almost the same time. Fortunately, this coincided with us having been in New Zealand just long enough to take out citizenship.[6] Another bit of good fortune. Soon after he visited us, our friend Doug Schmuck had sailed his own 28-foot cutter from Newport Beach to New Zealand and bought the cottage just 300 yards across the cove from us. He agreed to act as the rental agent for our cottage. We gathered all the charts for a voyage south of Australia and on to South Africa and locked the boatshed. Then we set sail, headed south towards the Marlborough Sounds and on towards Tasmania.

It was ten years before we settled into that cottage again. That was when we flew from Puerto Montt to edit the video project that we had now named *Storm Tactics*. Though the whole property looked shabby and neglected, though the iron roofs on both the house and the boatshed needed replacing, the property had withstood the rigors of being rented out for all those years. The rent money had covered the costs of insurance, property taxes (rates) and the few repairs that had been needed.

"Personalizing and upgrading the place will be a good project for us when we grow tired of cruising," Larry had said when we left to fly back to where *Taleisin* lay waiting in Puerto Montt. Despite the hard work I knew we were in for when it came time to "fix the place up," I was in complete agreement, especially as I could see no end to the cruising destinations we'd yet to explore.

But now, for the first time in our relationship, as we continued trying to beat under the Pacific High, the plans we dreamed of for our future didn't seem to meld. The discussions we had didn't come any closer to resolving the differences and often ended with one or the other of us retreating into a book. And gradually I came to realize, my biggest concern had nothing to do with Larry's mother or where we might live one day — it was Larry's intimation that he was tired of cruising.

"I am almost 65, been crossing oceans for more than 40 years now," he stated more than once during our discussions.

"I don't think this has anything to do with age," I'd said each time. "I think we are both tired of being at sea — all this passagemaking is getting a bit long in the tooth. We were at sea for more than half of last year getting from Virginia down to Cape Horn. And now we've spent most of the past

---

6   By obtaining citizenship we guaranteed our right to return to New Zealand at any time. We both retained our dual citizenships: Larry as a Canadian, me as a citizen of the USA.

three months at sea. That's a lot of time to spend offshore."

Larry's reply was always non-committal, usually something along the lines of "You might be right." Then he'd change the subject.

After six days of adverse winds, just when my mood couldn't have been lower, the afternoon report from WWV spoke of gale force westerly winds, driven by two separate deepening lows, 400 miles to the north of us. Strangely, instead of adding to the gloom on board, the need to get out on deck before it turned completely dark and prepare for the worsening weather seemed to break the spell that had been cast over us. As *Taleisin* heeled to the freshening wind, I used the downhaul to lower the working jib. Larry tied a safety line around his waist and worked his way out to the end of the bowsprit to remove the jib. As he undid each hank, I pulled the jib back along the foredeck onto the side deck. Larry clambered inboard from the bowsprit to help me store the jib away. When I stepped back into the cockpit, I happened to look down at the compass. "We've been lifted," I yelled. "We can ease the sheets and still lay our course." For the first time since we'd left Hilo 14 days previously, our bowsprit was headed directly towards our destination, and we were moving fast on a beam reach.

With the boat settled and moving across the growing seas at a satisfying clip, with the windvane steering, I went below and heated water and then, as soon as Larry came into the cabin, I handed him a steaming cup of hot buttered rum. The first words he said, words I faithfully recorded in our logbook along with our new course were, "You are probably right. Maybe I'm just ready for this voyage to be over."

———◆———

Twenty-four days out of Hilo, just at noon, I wrote in the logbook, "Cape Flattery abeam." The strong westerly winds that had given us 140 or 150 miles a day had been accompanied by gray clouds and lowering temperatures. Now we were wearing heavy sweaters even inside the cabin. I'd been concerned we'd have to heave to when we were nearing the coast as, for several days, Larry had not been able to get more than an occasional sun sight. But for the past two days he'd been spending every possible minute on deck watching for any thin spots in the cloud cover. His persistence had been rewarded. Larry had been able to catch occasional shots of the sun, enough to get a firm fix which showed *Taleisin* was now 100 miles from Cape Flattery. Our landfall was a good one and even better was the change of course we made soon after midnight to run down the Strait of Juan de Fuca towards Victoria. "We should see Mount Baker in the morning. I'm sure that volcano will be visible long before we get to Victoria," I commented as I climbed into the bunk.

When morning came, all I could see was fog. Larry had gone back into the cockpit after he shook me gently awake. I pulled on my foul weather jacket and went out to join him. Visibility was so limited the end of the bowsprit seemed to be poking into the mist. Our breeze had dropped off to a gentle eight or 10 knots. The seas were almost flat and for the first time in 25 days I could feel absolutely no ocean swell.

"Hear that?" Larry asked. I listened intently. At first all I heard was the gentle sound of *Taleisin* trickling through the water. Then I too heard it, the moaning cry of a foghorn calling clearly across the water.

"I know exactly where we are," Larry said. "I raced past that horn in heavy fog half a dozen times before I set off cruising. That's Race Rocks."

He put his arm around me and drew me close. "Let's not rush into any decisions, just enjoy cruising around here for the next year or two then decide what next. But I really do feel like I've come home."

Part Three
Assessing our Options

On board Taleisin

10

Another Kind of Cruising

2003 -2004 - British Columbia, Canada

I rush across the groomed gardens of the imposing Empress Hotel, clutching my shopping bag. I am almost out of breath by the time I reach the steps leading down to the marina. But still I rush onward. The docks are already crowded, my path blocked by people intent on inspecting every detail of the beautiful boats that have turned out for the Victoria Wooden Boat festival. When I finally reach the pontoon where *Taleisin* is secured, I realize I am too late.

For five weeks, from the day we sailed into British Columbia, Larry and I had devoted most of our waking hours to preparing for this moment. We'd found quiet bays where we could hide away and add a coat of fresh paint to *Taleisin*'s topsides and bulwarks, varnish her spars, hatches and cabin sides, refinish the interior of the bathtub, scrub the bilges. By the time we sculled into the marina in the heart of Victoria harbor the night before the festival was to open, she was ready for the Concours d'Elegance.

But I wasn't.

We hadn't been anywhere near a laundromat for the previous two weeks, and even Larry agreed none of my pants were clean enough to wear for the three-day event. I only had one shirt that didn't have paint or varnish on it. "No problem. Festival doesn't officially open until 11 am. Best department store in Victoria is just two blocks from the marina," Larry had said.

I liked the idea of treating myself to some new clothes and hoped Hudson's Bay Company would have a department for short women like me. I was already making a mental list of what I needed when Larry added,

Larry scraped and sanded the gray off the decks and all the bare teak in preparation for the wooden boat festivals. I sanded, then added a coat of varnish to all the exterior brightwork.

"It will only take you an hour. Besides, nothing much will start happening until later in the day." I couldn't think of any other solution. I had rushed off *Taleisin* without washing up the breakfast dishes or putting away the final bits of clutter from our morning ablutions. I figured I'd beat the crowds by being at the store the minute the doors opened, then come back in time to do the final bits of clean up before there was any chance of the Concours d 'Elegance judges arriving. I had been wrong on both counts. The store had been packed and it seemed the four judges had decided to start their work at the stroke of eleven. And, with more than 60 boats to judge, they had chosen to judge *Taleisin* first.

I spotted Larry standing on the foredeck watching for me. He must have sensed my concern as he immediately stepped off the boat and onto the pontoon when I arrived. "Like your new clothes," he said as he put his arm around me. Then he whispered, "Relax, I washed up the dishes and put them away." He must have seen my look of relief as he added, "And I stashed your stuff in the back of your clothes locker where no one would notice it. Judges didn't look in any of the lockers, but they sure made a fuss about the varnished bilges."

I paused for a few seconds to catch my breath and watched as the judges sat in the cockpit chatting quietly with each other while diligently making notes on their score sheets. "Is that John Guzzwell?" I whispered to Larry.

"Yep," he answered. "Blows my mind to think my hero is admiring my boat!"

Two days after I first met Larry, in the spring of 1965, he lent me his dog-eared paperback copy of *Trekka Round the World*.[1] "Read this," he had suggested. "Shows you what I plan to do."

I was immediately entranced by the book John had written. At the age of 22, while working as an apprentice to a boatbuilder, John rented a storeroom behind a fish and chip shop in the center of Victoria. Over the next two years he built a 21-foot-long yawl designed by Laurent Giles. Once completed, he bought a four-horsepower outboard motor and one-gallon fuel container. Then, John sailed *Trekka* right around the world and through some amazing adventures. He had completed his voyage while Larry was finishing high school. "I read about *Trekka* coming home, it was headline news in the local paper," Larry explained. "John told the reporter he set off with $500 in his pocket. When he sailed back into Victoria six years later, he still had $300 left. My first thought was: *That's for me!*"

Over the years, we had read about some of John's continuing adventures and seen photos of the beautiful 45-foot Laurent Giles cutter he'd built and sailed extensively with his wife and two sons. This was the first time we'd met in person. John is known as a soft-spoken and often shy person, but he and Larry formed an almost immediate bond over their mutual love of wooden boatbuilding. Every minute of the three-day festival seemed to be filled with showing old friends and festival visitors on board *Taleisin*. Yet, a half-dozen times a day, I spotted John and Larry sneaking away to a somewhat quiet spot to talk about boatbuilding, boat designs, or rigging details.

On the last day of the festival, when the judges' results were read out before a standing-room-only crowd, John was introduced by the festival organizers and asked to present various awards. I turned to see Larry's eyes fill with tears when John announced, "Best of Show goes to *Taleisin*, the most meticulously built boat I have ever seen."

The next morning, we left the marina to find a quiet anchorage where

---

1   *Trekka Round the World* was published in 1963, two years after John's return. It is out of print but still available on Kindle. One of the more amazing adventures recounted by John happened during a six-month pause in *Trekka*'s voyage when he joined Beryl and Miles Smeeton as they sailed their 47-foot yacht *Tsu Hang* from the Pacific to the Atlantic around Cape Horn. Their subsequent pitchpoling led to the greatest sailing adventure story I have ever read.

we could hide away and digest all the events of the past few days. As soon as we were anchored, Larry dug out the chart for Orcas Island. "John's going to be at the Port Townsend festival too. He suggested we sail over and anchor near his place when it's finished. He has two really interesting projects going on in his shed — wants my opinion on some rigging work he was doing."

The snow on the peak of Mount Baker glistened in the warm sunlight, and a light easterly breeze rippled the water as we approached Port Townsend three days after departing the Victoria Wooden Boat Festival, bound for the biggest festival of the season, less than a hundred miles to the south. Several dozen wooden classics were already at anchor in front of the town, waiting for their assigned time to move into the Port Townsend Wooden Boat Festival marina. Astern of us we could see several more heading towards the entrance to Point Hudson. Above the high seawalls protecting this historic man-made quarantine and clearance port, I could see the towering spars of boats that had already been secured inside the relatively small port. Several dozen people lined the breakwater. Many had settled in with binoculars and picnic baskets to watch the spectacle provided by 200 boats arriving to fill every inch of the port.

"I'll row in and find out if they are ready for us and where they want us to tie," I suggested to Larry. "You can have fun checking out those anchored boats while I'm gone."

We hove to and I used the main halyard to lift *Cheeky* off her chocks as Larry guided her clear of the lifelines and signaled for me to lower her into the water.

"Be sure to check the actual pontoon we'll be using," Larry suggested as I climbed into *Cheeky*. "It would be helpful to know how many cleats there are, where they are. You know the drill."

A half-hour later, Larry spotted me rowing clear of Point Hudson and tacked to sail closer. He eased out the mainsail till it luffed, then backed the staysail to slow *Taleisin* as he came alongside.

"They've given us a great spot, but there is a problem," I said as I climbed out of the dinghy. "Not only is it a downwind slip right in the center of the port, but even more of a problem — there is a big schooner already tied right ahead of where we'll be. It's got the most beautiful, varnished transom I have ever seen."

I knew that's all I needed to say — Larry and I were both picturing the tight squeeze: we had 30 feet of dock to tie to, but even if there were plenty of good cleats, stopping the boat with this tail wind would be problematic. The image of smashing *Taleisin*'s bowsprit through that transom was not something we liked imagining. Especially with so many people watching.

The festival harbor master had offered to send out two of the inflatable boats volunteers were using as tenders. The plan was to tie them alongside and use their engines to move us into position so our bowsprit didn't end up through the schooner's transom. I explained all this and watched as Larry glanced off into the distance, obviously mulling over our options. We had always avoided being towed. So that option was out.

A few minutes later, Larry shook his head and said, "I've got a better idea." Then, with a gleam in his eye, he added, "Do you want to do a bit of grandstanding?"

I couldn't resist the challenge. First, we sailed well clear of the boats that were waiting near the port entrance. Then we again hove to, and there we made preparations, getting out and securing the mooring lines and fenders, then preparing our stern anchor, which we jokingly called our emergency brake, plus the special gear we would now be using with it.

The boomkin[2] on *Taleisin* has twin stays leading down to chainplates which are just under her stern at the waterline. As we continued to lie hove to, Larry climbed into the dinghy and attached a snatch block to the shackle which secures the lower end of the starboard boomkin stay. I eased out the rode for the stern anchor, which we carry on a special roller at the end of the boomkin. Larry ran the line through the snatch block. We then lowered the anchor until it was about two feet below the water and out of sight. It would have taken a very keen observer to notice the anchor line leading from the cockpit seat locker, around the sheet winch, then along the inside of the boomkin and down to the anchor.

Larry climbed back on board and we had a short conference with a good deal of laughter. We exchanged looks — we were ready. I shrugged and said, finally , "If it all goes pear-shaped, we can round up quickly and you can drop the bow anchor. Then act nonchalant, like it's what we intended to do. There's just enough room for that."

The wind had increased slightly and was now blowing about 10 knots as we ran back towards the entrance to Point Hudson. The crowd of observers had increased substantially. I did one last tour of the deck to ensure all our mooring lines and fenders were secured and ready to use, the sail halyards ready to run free. Then, as we'd agreed, I took the helm.

---

2   The short spar projecting from the aft end of the deck to hold the lower end of the backstay.

As we sailed through the entrance — a mere 35 feet in width — Larry went forward, released the mainsail halyard, and pulled the sail down into the lazy-jacks. Now only the staysail caught the wind, but still *Taleisin* kept moving downwind at a speed that made me nervous. Only 300 feet of water remained between us and that schooner's transom. Then Larry wiggled his fingers in a prearranged signal. I eased off the staysail until it lost all its power and began steering in a series of zigzags to bleed off a bit more speed. A minute later Larry discreetly pointed his thumb down. I steered directly towards the designated pontoon, released the anchor rode and let it pay out slowly just until I could feel the anchor dragging along the bottom. Larry let go the staysail halyard and pulled the sail down. Fifty feet from the pontoon, I eased out a bit more anchor rode until I felt it grab the bottom, then continued letting the line pull through my fingers. Then, just as our bowsprit passed the tip of our pontoon, I snubbed and cleated the stern anchor rode, Larry picked up the amidships mooring line, ready and prepared to hand it to one of the dozen willing bystanders on the pontoon. All eight tons of *Taleisin* continued forward for a dozen feet more, then came to a gentle stop, bowsprit three feet clear of the schooner's transom as the anchor held firmly. I heard an audible sigh of relief from several of the people who had gathered to watch. Someone called out, "Nice landing. Had some of us worried but seems you've added an engine." I laughed but followed Larry's example: First, finish securing the mooring lines, with no further comment. Then, there was time to invite the man who'd made the comment, and the people around him, to take turns and come on board for a look around.

We couldn't have been in a better position for the festival. The biggest stage was on shore, just a few hundred feet ahead of us. All afternoon we watched as more than 200 beautifully maintained wooden craft, ranging from small rowing dories to classic launches, from brightly colored sailing dinghies to 85-foot schooners, were maneuvered into position. On shore a dozen food venders began setting up their trailers. An array of beautiful wooden kayaks and lovingly varnished trailer-able boats were wheeled into position on the grass verges of the marina, and the crowd of visitors kept expanding. At dusk, the festival officially opened and a parade of musicians took the stage: shanty singers, folk musicians, the local swing band. It was long after dark before the last musical act left the festival stage, the last revelers climbed on board their own boats, and the docks went quiet.

As we too settled in for the night, we were both suppressing giggles because not one person had figured out how we brought *Taleisin* to a stop. No one saw Larry climb into *Cheeky* to retrieve the anchor after dark; no one saw me as I stowed it back in its chock and coiled away the rode.

I tried to calm my head so I could fall asleep by once again considering our good fortune. We had chosen a boat that was more than just a vehicle we could use to wander off to distant places. It was more than our home. For us, *Taleisin* was also our hobby. She was our excuse to sail to interesting places where we could instantly make friends as we joined in festivals and gatherings of like-minded people. And, she was our toy, one we could take out for Saturday afternoon races or play games with and test our own skills as a sailing team, just as we had done that day.

The stern anchor we used to stop Taleisin is evident in this photo.

John Guzzwell was one of the other guest speakers at the festival in Port Townsend, and sailed in to a berth quite close to us on his most recent boat, *Endangered Species*, the varnished, cold-molded 30-foot racing sloop he had built on Orcas Island a few years previously. Once again, Larry and John seemed attracted to each other like magnets. I watched with amusement as they walked along drawing boats in the air, or answering questions posed by other show attendees who joined them in the cockpit of our boat or John's. I also noticed Larry's comments began to resemble those he'd made when we'd been voyaging for about eight years on *Seraffyn* and the dream of building another boat began to form. That was when we decided to sail back to California and build *Taleisin*. Now, Larry began dropping comments such as, "John has some friends who have some great yellow cedar that's been aging for years. They're looking to give it to someone who is building an interesting boat." Or, "John told me about a boat that's a write-off not far from Victoria. Owner's looking for someone to break it up. It's got a sizeable lead keel someone could melt down. Save us a lot of money if we decide to build a boat that's better suited to this area."

Slowly Larry appeared to be "stacking the deck" towards his idea of looking around for a home base here in the Salish Sea, somewhere with room for a boatbuilding shed.[3] Then, the day after the Port Townsend Wooden Boat Festival, we received a package of mail, forwarded to us from New Zealand. It contained distressing news, news that gave Larry more cause for his campaign.

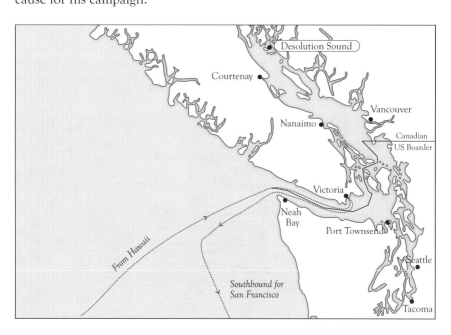

The waters from Tacoma to Desolation Sound are called the Salish Sea.

When we bought our property in New Zealand, we had not been blind to the physical problems that lowered its value to the point where we could

---

3   The Salish Sea is the inland sea that encompasses Puget Sound, the San Juan Islands and the waters off of Vancouver, British Columbia.

afford it. We also felt we had acted responsibly when we hired a respected lawyer to go over the legal aspects of the biggest purchase in our lives. The lawyer had pointed out a right-of-way we shared with 18 other property owners, one that led along the back boundary line of each property inshore of us, then crossed our property from the hill high above the boatshed and ended at the sea several feet away from the walkway leading onto our jetty. We couldn't envision the right-of-way being a problem as it led straight down a sheer 150-foot cliff and, due to being impassable, had never been used. But now, a notice had arrived from the High Court of New Zealand saying a suit had been brought against us and the local council. A would-be developer who owned several acres of land right at the far end of the right of way, and almost a mile from our island cottage, wanted to subdivide his property. Access to his land was extremely difficult. A recent change in the land laws of New Zealand had, he felt, opened a loophole, one he planned to use to force the council to create an alternate right-of-way which would actually cross within a few feet of our house, then carry on through our boatshed and on to our jetty. If he won, it would not only jeopardize our boat repair business permit, but mean our jetty could be available for him and 17 other neighbors at all hours of the day and night — *plus* it would be available for public usage too, even though it led directly onto private land. All this would no doubt be an expensive undertaking as the jetty would have to be upgraded, and a track and stairs built down the cliff face — and we would have to cover all the costs.

Larry had an immediate response. "That's insane. Let's put the darned place up for sale! I don't want to live in a country where we are forced to give up our privacy, our peace and quiet because of some dumb law change."

As upset as I was by this unwelcome news, I countered by saying, "The place won't be worth much if a lawsuit is hanging over it. Will be worth even less if the developer gets his way." There was only one way, that much was clear. I tried to hide my tears of frustration as I said, "We have to fight this."

We finished reading the court documents and called Hugh Gladwell. We had met many local sailors soon after we bought the property. We had common ground with them, as they owned and raced their classic wooden boats in the waters near our cove. Among them was Hugh, and a comfortable friendship developed quickly. Hugh was not only a sailor but also a solicitor who worked in the local village. His opinion was clear: "Yes, you will have to fight this." We discussed our options with Hugh, then he said. "And, yes, you will have to fly to New Zealand in May to appear in court," Hugh said. "Yes, I will have to hire a barrister to represent you." He briefed us on costs — "It will cost you a lot of money." But he was also ready to help in all ways, adding, "If that's a problem, I'll help out."

In Hugh's opinion, there was no legal basis for the suit. And, as one of only three local solicitors, he knew the developer had lost every previous case he'd brought to court. Hugh tried to put our minds more at ease by adding, "When you win, you'll get most of your legal expenses paid back, so just leave it with me. Try to forget about it for a few months and get on with life. Meanwhile, how's the sailing?"

Though we couldn't completely get this legal threat out of our minds, it was soon pushed from the forefront by two far more enjoyable prospects. Before us were dozens of islands and anchorages to explore, all within a few hours of sailing of each other. We had two months before winter set in. From November onwards, our calendar was filled to the brim with a seminar and boat show tour along a route that would let us visit friends and family we hadn't seen in several years. I knew the autumn weather in this part of the world could be quite changeable, meaning we'd have days when we'd be weatherbound. But that was perfect as it would provide the time we needed to prepare for the seminars we'd be presenting.

The Salish Sea is maze of more than 400 islands, some uninhabited, some set aside as parkland, others known for their art communities. Each has rocky shorelines where oysters and mussels are waiting to be harvested. Anchorages abound, many with docks and landings built just for transiting yachts. The waters around them are home to pods of orca and dolphin. The passing parade of commercial traffic, from ferries to tugs pulling huge log booms, adds interest to each sailing day.

When I look back over all the places I've cruised, the favorites that stand out have one thing in common — from Mexico's Baja California to Finland's and Sweden's island-studded Baltic coastlines, to New Zealand's Bay of Islands and Hauraki Gulf. They are places filled with a variety of islands and anchorages where we could meander for days without the thought of crossing an ocean. Each was sparsely populated but had interesting villages scattered along the shores, villages filled with history and stories, where we could restock, have a meal ashore, and easily meet interesting local people. By the time winter set in, the Salish Sea was worming its way onto the list.

Within a few days of departing from the festival at Port Townsend, we sailed over to Orcas Island to spend time with John Guzzwell and his wife, Maureen, at his boat shop and home there. The growing friendship between the two men deepened, and also led to Larry agreeing to join John for the

John Guzzwell, Larry's boyhood hero, celebrated his 70th birthday soon after the start of the Van Isle 360. All three of Endangered Species *crew were boatbuilders.*

next summer's Van Isle 360, an adventurous two-week race that took its competitors around Vancouver Island. Our visit with John and Maureen was the start of two months of meandering from one interesting anchorage to another. Along the way we made new friends and found several new fishing spots.

Neither Larry nor I are very keen fishermen. Me, because the idea of touching a slimy, squirming, fish makes me squeamish, Larry because he hated killing anything. And neither of us liked the mess that results from bringing a fish on board. On long passages, we often dragged a "meat hook" and when, infrequently, we snagged a fish and Larry successfully brought it on board, I'd hide below decks while he killed, filleted, then washed the bloody remains off the deck. I was much better with crabs — which I discovered on a much earlier visit to British Columbia, aboard *Seraffyn*, when I acquired a crab trap. I quickly realized I loved catching crabs and Larry was very willing to eat them (once I had cooked and picked the meat out for him).

Thus, within a day of arriving in Victoria on *Taleisin*, for the wooden boat festival there, I'd bought a folding crab trap which I stored on the cabin top, under the upturned dinghy. As we meandered slowly north through the Canadian Gulf Islands and later the US San Juan Islands, I had again found I was able to satisfy my appetite (and Larry's) for this delicacy. In a quiet anchorage at the north end of Shaw Island, I met a fisherman who suggested a new way to use my trap — and also indicated the best spot to do so. I convinced Larry we should sail right past several promising anchorages and on to Plumper Cove just north of Vancouver so I could try my luck catching prawns.

It was late in the day when we actually began reaching across Howe Sound towards Keats Island and I began preparing my gear. "That fisherman told me to tie the opening almost shut so crabs can't get into it," I explained as I unfolded the trap, laced the netting together, added the 300 feet of ¼-inch cord I'd purchased to act as a hauling line, and attached one of our boat fenders to act as a buoy. "He said to use canned sardines as bait, then set the trap in 250 feet of water when the tide is going out." Larry's skepticism was clear as he obligingly headed *Taleisin* into the wind about three quarters of a mile outside the cove. As soon as we slowed to a stop, I lowered the trap overboard, being very careful to avoid scratching the topside paint. "Only want it down for two hours," I said as we headed towards the anchorage just inside the cove. "We can sail back then and pick it up."

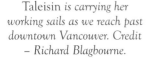

Taleisin *is carrying her working sails as we reach past downtown Vancouver. Credit – Richard Blagbourne.*

"Hell no," Larry said. "No way you can haul that trap on board without making a mess of the topsides. This is your crazy idea, not mine. When we get anchored, we'll launch *Cheeky* and you can row out and get it." He must have noticed I was miffed because he added, cheekily, "You'll enjoy the exercise."

He was right. Two hours later, as the afternoon was drawing to a close, I was humming happily as I fell into the rhythm of rowing. A feeling of peace and control came over me. I approached the fender I'd used to mark my trap.

The minute I had pulled the slack out of the trap line, my humming came to an abrupt stop. There was no tugging it further. *Must be stuck on a sunken log*, I thought. I put a bight of line right around my hand and tried again. This time I was able to pull in about two feet of line. I struggled to shrug off my sweater without letting any line slip back out, then used the sweater to protect my hands and kept pulling. Inch by inch, foot by foot, the trap edged closer to me. I had no watch but could tell I'd been working for more than an hour by the angle of the sun. It edged ever closer to the horizon as I continued pulling that line in. The growing pile of line in the bottom of the dinghy showed I'd made progress, but how much was hard to tell. As the time dragged on, I began to sweat despite the cold that crept in as the day drew to a close. My hands and shoulders began to ache. I felt like quitting and abandoning the trap rather than risk getting lost when it became dark. Then I looked towards where *Taleisin* lay, just visible behind a point of one of the tiny islands protecting Plumper Cove and saw Larry had put up the anchor light. "No excuse now," I said out loud, "Larry thinks this was a crazy idea, but when he's eating these prawns, he'll change his mind."

A short while later I felt the trap thud against the bottom of the dinghy. I quickly secured the line around one of the cleats we use when *Cheeky* has her sailing rig in place. I carefully maneuvered myself onto the aft seat of the dinghy. I looked over the transom and gasped.

There wasn't one prawn in the trap. Instead, it bulged with Dungeness crabs. Several dozen had ripped open the netting around the trap entrance to work their way inside. There wasn't room for even one more. A dozen extra crabs clung to the outside of the trap like hitchhikers. Some of the crabs were more than ten inches across. I used an oar to push the hangers-on off the trap, hoping that would lighten it a bit. But even with the hitchhikers gone, it was impossible for me to lift that trap on board. I took the only option I could see. I shoved the coils of trap line out of my way, put my feet against the rowing chocks on the floor of the dinghy and began pulling for shore.

The weight and drag of the trap full of crabs turned the rowing that had been a pleasure on the way out into near torture on the way back in. "I was getting ready to lift the anchor and sail out to see what was wrong," Larry called out as I slowly approached *Taleisin* in the growing dark. "Then I saw you start to row in and figured everything was all right. But that was a long time ago."

Only when I was a few feet from the boat did his flashlight reveal the reason I was making such slow progress. Then his laughter rang out across the still water. "Why didn't you let the crabs go?" he asked.

"Couldn't. Opening was on the far side of the trap. I'd have capsized the dinghy if I tried."

"So why didn't you just abandon it all?" he asked. Then he handed me the end of the main halyard and, once I'd secured it, hoisted the trap clear of the water and maneuvered it safely away from the paintwork and onto the deck.

I was too exhausted to answer as I carefully unlaced the trap opening and began sorting the crabs to select the ten largest ones as I whittled down my catch to the legal limit.

Larry went below and came back a few minutes later to hand me a glass of wine. Then he sat quietly on the cabin top as I took a sip of my wine before returning to my chore. I was putting the last of the keepers in a big bucket when he said, "Lin, you are the most determined person I have ever met."

Later that night I lay awake considering my blistered hands and aching shoulders, along with my underlying desire to enjoy just one more season in these attractive waters then sail away — because I wanted to cross another ocean.

Was I determined, or was I just plain stubborn?

11
Looking Back

2004 - Northern reaches of the Salish Sea, British Columbia

"A few spartan souls have been known to cross oceans in boats as small as 30 feet."

"What a stupid statement," I said out loud. From where I sat on the covered verandah of the Balboa Yacht Club at the entrance to the Panama Canal, I could see the whole cruising fleet. Half of the boats were under 30 feet in length. Most had already been sailed long distances to reach here, and their owners planned to continue onward.[1]

The year was 1971. Larry and I had been having a grand cruising adventure on *Seraffyn* for two-and-a-half years. On this day, we had come ashore to confirm our canal transit details and been stopped by a sudden tropical deluge as we prepared to head back to the boat. To pass the time, I'd picked up a copy of *Boating* magazine left behind by a previous cruiser. I turned to the article called "The Perfect Cruising Boat" and scoffed as the author extolled the virtues of his new 57-foot boat and implied others would be crazy to dream of crossing oceans on anything smaller.[2]

Larry laughed at my angry outburst and said, "So, write a letter to the editor."

I did.

Three weeks later, just after the canal pilot arrived to guide us into the first gigantic lock so we could begin our transit towards the Caribbean, the

---

1   In total, 31 yachts transited the canal in 1971. Seventeen were in the anchorage on the day I read this quote.
2   Several years later I met the author, Arthur Beiser, and thanked him for kickstarting a career and a passion.

yacht club tender pulled alongside. I immediately opened the telegram I was handed. The few simple words it contained changed my life.

Prove it. Monk Farnham, editor, Boating Magazine.

Before we set off cruising, I had never written anything other than literature class assignments — and those, only under duress. I did come to enjoy writing letters to family and friends as we meandered southward, sometimes filling two or three pages with descriptions of our encounters. But I was unprepared for Larry's reaction to that telegram. "Lin, I think you need something extra in your life. Something to keep that over-active brain of yours occupied," he said. "How about taking up his challenge. I'll help if I can."

I don't think either of us considered the possible financial benefit of taking up that challenge. Instead, we talked about how discouraging that article might be for people who, like us, could never dream of owning a 50-foot sailboat. And Larry was right, I did enjoy the challenge. It gave me a chance to use the skills I'd learned from being on the high school debate team. Almost immediately I began compiling notes for what I came to call "my rebuttal." Then, as we meandered through the San Blas Islands on the north side of Panama, and across the Caribbean towards Jamaica, I realized I was having fun gathering more 'evidence' from the scattering of cruisers we met along the way and filling the quiet hours of night watches noting down ideas for my rebuttal. Just a few months later, I received a payment from Boating Magazine Inc. that equaled almost two-and-a-half months' cruising funds, accompanied by an enthusiastic letter suggesting I call Monk Farnham, the editor, collect. "My readers will love what you've written. They'll want more," I was told. "I had the accountants give you a hundred dollars extra so you can buy a decent camera."

I put my good fortune down to timing and luck. The luck? Having a very photogenic boat, one that was of a size many sailors could dream of owning. Just as important, having the backup of someone like Larry who reminded me to include the technical details to help readers feel they were learning something from each story I wrote. And the timing? I was just 26 years old, and Larry was 31, which made us the only people under the age of 50 who were, at that time, writing about offshore cruising. Added to that was the recent but steadily increasing availability of fiberglass sailboats, bringing the cost of seaworthy boats into the range of many more sailors.

Within a year my writing was providing a quarter of our cruising costs. Then, one day I was speaking to an editor and mentioned an upgrade Larry did to our boat. The editor said, "Get Larry to write about that. Tell him I need just a few hundred words and a simple diagram." Larry soon started creating how-to articles. Four years later, after we'd sailed across the Atlantic and around the Baltic, then on to the Med, a New York publisher who loved sailing and had been following our adventures in *Boating Magazine* suggested we combine our articles, add a few more to create a book, which he titled *Cruising in Seraffyn*. It was an immediate hit among those who already had sailboats, as well as armchair sailors. Our book editor urged us to set to work as soon as possible and write a sequel.

The writing enhanced our lives, filling days when we were weather bound, giving us an excuse to settle into a secluded bay or particularly interesting village for several weeks at a time to finish a few more articles, and adding a further reason to meander through boat yards looking for interesting solutions people found to make their boats easier or more enjoyable to use. We'd then take some photos and write another article which could eventually be incorporated into a book. The gradually increasing financial gain meant we could be far more selective of the delivery jobs, the boat renovations, and rigging work we took on. And now that we didn't have to plan a route based on being in places popular with other cruising sailors, where we could find jobs to top up the kitty, we were free to explore more out-of-the-way places.

The year after we arrived in the Cheasapeake Bay, Wayne and Norma Tillett, Seraffyn's third owners, sailed her from Beaufort, South Carolina to cruise in company with us. The editors of Sail Magazine hired Starke Jett V, a well-known Reedville, Virginia photographer to capture photos of Taleisin and Seraffyn during that delightful summer.

Looking back from this age of YouTube sailing channels and on-line sailing bloggers where "followers" expect almost daily interaction and immediate access to creators, I realize how fortunate we were. We could clearly separate our cruising life and our writing life. No one expected to know what we were doing on each day, no one expected to have another story each week. In fact, we only needed to write seven or eight articles over the course of a year to supplement our income. These could be about experiences we'd had months, sometimes even years, previously. This allowed us to savor and distill each adventure before trying to capture it in writing. Furthermore, in direct contrast to the experience of those who create YouTube channels or blogsites today, the growing popularity of our writing had little effect on our day-to-day life. The magazines we wrote for were far away from where we were cruising. We tended to voyage away from popular routes and rarely visited larger ports where we were likely to meet folks who had access to our stories. The only contact we had with our writing world was through bi-monthly letters or phone calls with our editor or publisher. Only occasionally was there a letter to the editor which required a reply. Thus, it was almost five years after I wrote my first article that we realized we and *Seraffyn* were gaining what might be called a "following." And that happened far off the beaten path when we had a strange encounter that woke us up to our new reality.

We had sailed out of the South China sea into the main port in the Sultanate of Brunei, only a short distance from the capital, Bandar Seri Begawan. Brunei was still seven years short of becoming an independent country. Its police and military affairs were still being run by the British. There were no other yachts in sight, and only a few rough-looking local boats lay at anchor. We could see a freighter secured at the large commercial wharf at the far end of the port area. But we spotted a smaller unused-looking landing near a shed marked *Police*. Across an empty parking lot we could see the entrance to a British military base. We decided to come alongside to find out how to get inbound clearance. And as soon as we had secured our lines a policeman, sweating in an immaculate British-style uniform, marched over and politely asked for our boat's name. He then escorted us to his car and drove us into the capital. Two hours later we had been issued a visa after being served a tasty plate of pastries and very sweet milky tea. When we returned to the landing, we were slightly shocked to see only the top of *Seraffyn*'s mast showing above the landing. The tide had fallen almost 15 feet and was still ebbing.

A British military officer was standing on the landing, staring intently down at our boat. Larry stopped alongside him, looked down at *Seraffyn* to ensure everything was okay. then asked, "What are you looking at?"

The officer turned and stated, "I hear this boat is an exact replica of the *Seraffyn*."

Larry replied, "You must be putting me on. This *is* the *Seraffyn*."

The officer looked directly at him for a moment then, in a dismissive voice replied, "You are putting me on," as he turned on his heel and marched away.

We never saw him again.

But within a day we'd been befriended by several other people who worked on the British military base. They explained they had recognized *Seraffyn* because the base library had a subscription to *Practical Boat Owner*, a British publication which bought stories from us. The interesting excursions and dinner gatherings we were invited to by these new friends were an introduction to an unexpected bonus provided by our writing career.

As we sailed on to Canada and then south California to complete an 11-year-long circumnavigation on board *Seraffyn,* we were asked to be speakers at yacht clubs along the way. And, over the next few years while we built *Taleisin,* we wrote four more books, which made us more recognizable in the cruising world. To add to our income so we could set off cruising as soon as the boat was launched, we began giving seminars at various boat shows and meeting people who followed the stories we wrote. They showered us with both compliments and questions. I probably was on the verge of getting a swelled head, feeling ever more like a celebrity. Then one day, when we were walking into a seminar room at a boat show, a stranger rushed up and said, "I'm a big fan of yours."

Larry didn't pause before saying, "No, you're a friend we haven't met yet."

Later that evening, after a very busy day full of seminars and chatting with boat show attendees, I thanked Larry for his clever response. "Well, that is how I think of every one of them," he said. Then Larry highlighted the responsibility that went along with the role we'd taken on in life by adding, "Lin, we have to be very careful about the way we answer the questions these folks ask us. Remember, they really listen to what we say. The wrong words from us could ruin their dreams."

And it was true. Now there was a new responsibility. Along with it came infrequent but sometimes harsh criticism when readers disagreed with something we wrote, or a magazine editor wanted us to be less candid about the flaws in products promoted by their advertisers. There were occasional disadvantages. But I truly loved the writing I was doing. Larry, on the other hand, began to find writing was becoming a chore. He still was willing to edit what I had written and still added excellent ideas for me to incorporate. He was still an enthusiastic participant as, every third or fourth year we interrupted our cruising to return to the US, where we presented seminars and sold our books at boat shows and yacht clubs around the country. But, after completing his 520-page boatbuilding book, a project that took almost four years, he became more reluctant to write. "Don't worry about the finances," he said. "When our cruising kitty gets low, I'll look for some boat repair work."

I wasn't concerned about how this affected our finances; we were still living simply and spending less than we earned. But by the late 1980s, eighteen years after I wrote my first article, I was finding Larry far less interested in joining me to gather photographs, less inclined to meander around marinas and anchorages and meet other sailors to gather new ideas to write about. But my interest and pleasure in writing never seemed to ebb and I began to worry about how to overcome the conflict this might cause in our relationship. Then, luck, good timing and changing technology presented a new endeavor.

———— • ————

In late 1989, we set sail to explore the Marlborough Sounds between the North and South Islands of New Zealand, then headed onwards towards Australia, where Larry had contracted to restore the interior of a 115-year-old cutter called *Kelpie*. The job came complete with a free marina berth and, as a bonus, an office where I could write quietly between applying five coats of varnish on *Kelpie*'s new interior woodwork. Five months later, our finished handiwork became one of the centerpieces of the first Sydney Wooden Boat Festival. Just as we had at other festivals, we presented two evening slide shows about our voyaging. "I think your show would make a great video," said an eager young sailor named Roy Blow. He was also a professional video producer. "All I'd need to do is video you presenting your slide show tomorrow, then get inside *Taleisin* next week and take lots of interesting shots to add to your photos."

Larry's immediate reaction: "Not doing that again." We had had a television crew film inside our boat for a human-interest story on the TV New Zealand Evening News during the previous year, and Larry had failed to see the advantage of doing it again. "I spent the whole time trying to protect the varnish work from their cameras."

The next morning, even before the festival opened, Roy was standing on the dock next to *Taleisin*. He handed me a box of pastries. Minutes later he was sitting in the cockpit showing us the magic of the first Hi8 video camera. "This little devil records TV quality video and sound," he explained as Larry fondled the camera, which was about the same size as two thick paperback books. And so, even if we weren't interested in Roy's idea of recording our slide show, we found ourselves agreeing to spend the next two weeks learning about how to create a video and scripting out a program Roy could record as we sailed around the Pittwater, just half a day's sail north of Sydney.

A few weeks later, when we set sail south towards Hobart and eventually westward across the Australian bight, we were proud owners of two Hi8 video camcorders and a list of sailing shots Roy hoped we'd record for another program he felt viewers would enjoy. "As soon as you get to western Australia, call me," Roy said. "I'll arrange to fly over and shoot another program."

Larry glowed with enthusiasm as he learned to use the video camera. He reminded me of how, just a few weeks after he first set off to find a cruising boat, he had signed on as first mate on an 85-foot schooner, the *Double Eagle,* for a voyage from Newport Beach, California, towards Hawai'i. The schooner was under charter to a TV company. For the next several months, Larry watched and occasionally worked as an extra as the film crew and actors gathered the sailing footage they needed for a TV series called *The Wackiest Ship in the Army.* "Never wanted to be an actor, but, after watching them, I always thought being a filmmaker would be great fun," he said as he wrote down yet another idea for a video shot Roy might like.

We'd helped create two more videos with Roy while we were in Fremantle.[3] When we voyaged across the Indian Ocean, and continued eastward towards the Atlantic, the travel cost and time involvement made it difficult for him to work with us. But Larry didn't lose his enthusiasm for video storytelling, and he considered how he'd one day make a video to help people understand how we weathered storms at sea in a relatively small boat. All this came into play when, six years later, after we rounded Cape Horn, Larry declared, "Heaving to definitely got us through those storms without any damage. That makes me even more determined to make a video program explaining what we've learned." I agreed but started mentally calculating the equipment we'd need, the contacts who might help us with it. Larry was clear-minded. "Let's forget the expense," he said. "Let's put our own video together."

Thus, we'd spent the winter after our Cape Horn rounding (and the majority of our savings) in New Zealand, learning just how complicated,

---

3   These three videos were eventually re-edited into two called — *Get Ready to Cruise* and *Get Ready to Cross Oceans.* They are available, along with our other three videos through https::://thesailingchannel.tv

time-consuming and costly it is to edit and produce an 81-minute video. We were lucky to know Chris Gurr, a keen sailor and a well-respected TV editor who reduced his rates substantially for us. We had further good fortune when the Auckland production house that was owned by one of the men who supported New Zealand's America's cup team also reduced their rates. In 2003, we sat down with Chris and learned just how hard it is to produce any video, especially one shot by amateurs like us. For his professional editing jobs, Chris told us, he allowed one hour of editing for every minute of finished program. Unfortunately, our inexperience meant it took him double that time. Our *Storm Tactics* video, finished just before we set sail from Puerto Montt towards Canada five months previously, had been very well received at its sneak preview showing during the Port Townsend Wooden Boat Festival. And now, as autumn was ebbing towards winter and the wooden boat festivals were behind us, we meandered through the islands between Vancouver and Victoria, both of us excited about our upcoming seminar tour because we would be promoting our first, self-created video.

As we sailed north, days grew shorter, the winds stronger. We needed ever more layers of clothing to keep warm. We used our foul weather gear more frequently. We eagerly lit *Taleisin*'s kerosene cabin heater every evening and most mornings. My crab trap continued to earn its keep, even overcoming Larry's dislike of the rust stains it sometimes left on the cabin top. Because of the trap, we had wonderful repasts of fresh salmon and sometimes cod as fishermen we met along the way willingly traded catches with us.

Cruising out of season provides its special pleasures, pleasures that offset the challenges. We often had the most beautiful and desirable anchorages completely to ourselves. Sailing friends were actually in residence at their island homes and eager to take time entertaining us as we meandered from the Gibson's Landing on the Sunshine Coast north of Vancouver across the gulf to Nanaimo, then south through the Canadian Gulf Islands. An added bonus, now the tourist season was over, was that folks we met in the small towns along the way also had time for visitors like us.

The owner of a small marina near Nanaimo greeted us enthusiastically when I rowed ashore late one afternoon to inquire about tying alongside so we could top up our water tanks.

"Take any berth you want. Stay the night, won't charge you," he said. "I doubt anyone else will be sailing in until spring." Soon after we'd secured our lines, he insisted we join him for a ride into town that evening, to watch the highly competitive local lacrosse team as they battled for a place in the district playoffs.

"These are Senior A teams, the best of the best," Larry explained as I watched what looked like slightly organized, brutal chaos taking place below me in the Nanaimo sports center. He had mentioned playing lacrosse when we met. I knew he was good on ice skates. But I was a bit surprised when he said, "I was pretty good my last year of high school, a few recruiters suggested I come by for a chat." When there was a pause in the game, I asked why he didn't follow up on their suggestions. "Game was rough. Always came away with bruises from the sticks. In fact, that was where I got this chip on my front tooth." He pointed to his tooth — the one I'd always thought was chipped in some boyish prank. Then he turned back to the game and said, "But I'd never have been a match for any of these guys."

Many players on both teams were members of the local Snuneymuxw First Nations tribe. Their supporters filled the seats around us. Complete families shouted encouragement to their team, ribald comments to the opposition, all the while enjoying picnics out of baskets they passed from person to person. When someone noticed the three of us hadn't brought any food along, fully laden plates were sent our way. Fresh prawns, chunks of recently smoked fish, roasted potatoes, accompanied by cans of ice-cold beer. "It's all great fun," our host said as he drove us back to the marina. "Until someone disagrees with a ref's call late in the game. Tempers really can flare quickly. That is why I chose seats right next to one of the exits."

───────────●───────────

"Sunny, light northerly breezes, high 7° C." The radio broadcaster brought chilly news during the second week in October. I translated the temperature to about 42 degrees Fahrenheit as I huddled farther into the warm sleeping bag and tried to think of excuses to stay right there until Larry got the cabin heater going. The previous afternoon, we'd sailed south towards Dodds Narrows. Just before dark, we had come alongside one of the huge log booms which lay at anchor a short distance from the entrance. Larry had deftly jumped off *Taleisin* onto one of the hundreds of large logs that had been trimmed free of branches, then strongly banded together to form the football-field-sized log boom. He hammered two raft spikes into the cedar log next to us. I'd laughed when he came back to the boat with these steel spikes soon after we arrived in Victoria. But now I really appreciated them as he secured our mooring lines through the ring at the top of each spike. "Just like old times," Larry laughed as he climbed back on board.

He was truly excited about the sailing that was to fill the next day of our journey south towards the winter berth a friend had found for us just a 15-minute walk from downtown Victoria. "Don't have to set the alarm tomorrow," Larry told me. "Tide turns at 10 am at the narrows. Catch it right and going through the narrows is better than any four-ticket amusement park adventure." After once again reading the description of this infamous pass in the local sailing guidebook, my mood was closer to apprehension. But Larry bubbled on, "I sailed through Dodds twice when I was racing up here. Great fun, and when we get through it's only a short sail to Pirates Cove, probably my favorite anchorage in these islands. But we do need to time our approach to Dodds right," Larry added.

Dodds Narrows, between the cliff lined shores of Mudge Island and Vancouver Island, is almost a mile long and for most of that length rarely over 180 feet wide. With up to a 17 feet rise and fall of the tide, the currents through here can run up to eight or nine knots, and, even during neap tides rarely run less than six knots. I read about the whirlpools and overfalls that start to form within minutes of each tide change. Then there was the traffic. Fishboats, tugs towing half-mile-long log booms almost as wide as the pass. By the time we were ready to cast off our lines, I was truly apprehensive.

To add to my concern, the morning breeze did not fill as quickly as we'd hoped. It was almost an hour after our planned departure that we saw the water to windward begin to ripple. Then the breeze finally filled in and Larry said, "Come on, let's get moving," as he jumped down onto the log boom to cast off our lines. As soon as we sailed clear of the log boom, we settled onto a beam reach and Larry suggested we put up the nylon drifter to get moving more quickly. Despite the extra sail area, instead of arriving a few minutes before the tide would turn in our favor, we didn't turn south to enter the pass until 20 minutes after the tide had begun its southerly charge through the narrow and shallow channel.

Larry stood in the cockpit, holding the tiller between his legs and at the same time easing out the mainsail sheet and hauling on the boom vang line to pull the boom well out to starboard. Meanwhile, I was on the foredeck working as quickly as I could, setting the 20-foot whisker pole to hold the drifter out to port. The work would normally have been easy, but the rushing water had already created whirlpools that threatened to spin *Taleisin* first one way, then the other. The larger spread of sail got *Taleisin* moving at more than five knots, and for a few minutes I felt elated as the land seemed to buzz by ever faster, while the sound of the overfalls swishing and tumbling grew until I had to shout to be heard. In an amazingly short time, the tide increased its speed until it was carrying us south at the same speed as the wind. It became obvious Larry no longer had full directional control of *Taleisin*, but the rush of tide and his highly exaggerated tugs on the tiller seemed to carry us on a course down the middle of the pass and — miraculously — *between* whirlpools, not through them.

Larry had been right. It felt just like an amusement park ride. I began laughing out loud, jokingly screaming each time we bucked through another overfall and spray flew across the deck. Suddenly Larry pointed straight ahead. My laughter was cut short when I turned to see a large commercial fishing trawler had entered the pass from the south. Despite the tide rushing against it, with its powerful engines, the vessel was moving, quickly and steadily, towards us. Both of his trawl booms were fully lowered, and I quickly computed our combined width: his rig spread looked to be almost 60 feet; *Taleisin*, with its spinnaker pole set to one side and boom to the other, spread across 40 feet. That left less than a boat's length of clearance between us and the rocky cliffs that lined the sides of the pass. With the tide now carrying us south at more than five knots, the sails barely filled. Larry yelled, "I've got to haul the boom in, then try to ease over a bit more to starboard. You have to get rid of that whisker pole as fast as you can."

I rushed back to the cockpit as quickly as I could on the bucking, bouncing deck. Each time I looked forward I could see the trawler rushing closer. By the time I released the drifter sheet from the sheet winch and let it fly loose, the trawler was within a few hundred feet of us and closing fast. Without the pull of the drifter, we barely slowed down. But, with the pressure of the sail off, with no sheet pressure to hold it from flying forward, the whisker pole slammed against the headstay. I didn't care as the drifter snapped and shook, the pole banged merrily away, because now the trawler had an extra 20 feet of clearance. I had a minute's pause and looked forward to see the trawler crew had been at work too. Their boom no longer reached out across the pass, but had been hauled straight up into the air.

"Got any whiskey to spare?" one of the trawler crew yelled as the two boats rushed past each other so close the aroma of fish and wet, rusting steel wafted across to us. I prayed we wouldn't sail into a whirlpool which would swing us right into the trawler's metal side. "Sorry, only drink rum!" Larry shouted back. I just had time to hear one of the fishermen yell to another, "Wouldn't mind changing over to rum, not if I could be on that boat instead of this one. Bet the food's better."

Then they were whisked past. Larry eased the mainsail out and I set to work winching in the drifter sheet.

Minutes later, as the rushing tide and increasing breeze swept us clear of the narrows and into the calm waters surrounding the De Courcy Islands, I went below and made up two cups of hot buttered rum. "Yes Larry, it was wild. But fun? Not sure . . . "

"Wait till you see Pirates Cove," he answered. "No buts about it. Best spot in the gulf. I remember when . . . " I listened quietly as, over the next few hours, he pointed out familiar sights. Each seemed to trigger memories of the crazy stunts he and his crew got up to on *Annalisa*, the varnished mahogany 27-foot Tumlaren sloop he'd lovingly restored, then raced among these islands. His face glowed as he recalled wins, near wins and losses, the camaraderie of sailors like him who'd raced hard all day, then partied long into the night.

Three hours later, we rounded up and began beating into Pirates Cove. It was completely empty on this late autumn afternoon. Larry recalled race-end gatherings that had filled the cove almost to overflowing during his early days of sailing. He seemed almost intoxicated by the memories he recounted, memories of the sometimes idyllic, sometimes wild sailing he enjoyed when he headed home to North Vancouver once the weekend's racing was over.

Slowly it dawned on me. He was not only harking back to a time full of fine memories, but to a time when he felt fit, strong, and full of the vigor of youth. Then I began to wonder: Was his suggestion we look for a piece of land near here fueled by a desire to regain that youthful feeling?

12

Friendships and Family

2004 - Victoria, British Columbia

Larry sat with his back against the small wooden house, legs extended, feet against *Taleisin*'s topsides. With my feet braced against a big dock cleat on the marina walkway, I hauled on the line we'd attached to *Taleisin*'s windlass. When Larry yelled, "Now!!" we both put every bit of power we had into tugging and shoving our little floating home. The owner of the marina stood on the deck of the 45-foot ketch that we hoped would be *Taleisin*'s winter neighbor. He added his power, pulling, shoving, all the while tending fenders to protect the topsides of the ketch. Suddenly *Taleisin* popped free. We all let out a cheer as she began moving easily forward into the gap between the ketch and the deck of the pontoon which supported the wooden house.

We immediately set to work securing the web of lines that would hold *Taleisin* clear of the marina walkway and the ketch. Larry carefully adjusted her position to ensure, when she was heeled by the strong gusty winter winds, *Taleisin*'s spreaders wouldn't damage the houseboat's roof. The owner of a nearby boat walked past and said, "Never thought a boat could fit into that odd-shaped space!" I laughed and replied, "She almost didn't."

There was no shortage of boat storage yards around Victoria where we could have, for a very affordable price, hauled *Taleisin* onto dry land for the winter. But we had learned from hard experience that, unless the boat could be stored inside a shed and out of the wind, there was far less maintenance to do on our return if she was kept afloat. Unfortunately, there was a shortage of marina berths near Victoria, British Columbia. Having

*The music of Tony Latimer and Patsy Thomson livened our time together
at the Coal Harbour Wooden Boat Festival in Vancouver.*

*Each autumn over the next several years saw Taleisin wrapped up and secured
for the winter. We used shag carpet with the shaggy side against the varnish.
The varnish still gleamed each time we returned.*

a relatively small cruising boat had once again paid off. Despite his small marina being fully occupied, the owner of Hidden Harbour Marina found this triangular place near the bow of the big ketch for us. And, due to the berth being almost (but not quite) impossible to access, John was charging us far less than normal marina berth rates.

We had spent the previous week secured alongside the outer work berth at Hidden Harbour, preparing both *Taleisin* and us for the winter ahead. Half of November had passed. Our working hours, as we winterized the boat, were dictated by the ever-shorter days. We rose before dawn but still had only about eight hours of daylight. We filled every one of these to the brim and should have been exhausted when dark fell. But as often happens in a marina where liveaboards are allowed, we had quickly become part of the marina community.

Several of the people who kept their boat here planned to head off cruising. Tony Latimer and Patsy Thomson lived on the 48-foot wooden schooner *Forbes and Cameron* just down the dock from us. We shared so much about our lives, and our future plans, with Patsy and Tony that within a week they felt like family. Tony was a well-known folk singer/guitarist with a wonderful deep voice. His partner, Patsy, played the concertina and had a sweet but powerful singing voice which complemented Tony's perfectly. Tony had built the boat and named it after his two sons before he met Patsy. And now Tony and Patsy planned to set sail, bound for Mexico within the next two years. Every evening saw us sharing drinks or dinners either on their boat or ours, sometimes just the four of us, other times with a dozen or more sailors singing, laughing, telling stories.

By the end of that week full of preparation and new friendships, *Taleisin* looked forlorn but safe. Her water tanks and simple network of plumbing had been completely drained to protect them from cracking during freezing weather. Her windvane was disassembled and stored below decks. Her sails, along with all her cushions, had been removed and stacked up in the heated lock-up room the marina provided onshore. We'd covered all *Taleisin*'s exterior varnish work to protect it from the hail, ice, and snow, and we'd installed a very safe small tube heater designed to ensure air kept circulating inside the boat. This, plus three dorade ventilators and two ports that could be left open in all weather when she was in a protected spot like this, would work together to prevent mildew from forming inside the boat. Tony and Patsy assured us they would check *Taleisin*'s mooring lines for chafe and wash her decks down with salt water at least once every week. Tony explained his plan to set up a bubbler system to protect *Taleisin*'s wooden hull from cuts and abrasions if there was a threat of serious ice forming around her. By late afternoon, we'd gathered up our suitcases and set off for the airport, bound for sunny Southern California.

We chose to start our winter seminar tour in Southern California for several reasons. With a dry climate and very large population, it is the perfect place to buy an affordable, rust-free second-hand pickup truck, plus a slide-in camper to provide us with transport and serve as a simple, affordable home on wheels.

We had accepted Invitations to present daylong seminars we called *Priorities for Successful Cruising* and evening adventure sailing slide shows at several yacht clubs and sailing organizations between San Diego and San Francisco. All were scheduled for the last half of November and much of December. This meant we'd be within easy driving distance of many of the friends we'd made when we built both of our boats near Newport Beach. But best of all, most of my family lives halfway between San Diego and San Francisco. A brother, a sister, half a dozen nieces and nephews, and a very active mother in her mid-80s. With our truck and camper, we could visit everyone between seminar engagements, but sleep in our own bed and have our own traveling office. Nights could be spent parked in someone's driveway, or at a nearby seaside campground. We could work into or around our family's and friends' schedules. And, for the first time in years, we could savor Thanksgiving and the rest of the holiday season surrounded by people we knew and loved before setting off across the United States on the rest of our seminar tour.

Nothing could be more of a contrast than the cruising life we'd put on pause and the life of a touring "entertainer." Instead of meandering wherever our fancy took us, we had to bypass any intriguing side roads. Instead of lingering when we met someone interesting, we had to move onto the next date. Instead of heaving to when the weather turned adverse or we became over-tired, we had to keep moving, sometimes switching places every half hour to keep driving safely. There was the pressure of ensuring we arrived at the next destination on time, despite snowed-in mountain passes, heavy rain, traffic jams, and blown tires.

As we worked to introduce our *Storm Tactics* video, we gave presentations to audiences in 28 different cities, sometimes with several hundred attendees. We drove from the snow-bound mountains of Colorado to the icy cold of Chicago, from the tropical heat of Miami to the windswept shores of Connecticut. Inevitably, there was the rush once we arrived at each yacht club or venue. We sometimes had only an hour or two to ensure the sound system and projector worked for us. At the same time, we also knew that each of the volunteers who had done the work of organizing the evening or weekend presentations and were now helping us get ready for each program were potential voyaging sailors. They each wanted to ensure we had an enjoyable time but also hoped to discuss their cruising dreams with us. Then there were the attendees who came not just for a few hours of entertainment, but also for encouragement and information. After every presentation there were a dozen or more people who stayed behind wanting to take us out for drinks, a late dinner, or to show us the boat they were building or hoping to buy. We could have enjoyed stopping for a week to get to know each of them but had to be on the road the next morning to stick to our schedule. We also worked at boat shows in another four cities where we presented two or three one-hour seminars each day and met with show attendees for the rest of the time, rarely having more than a few minutes to grab a quick lunch. It was fun. It was also hard work and tiring.

When I thought of how hard it was to balance our need for some down time with sharing as much as we could with these "friends we hadn't met yet," I gained a huge respect for pop stars and other famous performers who had to satisfy thousands of fans at a time, and also earn enough to pay for all the crew that traveled along with them. We didn't have that pressure — there was only the two of us, helped along by generous volunteers at each place we stopped.

We had two other definite advantages over those touring artists. We weren't "celebrities" or "influencers" being judged by what we wore, how we looked, each word we said. We were fellow sailors. And most important of all, we weren't "famous personalities" who were recognized everywhere they went. Unless we were within a mile of a sailing port, or at a yacht club or boat show, it was extremely unlikely anyone recognized us. And even within the limited world of sailing, we were known only by those who dreamed of setting sail for distant shores.

The hard work was balanced by the chance it gave us to successfully introduce and recoup our investment in our new video. It also enhanced our cruising kitty with the speaking fees and the profits from selling a surprisingly large number of the previous books we'd written, and the two videos we'd produced with Roy Blow. Another benefit came from meeting with potential voyagers, listening to the questions they asked — those conversations gave me a list of ideas for articles I could write over the coming year. But the real bonus was that it gave us a chance to catch up with some of the special friends we'd made during our cruising life. Among these was one of my absolutely favorite women and the man who still calls me Mom.

I'd first met Lillian Jarman (now Lillian Jarman-Reisch) in Mandraki Harbor on the Greek island of Rhodes. We had squeezed *Seraffyn* into an almost non-existent space between a 35-foot charter ketch and a 30-foot cruising boat. Lillian was the cook and first mate on the charter boat. As we had tied off our mooring lines, she invited me to come along to the Great Hammam, the stunning 400-year-old Turkish baths which were just a short walk away from the harbor. Her madcap sense of humor, and her intensity when conversations turned serious became apparent as we luxuriated in the ancient marble pools and poured warm water over each other, and we almost immediately became fast friends. We spent the next ten days laughing and playing together. Only a few months after we met, Lillian returned to her life as a respected academic in Ann Arbor, Michigan. Through the ensuing years we'd managed to reconnect half a dozen times in places as varied as the mountains of California and the crowded by-ways of Montmartre, Paris. Each time the conversation seemed to pick up as if we had only been apart a week or two.

The same has always been true with Peter Legnos, who joked that Larry saved him from being homeless when we met in Cartagena, Colombia in the early 1970s. Peter had been just 18 years old and crewing on a large schooner for a journey through the Caribbean Islands. He had signed off as he didn't wish to continue through the Panama Canal, but instead was looking for a berth to sail back towards the US East Coast. He got talking to Larry on the dock of the Cartagena Yacht Club and mentioned he needed a place to bunk down for the night. Larry left him for a few minutes to have a quick conversation with me before he offered Peter a bunk. That night turned into six weeks of pure enjoyment even though 24'4" *Seraffyn* only had one bunk long enough for someone six feet tall. That was the double bunk where Larry and I slept. Peter made do with the shorter pilot berth and never once complained. By the time he left, despite being only seven years younger than me, he felt like a son and came to call me "Mom." We kept in touch as Peter headed back to his hometown of Groton, Connecticut, and set up a small boatbuilding business. There Peter built small cat boats to his own design. With his ever-restless mind and uncanny design ideas, Peter went on to create a string of unusual and successful boats. Each seemed to lead to other interesting projects, including designing and building the special buoys used by NOAA[1] to track ice movement and currents in the Arctic.

And now, as April 2004 drew to a close, the end of our tour was approaching when we arrived at his home near Groton, Connecticut. Peter and I almost immediately set to work together making a big fish stew just as we had back in Cartagena, while he and Larry jumped right back into

---

1   US National Oceanic and Atmospheric Administration

the discussion of the boatbuilding and yacht design ideas they had been having every time we met.

That instant reconnection, that feeling of kinship with people we met while we were out cruising, made each of these visits feel like a true respite from our touring work.

This is in direct contrast to the experience many of our voyaging friends had when they moved back on shore and tried to rekindle all the friendships they'd left behind for two or more years. One example of this problem was gradually played out to us in a series of letters we shared with Jasper Shotts, an English sailor we met when he was a boy of ten years old. We had sailed in to anchor near his family's boat in Mahón Harbor on the Spanish Mediterranean island of Minorca. Larry offered to show Jasper how to sail our little tender, Cheeky. Soon Jasper was out sailing Cheeky every time we didn't need it. Jasper had been cruising along the coasts of Portugal and Spain with his parents and older brother Lucas for two years on a handsome and well-found 28-foot sloop. His parents, both teachers, had originally planned to be away from their home near Bristol on England's western coast for a year-long sabbatical. The income from renting their house helped with this plan. Inspired by the low cost of life on board and the pleasure the whole family expressed with their undertaking, they arranged to extend their sabbaticals for an extra year. Now, work commitments called. The whole family was comfortable with the idea of returning to England. As they sailed homeward, Jasper became a keen correspondent, sending us enthusiastic letters describing his excitement about getting back to his old friends. "Can't wait to tell them about all the things we've been doing," he wrote from the canals of southern France. "Sure will be fun to show my friends the photos my Dad has taken," Jasper wrote as he described meandering through Paris, then down the Seine towards the North Sea.

It was a few months after reading that letter that we picked up a package of our forwarded mail in Malta and found one more long letter from Jasper, postmarked Gloucester, UK. "What a disappointment," he wrote. "My friends made a big fuss about me when I walked into school. Asked me all about my trip before classes began. After that all they wanted to talk about was the latest football match."[2]

---

2   Although Jasper's correspondence dwindled soon after this letter, I did learn the rest of his story when we sailed to the south of England almost 20 years later. I was walking along the waterfront in Falmouth, Cornwall, when a tall man I didn't recognize came running across the street, grabbed me and held me tightly as he lifted me off my feet. "Knew we'd meet up again someday," said Jasper. It had taken him a few weeks to settled back into school. He had begun playing "footie." A few years after his family returned to

Jasper's name had come up several times during our conversations as Larry and I traveled onward across the US towards each seminar. Six months previously, when we were sailing from Hawai'i towards Canada, Larry had made a list of his boyhood friends; friends who had played rugby and lacrosse with him, the crowd that had fixed up and raced hotrods, his skiing buddies from before sailing became his passion. Soon after we arrived in Canada, we had arranged a date to invite them all for a weekend gathering at the Vancouver home of Larry's 13-year younger brother Marshall and his wife Elaine. I was amazed at how easy it was to contact every one of them. All it took was a look through the local phone directory. We realized only two of the people on his list had moved far from their childhood homes.

As soon as the gathering began, I could see why Larry had such fond memories of the two dozen men and women who joined us. I laughed until tears ran down my face as they described Larry's early shenanigans: car transmissions falling out right on the main street of North Vancouver, fights over girls who it turned out weren't terribly interested in either of the men, the aftermath of a rowdy party that led to Larry becoming a sailor. At the age of 17, he'd had one drink too many, driven home and been arrested by the Royal Mounted Police, one of whom followed him right into the carport of his parents' home. (I was a bit disappointed when I learned there was no horse involved. This ruined my mental picture of the so-called "Mounties.")

Bonnie Holmwood, his "steady" for four years, described what happened next. "After Larry lost his driver's license for six months he was walking to work and spotted a small wooden dinghy for sale on the side of the road. Owner was asking just $75," she told us. "Larry bought it, fixed it up — and sank it the first time we tried to sail it."

Larry heard us talking and piped in. "Gave me something to keep me out of mischief while I couldn't drive." It also kindled his love of sailing.

"Didn't see him near as much after that," someone at the party said. This comment echoed through the rest of the evening's conversations.

Later, Larry said, "Sort of disappointed Roland and some of the other guys couldn't bring their families along and come down to the boat when we were near Vancouver." We were careening down the seemingly endless freeways towards our next speaking engagement at the Lake Granby Yacht club in the mountains near Denver, Colorado. "Would have been nice to

---

Gloucester, they had relocated to the south of the UK to be closer to an enjoyable sailing area. Both he and his brother Lucas were now involved in the boating industry. Jasper and his wife were also fixing up a boat to take them offshore.

take some of them out on the boat, show them a bit about my life. Guess with work, families, hard for them to do spur-of-the-moment things."

Gradually Larry came to realize, just as Jasper Shotts had found, the friends of his youth had moved on. The space he had filled as a young compatriot had become filled by other obligations, other relationships. "Some of the guys meet up occasionally. If we settle down somewhere in the Gulf Islands, I can get over to Vancouver to catch up with them," he commented. Then he paused and quietly added, "But not sure I am interested in talking about cars all evening long. Guess that's one of the real costs of choosing the life I've led. You do risk losing a lot of your old friends."

"What makes you think you'd have nurtured and maintained all those old friendships even if you never went off cruising?" I asked. "My brother used to bring home lots of his favorite university friends. I dated a few of them. Now when I ask about those guys, he tells me he only sees them maybe once or twice a year, when someone suggests a meet up for drinks. Most of his social life now revolves around people he's met far more recently."

As we traveled onward, these discussions peppered our conversations, along with the dilemma of Larry's mother and her place in our lives. Beryl's welcome had so far been icy.

"I'm not feeling very well. Doctor says I should take things easy," Larry's mother had said when, the day after we sailed into Victoria, Larry called to invite her to join us at the Empress Hotel for a reunion dinner. "It would take me almost an hour to get there, and I don't feel up to driving this week," Beryl told Larry. "Why don't you come here? But best if you come by yourself this first time."

Larry rented a car the next day, saying, "Lin, I don't like leaving you out of this. But probably a good idea not to push things too hard."

In a way, I was relieved to hear this. Over the years I had tried hard to break the ice with Beryl, ignoring the barbs she threw my way each time, pretending not to hear the antisemitic comments. I tried to believe when he explained those away, telling me, "Never saw her insult any of the Jewish guys I hung out with. You probably misinterpreted what she said."

It was only a year after Larry and I met that his mother had told Larry he should "be sensible, get rid of Lin, come home and be a proper son." Ever since, I had tried, time and again, to engineer a reconciliation. I never wanted Larry to feel I might be the reason he and his mom couldn't rekindle the warm relationship he'd had as a youth. But each time we got together with his parents, it happened again. Beryl was all smiles when we first met, then she would begin making snide comments, and a few drinks later the insults would begin — and Larry would suggest we leave. Communications would stop for a week, a month, a year. Beryl's difficult behavior had grown even worse after her husband died. I couldn't imagine this reunion being any different. I had come to the conclusion this was one problem Larry had to resolve by himself.

Larry drove 25 miles to the Pender Island ferry. His mother drove down to the ferry landing to meet him. When he arrived back at *Taleisin* later that afternoon Larry described the warm reception he had, the pleasant afternoon he'd spent at his mother's home. "But the minute I mention your name, she changes the subject. Maybe it is best if I visit her on my own a few more times."

He had arranged two more visits with his mother before we set sail from Victoria towards Port Townsend. He found the same pattern: He found his mother warm and welcoming, but the minute he brought my name up and suggested all three of us get together, Beryl's reaction turned negative.

Larry's telephone calls to her seemed to dwindle as we spent the autumn months exploring the islands of the Gulf. Soon after we had sailed through Dodds Narrows and were headed south, I asked if we were planning to stop in Thieves Bay and spend a few days visiting with her. Larry's father had helped build the small community marina which was only a half-mile walk from Beryl's home. We would be sailing right past Thieves Bay on our way to our winter berth in Victoria.

"Nope." Larry's response was definite. "Don't want to ruin the last week of this season's sailing. I've tried to make it all work. I know you have been trying for years." Larry put his arm around me and pulled me closer, and added, "I've had enough. If my mother won't welcome my wife, she is the one who loses out."

I was saddened by his obvious disappointment, but relieved by his decision. And I can't deny that I also saw this as a possible weakening of Larry's image of the life he'd recreate by finding a home base in the islands near Vancouver – and I hoped it might turn his mind back towards planning another ocean voyage. Fortunately, the work and pleasure of presenting seminars, and the friends we visited along the way, gradually filled our minds and conversations until we rarely had time to think about social problems, future sailing plans, or the most troublesome concern: the need to fly to New Zealand and appear at the High Court. That date had been looming and we'd put off thinking about it most of the season, but with each passing month, we knew we'd have to get back to Kawau Island and fight the developer who was threatening the peace of our little home there.

13

Resolving the Big Issues

2004 - Salish Sea, British Columbia and Kawau, New Zealand

I reach over the companionway sill and carefully set the platter of freshly steamed crabs next to a bowl of Greek style salad. Then I carry a bottle of chilled Sicilian Soave wine out into the sun-washed cockpit and join Larry. Overhead the nylon drifter and mainsail undulate gently as they pull *Taleisin* through the water at a comfortable six knots. Astern of us, the windvane barely seems to move as it keeps us on a steady northerly course, bound from Vancouver towards Desolation Sound. I settle down onto the cockpit seat and fill two glasses with wine. My phone begins to ring.

"Ignore it. They'll leave a message," Larry suggests. "Been looking forward to my first crab feast of the season. How about handing me the salad, too."

I almost decide to ignore the phone. But when I pull the phone out of my pocket to silence it, I notice the caller's number — Boston. I had recently sent an article to a magazine based in Boston.

I push answer. It isn't a magazine editor.

"Hi, this is George," rings a voice of bold familiar tones. "It's a gorgeous evening here. Pam and I are sailing home from a weekend gathering of wooden boats just outside of Boston. *Seraffyn* is moving at five knots on a beam reach. Windvane is steering perfectly. We're sitting in the cockpit eating fresh lobster dipped in melted butter, and drinking a very good Pinot Gris, couldn't be more perfect. Wondering what you two are doing?"

I am truly delighted I ignored Larry's suggestion. During the first 20 years after we sold *Seraffyn*, she had three different owners. Then we received a phone call from George Dow. Unaware of her history, he had fallen under

Seraffyn's spell the first time he saw her, one day after the 9/11 Twin Towers catastrophe. Norma and Wayne Tillet, her owners, had been sailing south past Manhattan Island, headed from Maine towards the Chesapeake Bay on that fateful day. The US Coast Guard immediately diverted them into Brooklyn Marina just opposite the fallen towers. A major US publication had hired George, a professional photographer, and arranged for him to be taken to Manhattan from this same marina. He was waiting for his boat to arrive and walking the marina dock and, by good fortune the Tillets were on board, so he stopped to talk with them. The boat was not for sale, at least not until George (a very persuasive man) decided he had to have her.

The moment he took possession, George contacted us. And as he spent time sailing on *Seraffyn*, we gained a wonderful and loyal new friend. We never again worried that she might end up neglected.[1] That was reinforced when we had spent three days enjoying a pause in our seminar tour at Pam and George's home just south of Boston. As a special treat, we'd all gone out for an afternoon of sailing on *Seraffyn*. She looked wonderful, varnish gleaming, paintwork shining. I reveled in being back on board that little boat. Each piece of wood, each bronze fitting I touched, brought back memories. As we sailed *Seraffyn* out between the breakwaters of Scituate Bay, my feet seemed to know exactly where to settle when I nestled into the corner next to the chart table and helped Pam serve snacks. My hands remembered each cleat, each winch placement when I helped lower the sails as we came gently alongside *Seraffyn*'s mooring buoy to end a perfect sail.

Now, two months after that fine visit, George's hearty laughter rings out from the far side of the American continent when I answer his question by saying we are enjoying an almost identical experience. Our conversation ends when George says, "Aren't we privileged. We're all exactly where we want to be, sailing through calm waters on a delightful boat, sharing a fine repast with a wonderful partner."

I couldn't have agreed more. I truly was where I wanted to be, both physically and mentally.

We finished our successful and generally enjoyable seminar tour in Maine near the middle of May. Undecided as to whether we should sell

---

1   On October 31ˢᵗ 2024, *Seraffyn* will be 56 years old. George Dow will have owned her and sailed on her between Maine and Scituate, Mass., for 23 years. She still looks delightful.

the truck and camper, we nestled it into a corner of Peter's boat yard in Connecticut, then flew to New Zealand for our day in court.

In the ten months since we'd received notice of the trial and all during our seminar tour, we had tried to push it to the back of our minds and, much of the time, we succeeded. But as we flew towards New Zealand, three weeks before the trial date, we could think of nothing else. If we lost this case, we couldn't legally continue to repair boats in the boat shop or alongside our jetty. We'd have a track running right along our porch, one that dozens of people could use at all hours of the day. And the property we had worked so hard to fix up would have almost no resale value.

We landed in Auckland before daybreak and, as arranged, were sitting outside the office at 7 am, waiting to meet with the barrister who would actually speak for us in the courtroom. This would be the very first time either of us had been in a courtroom other than on the day we were married by a judge at the Santa Ana, California courthouse back in 1968. Our barrister arrived at 8 am and spent an hour discussing how he planned to proceed. He again assured us there was only a five percent possibility the decision would go against us. Despite his optimism, Larry and I both felt uneasy, up and down as if we were living on a seesaw.

In the days leading up the trial, we tried to keep busy, Larry cleaning up the boatshed and tools, fixing the long wooden walkway leading to the jetty, me ripping out the ivy and weeds that threatened to engulf the cottage, both of us taking walks along the crest of the heavily wooded island. We talked about the good times we'd had here, the improvements we had considered before this legal threat entered our lives — but inevitably, one or the other of us would bring up the impending court case, putting a damper on the conversation.

The New Zealand winter had set in, and the cove was very quiet; most houses on the island emptied of their summer residents. The only neighbors were the three who had joined in the case against us. But we only saw them in the distance as they rowed down the far side of the cove and pointedly ignored us on their way out to the community landing to catch a ferry.

Our moods seemed to yo-yo, but fortunately not in sync. This had been the same throughout our lives together. The minute I began feeling down, Larry seemed to jump into cheerleading mode, encouraging me, reminding me "nothing is ever as good as it looks or as bad as it seems." I'd notice him having a bad day, and I'd find some way to distract him. It became such a joke between us that one day I said, "If we both get down at the same time, the world will end."

Now, as we nervously waited for our court date, we had almost reached that point.

Just at a crucial moment, Hugh Gladwell, our solicitor, invited us to join him and several of his non-sailing friends for a day of racing on his 48-foot ketch. The need to haul in sheets, reef sails, set the spinnaker, act as coaches for a crowd of neophytes who were eager to learn (and to laugh) lightened our moods. As the day was coming to an end, one of the guests took me aside. Sarah explained she had bought a very handsome, wooden Buzzards Bay 25. (The 25 refers to the waterline length, the length on deck is 34 feet.) *Jonquil*, with her gaff rig, was built in 1973 in New Zealand to the original design from 1914 by Nathanial Herreshoff. Sarah had meant it as a gift for her boyfriend. She had since parted ways with the boyfriend, but she'd kept the boat.

"I want to learn how to sail *Jonquil*. I want my daughter to learn too. But I want another woman to teach me," she had explained. "There is a whole series of classic boat races planned over the next few years. I'd love to get out in a few."

I briefly pondered the proposal. Sarah added, "If you come back here for the summer, you could be that woman. You could keep her at your place and use her between races."

Two days later, we sat in the crowded courtroom listening to the plaintiff demand that a new right of way be formed across our property – the jetty needed to become a public thoroughfare, so the argument went. Never mind it was the jetty to our private workshop. But no one seemed to take this into account – nor did they consider the loss we'd incur with such a change. I looked around the room and felt saddened to see the pleasure a few owners of neighboring properties showed as they listened to these arguments. It was encouraging, then, when, at the first break in the proceedings, we went out into the court lobby, and discovered there were far more property owners who had turned up to support us, or to learn how this case might affect their properties. We knew all of them from occasional meetings on the ferry and appreciated they were expressing support for us.

After the first day of court proceedings, Larry said, "I need some fresh air. Let's get away from all this court talk." He suggested we locate the yacht club where Sarah kept *Jonquil* stored on shore. "It is just a few miles out of the city. Let's go take a look just for something to do." His reaction when we located *Jonquil*, sitting on a cradle looking a bit neglected, was just like mine.

"She's a real sports car compared to *Taleisin*. Probably a handful to sail," I said as I took in her amazingly sweet underwater lines, the large centerboard that slid through a solid lead keel, the boom that was so long it extended several feet beyond her transom. "She has a huge mainsail according to the photo Sarah showed me."

I noticed a change in Larry's mood as the second day's proceedings continued. By mid-afternoon the facts had all been laid out, the judge had announced he would delay his decision. Our barrister explained we probably wouldn't see the judge's final decision for two or three months and if, by some slight chance, it went against us, we could appeal. That night, we lay awake for a while, each lost in our own thoughts. Then, Larry pulled me close and quietly said, "I think the barrister is right, the decision will go our way. And the past few weeks have reminded me why we bought the Kawau place. We could never duplicate it anywhere else."

"What about your idea of a place near Victoria or Vancouver?" I asked. "It was all you talked about when we were sailing from Hawai'i."

"I was probably feeling worn out by all the passagemaking we did. And I was feeling nostalgic," he replied. "I am enjoying meandering around the gulf, but with the tides, the flukey winds, not many really good sailing days." I listened quietly, feeling optimistic about the path his thoughts were following.

"The whole Pacific Northwest is more like motorboat country," Larry said. " I think it would be good to spend a few summers exploring Desolation Sound, maybe even go farther north. Then we could fly back to New Zealand when the weather turns cold around Canada, take up Sarah's offer."

I smiled as I listened to Larry's musings. "I think sailing *Jonquil* could be a real kick. Her rigging definitely needs an upgrade, I could easily do that with a few days' work," he said. "And eventually we can sail *Taleisin* home and explore New Zealand, buy a little boat to keep near Victoria and continue to enjoy some endless summers."

I never would have suspected the impact our visit to *Jonquil* might have had on Larry. And I didn't say a word as I cuddled closer to Larry. Instead, I lay there realizing I would forever be indebted to Sarah for, just as he was drifting off to sleep, he said, "Win or lose, it is worth fighting for our place here in New Zealand."

Part Four
The Route Towards Our Future

On board Taleisin

As we waited for a break in the weather before making our second attempt to round Cape Horn into the Pacific, we lay secured alongside the southernmost yacht club in the world, the Club de Yates Micalvi. Astern of us are the towering peaks of the Dientes de Navarino

When Cape Horn lay directly on our beam, I brought out the bag of confetti I'd hidden on board just for this occasion

I thought Larry was joking when he suggested we add a reef to our storm trysail before heading for Cape Horn. When we lay hove to in winds gusting to 85 knots a week after we rounded Cape Horn, I no longer doubted his wisdom.

The most amazing sight in my life: momentary glimpses of sun shining through the tops of the marching gray beards off Chilean Patagonia.

The forward cabin on Taleisin is open right to the stem of the boat. Makes it lighter and larger feeling. There is a removable curtain to protect the cushions from any saltwater or mud that might come off the anchor chain.

The upper two steps of Taleisin's companionway ladder lift off to give access to the cedar sitz-tub.

My favorite photo of Larry. He is repairing some stitching on the mainsail as fresh tradewinds propel us towards the Marquesas Islands.

With Big Blue (the 1.2-ounce nylon drifter)
and the Red Baron (a 1-ounce nylon
staysail) Taleisin eats up the miles on light
wind days.

Thanks to Ben Mendlowitz, I have this great photo of Taleisin sailing off Brooklin, Maine.

Taleisin's bowsprit worked as a light air sail extension. Once winds gusted over 22 knots,
we usually removed the headsail and relied on the staysail to keep us moving.

Jonquil, *the Herreshoff Buzzards Bay 25, reaching into the finish line at the Mahurangi Regatta. Photo Roger Mills www.hummingbirdvideophoto.com.*

Nick Compton took this photo of Larry and I when we were racing in the Falmouth Classics Regatta.

Jill Dingle was on board the boat ahead of us when she took this photo of Thelma moving at 10 knots during a classic boat race near Auckland Harbour.

Thelma is secured alongside the pontoon at Mickey Mouse Marine. Taleisin is dried out on the tidal grid next to the workshop. To the left you can see the cottage Larry named Hove To.

(Opposite) Thelma was 115 years old when Larry
bought and restored her as a birthday gift to me.

I took this photo the first time David Haigh joined me
for a sail on Felicity, my Herreshoff 12½.

The sign next to David was made for us by Leigh
Gillard, a friend and boatyard client. It was supposed to
be a joke, but the name stuck.

I needed a step stool to be able to see over the doghouse
on Sahula.

The most important boats in my life. Taleisin's owners brought her onto the grid alongside the boatshed to scrub and antifoul her. Sahula is alongside the pontoon on one side of the jetty, Bubbles, our run-about on the other side. Felicity can be seen on her mooring just off Sahula's bow.

David spent several years as a deck officer in the British Merchant Marine. "I saw how hard it was to spot a white yacht at sea. That's why I painted Sahula bright red," he told me.

14

The Turning Point

2006 - Salish Sea, British Columbia and California

"Neah Bay — Heavy fog, wind southeast five to nine knots, low 54 degrees, high 60."

I listen to the early morning forecast, turn off the radio and quickly climb back into the big forward bunk to warm myself by snuggling up against Larry. There are generous-sized round portlights on either side of *Taleisin's* bow, just a few feet from my pillow. Through them, I can see clear skies and bright sunshine. But, from yesterday's experience, I am not going to doubt the forecast.

It had taken us four days to sail from Port Townsend to Neah Bay, a distance of just 80 miles. Forecasts that promised clear skies and pleasant sailing breezes turned out to be overly optimistic. Fog plagued us. The breezes never seemed to fill. Because the sailing was so slow, instead of catching a fair tide our westward progress had been slowed by tides which ran against us. Despite sailing all day, we were only able to gain 18 miles the first day out and when the tide again turned against us we held onto our gain by anchoring for the night behind Dungeness Sandspit. The next day we tried to sail onward. After six hours we'd only made six miles and the tide had once again turned against us. We retreated. With the tide flowing with us, it took us only two hours to beat back to the previous night's anchorage. Our third day out, the forecast again misled us. But, sailing in and out of thick fog patches, we reached Port Angeles and were lured out early the next morning when the forecast came over the radio: "Fog patches clearing mid-morning."

We'd set off to cover the 60 miles towards Neah Bay only to find patches had turned into a solid wall of nearly impenetrable, unrelenting fog. Regardless, commercial fish boats and cargo ships charged through the straits at full speed, bound to or returning from the Pacific Ocean. We could hear their foghorns blaring as they approached. Minutes later we could feel their wake as they passed. To keep clear of the shipping channels, we had worked into the shallow waters close to the coastline of Washington state, keeping an eye out for kelp. We were close enough that, through the drifting fog, we could catch occasional glimpses of surf breaking against the rocky shores.

Just after midnight, during my watch, a sport fishing boat had appeared out of the fog, headed directly towards us. "You guys have radar?" the helmsman asked as he slowed down to match our drifting pace.

"No, why?" I replied.

"Fish are running. Best run of the year so far. It's brought a lot of extra Clallam Bay folks out here. You are sailing right through a fleet of anchored sport fishermen. Heard some guys on the radio wondering if you saw them. I thought you might like an escort." He generously stayed with us for more than an hour, using his radar to guide us past more than two dozen boats full of determined amateur fisherman. Though we couldn't see most of them as we passed, we were often close enough to hear their onboard chatter. "That's the last one I can pick up on my radar," our escort said when he took leave of us. "Fishing isn't usually very good west of here."

After those close encounters, both of us stayed on deck almost every minute through the dark of night, one on the helm, one on the foredeck with foghorn in hand and spare canister of foghorn gas at the ready. Daylight showed the same thick blanket of fog surrounding us.

Still the breeze hadn't increased. *Taleisin*'s nylon sails, soaking wet from the fog, could only keep her moving at a little over two knots. I kept updating our position on our chart using dead reckoning,[1] checking the taffrail log, taking bearings on the rocky outcroppings we could occasionally glimpse through the fog, noting the position of the kelp beds we passed as most were shown on the chart. It was almost noon when, with a sigh of relief, I heard the occasional clangs of the bell on the entrance buoy at Neah Bay. A ship's wake rolled under us moments later; disturbed by the same wake, the bell tolled more loudly. Larry changed course directly towards the sound. We were within 100 feet before we could clearly see the green banded buoy. It was with a sense of relief that I went below and plotted a

---

1   Dead reckoning - the determination without the aid of celestial observations of the position of a ship from the record of the courses sailed, the distance made, and the known or estimated drift. 2. guesswork. Merriam-Webster dictionary

safe course for Larry to steer into the anchorage.

"The minute we get 100 feet inside that bay, let's just anchor," I said to him when I came back on deck. "I don't care how deep it is, I am tired of worrying about hitting someone or something. In fact, I'm just plain tired."

Only a few seconds later I was laughing. One minute we were looking at a blank white wall of fog. The next minute we were sailing in clear, bright sunshine, through sparkling wind-kissed waters with a crystal-clear view of bright green heavily forested foothills which lead up towards the glistening snowcapped peaks of the Olympic mountains.

Rereading my logbook entries for the three days fog kept us at anchor in Neah Bay confirms how relaxed we both were with this delay. We still had more than two weeks before the autumn equinox, the time of year when the risk of gales increases dramatically along our route to San Francisco. Though we had lots of ideas for how we wanted to spend the next year or two, we had only one date we had to meet, and that was more than six months in the future, in Oakland, California, on the eastern shore of San Francisco Bay — just over 600 miles south of Neah Bay. Other than that, we had no obligations and no need for a calendar. This weather-induced pause gave me time to reflect on the three years that had passed so quickly since we first sailed out of the Pacific Ocean and through the Strait of Juan de Fuca into the Salish Sea.

Wooden boat festivals and boat shows, reunions with friends, exploring the San Juan Islands — we'd had much to fill our first months here. Then we'd winterized *Taleisin* and left her in Victoria harbor to spend six months handling reality: seminars across the country, the business of publishing a new book, legal problems in New Zealand. When we returned to *Taleisin*, we'd gratefully set sail northward.

The three months we spent meandering through the multitude of islands and stunning fiords of Desolation Sound had proved to be just what we needed after the highly regimented seminar tour followed by the stress of flying to New Zealand and spending a month preparing to appear in the High Court — as yet still undecided. The Sound also provided challenging sailing. We often had to use Taleisin's 14-foot-long sculling oar to get us clear of quiet anchorages in time to catch the tide.[2] The oar worked to keep us

---

2   A scull is an oar which you use off the stern of a boat, moving the blade in an athwartship direction. By using a Chinese style lanyard to control the upward thrust of the oar, Larry could attain speeds of up to 1 ½ knots in smooth water and comfortably sustain this for an hour at a time. I found I could work the sculling oar for about 20 or 30 minutes without needing a break. For more about using and building sculling oars refer to our book, *The Self-Sufficient Sailor*.

moving past the calms we often encountered in the lee of steep headlands and into the nice breeze we could see just ¼-mile ahead. Climbing in and out of foul weather gear became a normal part of our cruising days. And I'd come to recognize why most local cruising boats had enclosed doghouses, large motors and generous-sized radar equipment. But we were rewarded for the hard work by stunning vistas and beautiful anchorages. And, just as I've found in other parts of the world where the cruising season is limited, when we stopped near isolated villages, or anchored anywhere other sailors congregated, we were invited to join gatherings on shore or afloat. Sailing friends we'd met in other places planned their summer holiday routes so they could join up with us. They led us to their favorite spots throughout the sounds. Between sailing to new places, joining local rendezvous, setting my crab trap, harvesting mussels or clams, socializing, or drifting through quiet days completely on our own, we only rarely thought about the outcome of our New Zealand legal problems.

It was ten weeks after our return from the New Zealand trial. Autumn was just beginning to empty out all the anchorages around Desolation Sound when we set sail, bound across the gulf for Courtenay on Vancouver Island. It is the largest town near Desolation Sound and there we found an internet café to check our mail and send off a few articles I'd written during weather-bound days. An email from our barrister awaited us. The news was excellent. The claimant had lost his case. He also had been ordered to pay us more than $25,000 for all the costs we had incurred because of the trial. "The claimant has indicated he will be appealing this decision," our barrister wrote. "But I can see no grounds for his appeal. The judge has carefully backed up all aspects of his decision and it is an important one. In the future I am sure this decision will be referenced in other trials to clarify the wording of the Resource Management Act."

"What a relief," Larry said as he gave me a big hug.

"Come on, let's find the best restaurant in town and celebrate," I said. "After that, we could take a walk and look around here for possible winter berths. Might be cheaper than Victoria and we'd be closer to Alaska when spring comes." I had heard the rainforests of Haida Gwaii were amazing and Alaska was even better.

Though Larry readily agreed to the celebratory lunch, I was surprised when he said, "No Lin, I wouldn't mind spending next season around the Gulf Islands, but then I want to head south. Not really interested in going onward to Alaska." I must have looked perplexed because he added, "Not much fun doing it under sail, just too much work."

"You never called it 'work' before," I countered. Then he quietly said something I tried to ignore: "But I wasn't 67 years old before."

This reminded me of another incident that happened at the very end of our seminar tour. It seemed inconsequential at the time. We'd been presenting a talk about how we handled heavy weather at sea. The evening had been moving along well. The room was full, probably 150 attendees. I'd spoken first. Then about 20 minutes later, Larry took over. He set his notes on the lip of the whiteboard he was using to illustrate his points, then picked up the mic and a marker. He began speaking as he sketched a simple sailboat with a storm trysail on the whiteboard. I left the stage and walked quickly to the lady's room. I came back only minutes later, just in time to notice Larry stop speaking. He looked confused as he turned to where I had been sitting, before I'd left the stage. I glanced at the drawing he had been doing, took the mic from him and, as this was a seminar we'd presented many times before, continued as if nothing had happened. Larry picked up his notes and began reading them. A few minutes later he indicated I should hand the mic back. The attendees appeared so involved with the information they were hearing, I don't think any of them noticed this slight hiccup. And when we mingled with them after our talk was over, Larry acted generous, warm and comfortable. But when we left the hall and were out of earshot, Larry turned to me and angrily said, "That's it. You deserted me. I couldn't remember what I was supposed to say, and you weren't there to help out. I was completely embarrassed. I am never going to do that again."

I countered, "Anyone can have a temporary mental glitch. No one but you and I noticed anything. You heard everyone telling us the talk was good."

Larry firmly stated, "Sorry, Lin – I know you love doing this. If you want to do more seminars, I'll come along and chat with people one on one. But that's it. I mean it. I am never again going to stand up in front of people and talk into a microphone."

"That is going to eat into our savings. Seminars are a good way to keep topped up," I said.

"So, I'll take on boat repairing work if we need more money. Classic boats are getting a lot of attention lately, everywhere in the world. And the rigger in Port Townsend asked if I was looking for some work. Or, we can just tighten our belts." He looked directly at me and said, "But no more seminars, no more slide shows for me."

Larry had been right about the increasing interest in classic boats and the opportunities this opened for him. That had become apparent when we decided to leave *Taleisin* secured next to the floating house at Hidden Harbour a second time. Thus began a series of endless summers, flying down to enjoy our home base in New Zealand part of the year, then returning to *Taleisin* for the rest.

Larry was also right about *Jonquil*. She did add real spice to our next three southern summers as we taught Sarah and her daughter Sybil how to sail her and, between regattas, played with her ourselves. We hitched a ride from our island home only two days after we returned to New Zealand to bring *Jonquil* to our Kawau boat yard and prepare her for the racing. I'll never forget the first sail we had on her. The 30 miles from Auckland to our home base provided a wonderful introduction to sailing this slightly neglected but beautiful and nimble sloop. With just the two of us on board, we were on a beam reach in only 15 knots of wind, but we had tucked a reef in her mainsail, not because of the wind strength but because of our unfamiliarity with boats like *Jonquil*. Much of her stability depends on her large centerboard which slots through her 1 ½-ton lead keel, which means she doesn't have the same stability as a deep-keel boat. And this 7,400-pound boat, with her oversized gaff mainsail, has the same sail area as *Taleisin*, which weighs 17,500 pounds. Furthermore, she is an open boat. There is no self-draining cockpit. At first, I worried each time a gust of wind made her heel until water lapped against the sides of the cockpit coamings because I realized, if she heeled more, she could quickly fill with water and sink. So I learned to keep the mainsheet in my hand, uncleated, clear and ready to run out smoothly. The instant a gust hit her, I learned to let go of the mainsheet and dump the wind out of the mainsail before any water could rush over the cockpit coaming.

Within three weeks Larry had upgraded *Jonquil*'s rigging and repaired the centerboard so it could be raised and lowered easily. Then Sarah, Sybil and an interchangeable crew of other women got out practicing or racing with me. Each time, the person in charge of the mainsheet was reminded, "Never cleat that mainsheet. Make sure it's ready to run. Remember — it's dump or die."

Between bi-monthly regattas, where sometimes over a hundred truly classic sailboats and launches came out to vie for racing honors, or just for a fun day on the water, Larry and I enjoyed using *Jonquil* on our own, as a daysailer. We'd explore the various anchorages around our island. We'd sometimes camp overnight in her tiny cabin. At the end of the summer, when it was time for Larry and me to return north to *Taleisin*, we sailed back to her mooring near Sarah's house in Auckland Harbor. "Pick *Jonquil* up when you get back," Sarah said, "Thanks for getting my daughter excited about sailing."

Not only had sailing on *Jonquil* added to our New Zealand summer, but she had gotten us involved with an eclectic assortment of local sailors, some new to us, but many we had come to know during the almost five years we'd spent fixing up the boat yard and jetty when we first bought our island property. Soon the weekends when we weren't off racing turned into instant parties when half a dozen fellow "boat nuts" sailed in to anchor near our place, then rowed ashore with a bottle of wine plus something to put on the barbeque during their weekend getaways or when they headed north for longer holidays.

Jonquil's extremely large mainsail made her challenging to sail when the wind began to freshen. Credit – Roger Mills.

Larry quickly gained a pleasant line-up of repair projects which helped keep our kitty topped up so we could buy the materials to upgrade first the boatshed, then the cottage. Between jobs on our place, he set to work on paying jobs like building a new gaff spar for one classic yacht, or creating a pair of bookshelves to match the ones built almost 100 years previously for a classic launch. I enjoyed watching Larry sharpen tools that had lain unused for several years or helping him dig through the pile of teak and cedar and local hardwoods we'd gathered through the years. I marveled at how he could spot the perfect piece of timber amidst a dusty jumble of weathered, gray-looking rough-sawn timber, then with amazing speed turn it into a velvety smooth spar or bookshelf or blend the wood into a damaged part of a boat until it was almost impossible to notice the repair.

We slowly converted the very plain little cottage. The first big addition was to add a wide verandah and rebuild the house in plantation-grown Lawson cypress (yellow cedar) which we helped harvest in the Waikato, about 100 miles south of Kawau Island.

We settled into an easy rhythm during these island days. We split our time between upgrading our cottage and the land it stood on, getting out sailing, and spending several days a week earning the funds to pay for it all. On working days, after I'd spent much of my time at my computer updating and writing new chapters for a revised second edition of *Self Sufficient Sailor*, I'd join Larry in the workshop. I'd get a few sheets of sandpaper and set to work removing any pencil marks Larry had missed, any slight imperfections. Just before we called it a day, I would lay on the first coat of varnish. And each time I realized how much I enjoyed watching the finished timber darken into glorious color.

By the time we rejoined *Taleisin* for our third season in the Pacific Northwest, any doubt we'd had about keeping our Kawau cottage as our eventual home base had been dispelled. Larry no longer looked at "Property for sale in the Canadian Gulf Islands" advertisements. I no longer worried about adapting to life where winters could be harsh. But I did have twinges of regret as I thought of missing the chance to explore the islands and fiords to the north of Vancouver Island then sail on to Alaska. But I had come to agree with Larry, it was time begin cruising towards New Zealand where, as he often reminded me, it was only a short easy sail to places like Fiji or Tonga or New Caledonia.

It was during this last summer of cruising around the Salish Sea that we finally sailed into Thieves Bay Marina on North Pender Island. On *Taleisin*'s foredeck lay a thick slab of solid granite. Larry and his brother Marshall had decided to put a memorial bench at the place where their parents had enjoyed sharing many quiet times fishing or having sundowners, the green grassy picnic spot right at the end of the breakwater protecting the cove. Engraved into the stone was a short dedication to Beryl and Frank Pardey. Beryl had died two years after we arrived in Canada from Hawai'i, while we were spending the northern winter season in New Zealand. Marshall had been in the middle of the Sea of Japan, working on a drilling exploration ship. Now Marshall had returned to the US and with his wife Elaine had flown in from their home in Salt Lake City for a memorial gathering. As we worked together mixing cement for the base of the seat, then assembling and securing the bench, I looked over to where *Taleisin* lay, alongside one of the pontoons Frank Pardey had built many years before. A sense of disappointment twinged with relief washed over me. Larry's father had always wished we could be a bigger part of his life. For years he'd paid extra money into the community-owned marina maintenance fund so we could have a berth here if ever we sailed to Thieves Bay. More than once he'd told us, "I'll get your mother to come around. Then you and Lin can build a little cottage just below our house and make this your home." I know the idea had appealed to Larry. But I had held my counsel, secretly praying it never came to pass.

Now, several of Beryl's neighbors joined us on board *Taleisin* as we sailed out of Thieves Bay on a light southerly breeze and spread her ashes. As we were sailing back into the marina, one of the local women took me aside and quietly said, "Sorry, but can you let Larry know, now that Beryl's house is sold, she is no longer part of the Magic Lake Property Owners Association. So you can't hold onto the right to have a berth at the marina here." Only then did I realize Beryl had, for the 13 years after Larry's father died and right up until the day she died, paid money to hold onto her dream of having Larry "come home and be a proper son."

Our fog-induced rest days in Neah Bay came to an end when, after four days, the evening forecast didn't mention fog at all. During our stay, two other cruising boats had come to anchor near us, one 28 feet long, the other 35 feet on deck. Larry rowed over and invited the crew of each of these boats to join us for sundowners. They were all southbound, on their first foray offshore. The excitement and slight anxieties of the two couples were apparent as we toasted the setting sun and talked of our planned departure, set for early the next morning, an hour before the tide turned, to run towards the west.

"What's your plan?" one of them asked.

"Get out of the strait and head offshore," I said. Then I went below to get out our passage chart and show them the general course we planned to follow, one that saw us heading slightly west of south until we were 100 miles offshore, and only then turning towards San Francisco.

"That adds a lot of extra miles," one of them commented. "And you'll miss out on some interesting ports."

"Helps us avoid some of the counter currents that run near shore, and usually there are better winds out there," I replied.

"If any fog fills in," Larry added, "I'll feel a lot more comfortable being well outside the shipping lanes and far away from any rocks."

There was a lot of banter between the crews of the three boats the next morning as, within minutes of each other, we hoisted our sails, then lifted and stowed our anchors. An impromptu race ensued as all of us sailed towards the west and the open sea, sun shining, clear skies but a nip in the gentle southwesterly wind to remind us winter was on its way. It was just after noon when we cleared Tatoosh Island, just north of Cape Flattery. I watched as the two other boats tacked to head due south while we continued on our offshore course.

The farther offshore we traveled, the more the wind increased and the more it headed us. By midafternoon we tacked but lay close hauled to continue working away from shore. Just before dusk, the promised northwesterly filled our sails. We eased sheets. *Taleisin*'s taffrail log began to hum as her speed increased to six knots. We settled into our nighttime routine. As Larry lay in the pilot berth gently snoring, I lay in the cockpit, my head over the taffrail, watching the green glow of bioluminescence stirred up by our passage. *Taleisin* ate up mile after mile. I was glad to be in the place where I most felt at home, at sea, where I could avoid, or maybe just ignore, the emotions that life on shore seemed to stir up.

Our offshore course provided us a fine passage and no fog. I was a bit surprised when Larry asked me to take a round of sights two days out, before we made the turn directly towards San Francisco. "Good for you to keep in practice," he said. So, after he had taken his sights, I picked up the sextant and did the same. Our calculations put us both within a mile of each other, showing us to be 100 miles offshore of the entrance to the Columbia River. We turned directly towards San Francisco and continued our romp southward. Though the wind varied in speed, sometimes blowing less than 10 knots and sometimes up to 25, it never changed direction. As I'd found in the past, offshore sailing always seemed much more predictable than coastal routes. I thought about the two crews we'd met in Neah Bay as they worked south close to shore. The local radio broadcasts I was picking up on my shortwave radio spoke of both fog and strong winds in towns along the Oregon coast. [3]

At Larry's urging, I continued taking sights and comparing my results with him. And as expected, not long after midnight, five days out of Neah Bay, Larry picked up the light at Drakes Bay. By the end of my watch, at 0500, I had identified the light on the Farallon Islands just off the entrance to San Francisco. With our position firmly established, I changed course to work inshore, and we were soon sailing in smoother water as the point of Drakes Bay blocked the big northwesterly swell. The wind began to ease. We were still running comfortably but now making only about 4 ½ knots. I prepared to climb into the bunk when Larry called down, "Greeting committee has arrived."

I laughed out loud when I climbed on deck. Whales surrounded us — big ones. I counted more than a dozen, slowly moving in a large circle with *Taleisin* right in the middle. They stayed with us for the next hour. But there always seemed to be a clear path for *Taleisin* to keep moving onward. When the Golden Gate Bridge came into view our wind dropped off, our speed slowed to a sedate three knots. Our giant escorts turned northward and were soon out of view.

Just five days out of Neah Bay we sailed under the impressive center span of the Golden Gate bridge and soon came to anchor near Sausalito. "Looking forward to exploring more of the bay," I said to Larry as we worked together putting *Taleisin*'s sail covers on. "Maybe there are some classic boat races around here — would be fun to join in."

Larry had always jumped at any chance to join a race. He continued flaking the staysail, then replied, "Not really interested in racing around here, especially not in this boat." It was a surprising response, but his next

---

3   We later encountered one of these couples at a sailboat show in Jack London Square in Oakland, California.. They had encountered headwinds and commented on rough seas along their route, the difficult entrances to the ports they'd chosen. It had taken them almost four weeks to reach San Francisco. Fortunately, none of this dampened their enthusiasm for cruising onward.

statement was even more of a departure from our usual frame of ideas: "Want to keep the gear in good shape for our voyage home."

I mulled over Larry's comment. Until now he had always referred to *Taleisin* as his home. Now I realized, instead of thinking of Kawau Island as our "home base," something important had shifted. In his mind it had become his *home*, and something within him was making him eager to reach it.

15

Personal Stories: People and Places

2007 - Southern California

"The only thing wrong with endless summers is the endless packing," I joke as I climb out of the cabin to see how Larry is faring.

He laughs as he says, "Glad that's your department." But he doesn't miss a stroke as he continues sculling down the channel between Alameda Island and Oakland. Then he adds, "Please don't worry about having the boat perfect. People will love her just the way she is."

I don't answer. Instead, I look around then calculate it will take another 20 minutes to reach Jack London Square, just a half mile from where *Taleisin* has spent the winter tucked in a corner of Alameda Marina. There had been absolutely no wind when we worked clear of her berth. Now, in the calm water of the channel, she is moving along nicely as we head towards the marina where *Taleisin* will be front and center at Strictly Sail Pacific at the Jack London Square in Oakland. We had attended this boat show a few years previously, but this would be the first time we would have *Taleisin* with us. We have set a goal of using her to raise at least $5,000 for the Bay Area Association of Disabled Sailors (BAADS). Several BAADS members are waiting for us to arrive. We will have them on board for a pre-show briefing as soon as we secure our lines. This is my last chance to get *Taleisin*'s interior looking as good as her exterior. I leave Larry to his work and head below.

It has been only four days since we had flown back from New Zealand to rejoin *Taleisin* after another endless summer. This morning I'd finally stowed our travel bags in the farthest reaches of the big locker under the forward bunk. Now I rush to check every visible corner of *Taleisin*'s interior for signs of mildew. So far, I find none. The preparations we'd done five months earlier, when we closed her up, have paid off.

About ten years previously, we'd begun an interesting correspondence with Don Backe. He had been a highly competitive racing sailor before a late-night car accident left him in a wheelchair with a severe spinal injury. During his rehabilitation, and determined to get out sailing again, Don founded CRAB (Chesapeake Region Accessible Boating). In 1991 it was only the second of the groups in the US created to get people with disabilities out on the water. By the time he wrote to us, CRAB had a growing fleet of boats specially adapted for people with disabilities. The State of Maryland had provided a dock at a park near Annapolis with a hoist to help lift people with physical limitations onboard for a day of sailing. But Don wanted more.

His first letter asked if Larry could help him with a rigging problem. "I dream of actually getting down below in a boat once more and having a glass of rum," he had written. "Any ideas on how to rig up something to help me achieve that?"

I wasn't the least bit surprised at Larry's reaction. "There must be a way we can do more to help Don and his group than just exchange letters full of diagrams," he had said.

A few months later a perfect opportunity came up.

After the letter exchange had begun, we sailed across the Atlantic from England to spend a summer cruising the waters of Maine. When autumn approached, we planned to sail south to the Chesapeake Bay and warmer weather. We had also agreed to present a series of seminars sponsored by *Sail* magazine at the U.S. Sailboat Show and greet their subscribers in the magazine's booth. This was a win-win situation for us as it meant we could promote our newest book, *Cost Conscious Cruiser*. In a phone conversation with Don, we learned the organizers of the show provided a space for CRAB to have their boat floating in a berth right at the center of the action and not far from where we would be working. They also gave his group space for an information and fundraising stand onshore behind their boat.

"Maybe you could stop by our stand and talk to a few of our visitors," Don had suggested.

"I've got a better idea," Larry said. "Let's moor *Taleisin* alongside the CRAB boat and have her open to the public. CRAB people can show folks down below. Then we'll put a donation bucket right where the visitors step off the boat."

The organizers of the show were reluctant at first. "Not sure if it's fair to the vendors who pay so much for their space," the show coordinator said. "What will they think when they see a funky old wooden boat right in the center of their shining new offerings?" But Don set to work and when the show opened, *Taleisin* was there, dress flags flying, secured right next to the CRAB boat. No one kept formal track of the number of people who left their shoes on the dock to clamber on board then climb below decks under the careful direction of a crew of sailors with various disabilities, but the show organizers said the lines to climb on board were among the longest at the show.

Having *Taleisin* right at the show, presenting seminars and working in the *Sail* magazine booth turned the event into an exhilarating, exhausting weeklong party for us. By the end of the show, she had earned $18,000 for CRAB. I gained something far more important. I learned to be utterly comfortable working and socializing with people with disabilities. Both of us also learned a lesson by watching the grace and humor with which CRAB members negotiated their disabilities, carried on with life, and got out sailing any way they could. This was a lesson that would echo throughout the coming years. A long time after our time at the Annapolis boat show with Don and CRAB, when Larry was nearing his 69th birthday, the two of us went for a walk together, just to get some exercise, and I expressed my frustration with Larry's ever-slower walking pace. Larry reminded me, "Don Backe would have been thrilled if he could walk at all."

After our first introduction to this method of fundraising, whenever the opportunity arose, we arranged to bring *Taleisin* to similar events on both coasts of the USA. The morning after our latest fundraiser at Jack London Square ended, we said our farewells to all the BAADS helpers then hoisted *Taleisin*'s mainsail to reach clear of the docks. Less than an hour later we came to anchor at Angel Island. The only signs that several hundred people had been on board was an eclectic collection of small gifts people had left for us: home-baked cookies, jam, preserves, a beautiful handmade canvas ditty bag, some bottles of wine, and floorboards that needed a wipe down with a soapy rag to regain their normal color. Larry and I were on a high. We'd reached our fundraising goal, made a lot of new friends, and now had no dates at all on our calendar.

In the quiet of the anchorage we finally had time to recall all the friends who had stopped by to greet us, the new friends we'd made. We both agreed our favorite memory from the week showed the wide-ranging effect of groups like BAADS and CRAB, who did more than just help people with disabilities get out on the water. They also invited able-bodied

people who could never dream of having a boat to come along for the ride.[1]
Andrea had been among the first of the BAADS volunteers to greet us as we
sculled *Taleisin* into her boat show berth. A warmhearted 30ish fully abled
woman, Andrea introduced herself as the BAADS volunteer with the job
of making sure there was always at least one well-briefed minder on board

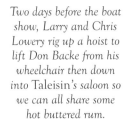

*Two days before the boat
show, Larry and Chris
Lowery rig up a hoist to
lift Don Backe from his
wheelchair then down
into Taleisin's saloon so
we can all share some
hot buttered rum.*

Taleisin. The day before the show opened to the public, her 11-year-old son
came rushing directly from school to the boat show looking for Andrea and
the BAADS boat show stand. Andrea, who is a single parent, introduced
us to Jason and said, "You are the reason my son has found something he

---

1   Weekend open sailing days are offered by all the groups we worked with. Anyone who
is interested in learning to sail, not only people with disabilities, is invited to participate
both on the water or as a volunteer on shore. Here is a complete list of accessible boating
opportunities in the USA - https::/www.ussailing.org/education/adult/adaptive-sailing/
sailor-resources/ For BAADS - https::/www.baads.org/sailing/

loves more than hanging out on the streets after school. And I've found a great group of new friends."

She explained she had been trying to find something interesting to add to Jason's life. Then, one day, as she drove across the Golden Gate Bridge and into downtown San Francisco, she noticed the sailboats below her and on a whim chose to listen to a podcast on sailing. By chance, it was an interview Larry and I had done just a few months previously. The podcast ended with the interviewer asking about our upcoming visit to the boat show with BAADS. I had described how, like most similar groups, they offered to take sailors without disabilities out for an afternoon afloat at no cost. Andrea had taken her son along to the next free sailing day and he was hooked. Now he spent many of his after-school hours working alongside BAADS members, helping maintain the fleet. Weekends found him out on the water, gaining sailing skills.

We began sailing south after a few weeks of meandering around San Francisco Bay. Half Moon Bay, Santa Cruz, Moss Landing, Avila Beach: Each one brought back memories of the good times we'd had along this coastline during previous forays both by sea and by land. This was where Larry first introduced me to sailing, where we'd moved boats north or south for owners who had more money than time, where we did sea trials on both of our boats after we finished building them and before we set off across oceans. As we'd expected, summer brought light winds and early morning fog, fog which was usually blown away by noon as the fresher sea breeze filled in. The northwesterly swell, created by fresher winds far to the north of us, rolled gently and unceasingly under us. I could have spent more time lingering along this coastline. Instead of spending just a few days each in Half Moon Bay and Santa Cruz, I could have enjoyed day-hopping south, seeking out the shelter of various headlands, going into each cove or bay.

But Larry was on a mission. "Your mom is 86 years old. She has always been great to us. She won't be around forever, you know," he said when we sailed out of Santa Cruz. "We should get down to Ventura as quickly as possible so you and I can spend some serious time with Marion, you can have some girl time together, invite her to bring her friends down to the boat. I can get her out dancing, take her to a few plays like I promised when we last spoke."

Two days out of Santa Cruz, as we approached Point Conception, I expected the wind to accelerate as it usually did around this headland where currents swirled and cold water upwellings and nearby coastal mountains disturbed the weather patterns. Here, the winds frequently blew at 30 knots or more. But our winds continued to be light, moving us along at just over four knots, and all during the night, the fog thickened. By morning, as daylight crept in, the VHF weather report reported visibility at less than a quarter mile. On board *Taleisin,* my estimate was more like 150 yards.

"I suggest we continue another twenty minutes or so, get another mile south before we turn east," I said when I finished consulting the taffrail log and plotted our latest position on the coastal chart. "That should put us two miles south of Point Conception. Then we can turn and reach eastward a few miles off the coast until the fog clears." I knew the fog always cleared as soon as we entered the Santa Barbara channel. I thought my plan to keep clear and use our knowledge from years of knowing this coast was sound.

I was utterly surprised, then, when Larry firmly stated, "I suggest we get out the GPS I bought at the boat show and use it. If it means we can turn sooner, we'll do it. I am ready to find a calm anchorage, get the pick down, and get some rest. This fog is wearing me out."

I had been very reluctant about this handheld, battery-operated GPS Larry asked me to buy during the boat show. We had used electronic navigation gear occasionally when we delivered other people's boats, but never considered adding it on board *Seraffyn* or *Taleisin* for several reasons. First, we didn't have any way to power the gear. Secondly, until the late 1990s the cost for even the simplest electronic navigation gear was beyond our budget. Later, when the cost of this gear came down and we had added a solar panel on *Taleisin* so we could use video cameras, the power consumption was well beyond the capability of our 31-amp storage battery. Beyond that, both of us were totally comfortable with our non-electrically complicated life and enjoyed the routine of plotting our course using a hand-bearing compass, taffrail log, and sextant to gather the information we needed. To do this, we had to get out on deck frequently, which kept me more connected with the changing weather and sea conditions. Taking sights, recording them, updating our position every few hours added a special routine to our days at sea and in many ways made us feel connected to those who had plied the seas for centuries before us. There was also the extra care we were forced to take when nearing our landfalls, which contributed to our staying safe through the years. And the real bonus: the magic of sighting land and realizing you had found it without any outside assistance. After nearly 40 years of sailing together, neither of us had expressed the need to change things.

Larry's request caught me by surprise.

"I want it for next winter when we fly back home. Want to use it on

Jonquil to improve her speed. I'm never quite sure if I'm adjusting her sails right," Larry had explained when he insisted on the purchase. "If we had a really accurate way of gauging her speed through the water, we'd know if tweaking the sails, easing the gaff, or letting her carry a bit of a luff in the mainsail instead of reefing down the mainsail has paid off." With a boat show special price of just $79 for a brand named, battery-powered GPS, I couldn't use cost as a reason to avoid buying it. The GPS, its box unopened, joined a growing stash of "stuff for New Zealand" right next to the luggage in the most inaccessible locker on board.

Now, I struggled to keep from saying what I was thinking: *Am I willing to risk our boat by depending on a seventy-nine dollar battery-operated gadget?* But I could see the man I always considered a pillar of strength was, for the first time in 40 years of sailing and voyaging together, feeling insecure.

Twenty minutes passed as I pulled out the forward bunk cushions and all our winter clothes to dig out the GPS, read the instructions, insert the batteries, then watch the display as it picked up first one satellite, then two more. When the longitude and latitude appeared, I plotted the results on our chart. "You can definitely turn east now," I called out to Larry. "GPS position shows us about a quarter mile farther south than my DR."

I plotted a course into Cojo Anchorage. A short while later, Larry suggested I use the GPS to update our position. But instead, I pointed out that, despite the fog, which didn't relent, it was easy to feel where we were. The swell had gradually begun to die away. The wind, influenced by the lay of the land, backed more to the west. Both changes indicated we had come into the shadow of Point Conception.

"No need to use that gadget," I answered. "Just carry on another ¼-mile and we'll be in Coho anchorage." Minutes later we were skirting the edges of the kelp beds that lay up to a half-mile offshore all along this coast. When a break in the kelp appeared, I checked the taffrail log. "Yep, time to head due north and sound our way in. Should have about ten fathoms under us right now. Lots of room between us and shore if we anchor at seven fathoms."

Larry went forward and lowered the genoa while I swung the lead. "Glad we had that GPS to back you up," he said in passing.

His sense of relief was clear, and it helped me realize, if I wanted to continue voyaging, I'd have to accept having "outside assistance." At the same time, I began to question my motives for resisting so strongly. Was I truly distrusting technology that had, over the past several years, grown ever more reliable, or was I caught up in my own dogma? Was I concerned by what other people might say, or was I concerned that I might become lazy and stop being as diligent if we came to rely on the GPS? Was I worried that we might lose the edge that had helped keep us safe?

Larry obviously sensed my thoughts. "Don't worry, Lin, even if we do use that GPS along the way, we won't depend on it," he said as we quietly slipped into the routine built by years of practice, settling *Taleisin* securely at anchor, then flaking and securing her sails, coiling her lines. Then he added, "We'll still stick to our normal routine. The GPS will just add one more bit of information to help keep us off the rocks."

16

Storm Warnings

2008 - North Pacific Ocean, bound towards the Line Islands

"You are right," Larry comments as he points eastward. "I can feel a definite swell coming from over there."

"Yep, been feeling it since mid-morning," I reply. "Yesterday the report on WWV mentioned two slow-moving depressions just off the coast of Mexico. Wonder if another one has formed somewhere nearer us."

Taleisin is running along at a sedate four knots on a light northeasterly, windvane in control. The low, smooth swell doesn't disturb the big blue nylon drifter, which shades us from the heat of the late afternoon sun. We have carried the pilot berth cushions out onto the foredeck and are lazing away the afternoon together. it's been seven days since we set sail from Ventura, California, bound towards Kiritimati, one of the Line Islands, which lies 1,100 miles due south of the big island of Hawai'i. We've covered 900 miles and have another 1,900 miles to go.

When I awoke from my morning off-watch, Larry invited me out for a date. Though he did it in a joking manner, I took him seriously. With the routine of watches, caring for the boat, navigating and handling the rougher seas we'd had until this morning, we hadn't really had an opportunity to spend intimate time together. After the morning routine of updating our navigation, and giving the inside of the boat a clean-up, we each enjoyed a long generous shower. I shampooed and conditioned my hair, and while it dried, I used some of the tuna we'd caught two days before, plus the last of our fresh lettuce, to make a large salad. A late lunch behind us, I'd joined Larry on the foredeck where we had talked for a while, then lay quietly together watching the sail above us undulate. Sated and content, I suggested I'd keep a watch for ships or squalls while Larry dozed off. I didn't want to change anything about this special moment, so I continued to lie there next to him, reflecting on the trajectory of our lives together.

Ever since we successfully rounded Cape Horn, and as we continued onwards towards Canada, there had been signs that age, and Larry's sense of fulfillment, had begun to dull his enthusiasm for long-distance sailing. Now, as Larry neared his 70th birthday, it became more obvious that this could be the last time I experienced the magic of crossing an ocean completely under sail. I also realized, once we had successfully sailed *Taleisin* westward across the Pacific and south to our home base in New Zealand, there would be an empty space in my life, one that had, for years, been filled with preparing for, then embarking on, yet another offshore adventure. These thoughts had begun occupying my mind when, during the previous northern hemisphere winter, we'd again secured *Taleisin* and flown towards summer in New Zealand.

Once we arrived at our home in New Zealand, Larry had eagerly jumped into upgrading the shabby little cottage and completely rebuilding the boat shop, the boat ramps, and tidal grids. It had been a long time since I'd seen him so content and emotionally involved. Even when a bandsaw blade unexpectedly snapped, or he accidentally cut a piece of timber a bit too short for whatever he was building, he took it completely in stride. He frequently shared his pleasure in working with his hands again, shaping timber to the vision he had in his head.

"It'll take me a couple of years, but this place will be really great when we're finished," he said when I commented on the scale of the work he'd sketched out. "Materials won't cost much 'cause I love this plantation-grown cedar you found for us. The two of us can do most of the work," he reassured me as another wall appeared where none had existed before and piece by piece he expanded what had previously been a small, rough, dirt-floored workshop under the cottage into a large area that would house a pool table and guest room under the 600-square-foot cottage.

It wasn't as if Larry had forgotten about sailing. We were often out on the water. With the help of the GPS we bought at the Oakland boat show, we did learn to tune a gaff-rigged sail. We did get a noticeable increase in speed as we joined the classic boat fleet to race *Jonquil* among the islands and estuaries between our island home and Auckland. But most of Larry's time was filled with rebuilding the boatshed and then the cottage. The only real break in his routine came about when an accidental gybe broke a spar on a local classic boat, or someone's ill-timed tack left another friend with a damaged hull. Then he'd take a break and launch, just as contentedly, into boat repair mode.

Just as we had back in Bull Canyon, when we were building *Taleisin*, I divided much of my day between being a writer, acting as project manager for Larry's building project, and working alongside him adding varnish or paint to whatever he was building. But I realized, with our changing circumstances, it would be wise to get to know and create ongoing friendships with the people who lived around us on the island.

An average of 120 people live full-time on this rugged, steep-sided island. Another 100 people have holiday homes they use frequently during the summer, less frequently during winter. Other than in two clusters of about 20 homes each, the majority are scattered along five miles of rugged coastline. There are no roads connecting these homes, just rough trails that climb steeply up from the shore to a meandering track along the ridge of the heavily wooded island. There is no communal landing spot; instead, there are 71 jetties scattered along the shores of seven different bays, each serving one or two houses. Socializing, even with nearby neighbors, means getting into a boat or trekking through the woods for at least a half hour. There is no central village, no shops on the island, no meeting house, so the only time I saw most of the other islanders was when we happened to be on board a ferry to or from the mainland. Larry and I had so often been away sailing, sometimes for eight or more years at a time, so we had only a nodding acquaintance with a few of our closer neighbors. Many cruising sailors from overseas, some old friends, some who came looking for us because they read one of our books, stopped by to anchor nearby for a day or two when we happened to be at home on Kawau. They, plus the friends we'd made on the mainland through sailing and racing, had satisfied our social needs. But if we planned to live here in the future, I knew the winter months might not be spiced with visitors. So I set aside time to do something completely new for me. I asked if I could come along to a meeting of the local ratepayers' and residents' association committee to offer my skill as a writer. Little did I realize this would be the first step towards doing more than just building island-based friendships; this would eventually lead to me gaining the title "Mother of Kawau Island."

"What are you working on?" Larry asked me as we were flying back to Ventura, where *Taleisin* lay waiting for us.

I turned my computer towards him so he could read the essay I was writing for the island association's quarterly magazine. "Hope to finish this up before we land," I said. "It's a fun mental exercise, write an essay — really different to the articles and books I've done before."

Larry laughed as he read my short story, then said, "Sure hope that's the only commitment you made to the folks on Kawau."

It wasn't, but I didn't tell him that until long after we'd arrived in California and began preparing for our voyage southward.

———————————

The previous two northern hemisphere warm weather seasons had felt like a true nostalgia trip as we meandered along the coast of Southern California, north from Ventura Harbor to Santa Barbara and its off-lying islands, south as far as San Diego then back again. Sailing and boatbuilding friends from our earliest years together, the years we spent building *Seraffyn* behind an old shed in the middle of Costa Mesa, welcomed us right back into their lives. Many of those we met when we finished our 11-year circumnavigation and were building *Taleisin* in an isolated desert canyon near Lake Elsinore came out to rendezvous and sail along with us for a few days at a time. Best of all, every member of my family worked to wrap us into the day to day of their lives.

When we were close to Ventura or Channel Islands, the area where most of them lived, someone would drive down to wherever we were moored and take us home to spend the weekend surrounded by family. When we were farther away, family members, ranging from my mother and her second husband to siblings, nieces and a nephew who were old enough to drive would seek us out and join us on board for a day or two on the water. My brother's youngest daughter, Cami, was the only member of my family who had moved far from home. I was delighted when she arranged to bring her family south from northern California to stay with her father so we could all be together for a long holiday weekend soon after we arrived in Ventura.

During a quiet moment, Cami brought up something I had observed through the years of my cruising life. "I really like what happens when I come home," Cami said. "Since I don't live nearby all the time, everyone actually makes an effort to spend lots of time with me when I am here. When I was here all the time, everyone said, *let's get together*. But it seemed they were too busy to squeeze in much more than an occasional meal together."

Maintaining a connection to family is often a topic of conversation when I meet people who are just preparing to set off cruising. I shared Cami's comment as it reflects what I saw within my own family. Though we missed the day-to-day give and take of family life, we were able to arrange a visit "home" at least every third year. Each time we came to visit became a special event. When my parents or other family members found a way to join us in some distant port, the link deepened. We did miss some important family events: the weddings of our siblings, the 21st birthdays. The best we could do in those cases was send a gift with the flavor of the country we were in or arrange for a long phone call the night before the event.[1]

By very good fortune, we were nearby when Larry's father died. Later when my father died unexpectedly, I was able to be with the family within hours. And, a few months before we set sail for New Zealand, I was with my mother when her second husband died. Now Mom asked, "Can you please stay around to celebrate my 87th birthday with me? June 6th is just six weeks from now. The whole family will be there. Having you with us for once, that would be very special."

This presented a difficult choice. The hurricane season in the northern hemisphere officially begins on the first of June. The pilot charts for the North Pacific Ocean showed tracks of tropical depressions that had, in past years, deepened to become hurricanes with winds raging at 70 knots or more. These tracks cut right across our proposed route. We had planned to set sail by the middle of May to be south of the danger area before the official start of the season.

My first instinct had been to flatly refuse my mom's entreaties. But Larry, who considered my mother to be his most steadfast supporter, immediately stated, "Marion, we wouldn't miss your birthday for the world."

Then my sister chimed in, "Great, Kurt's wedding is only two weeks after that. Now you can be part of my son's big day!"

Neither Larry nor I directly agreed to this proposal. But later that evening Larry asked me if I actually wanted to stay for the wedding. I was torn between the concern of hurricanes and my sister's feelings. She is several years younger than me. Her own wedding had been one of the many I'd missed through the years. But I decided to let Larry make the final decision. When we got back on board the boat we pored over the pilot charts. "It's a huge area of ocean, and June is just the beginning of the hurricane season. Chart for June shows most of the storm tracks fade away close to the Mexican coast," Larry noted. "Let's take the chance."

Between Mom's birthday plus Kurt's and Larissa's wedding, it was the 21st

---

1 Many cruisers have told me the internet and video calls have helped resolve this issue. But I wonder if it has in some ways aggravated the situation, emphasizing the day-to-day family moments you are missing as you cruise, and giving people back home the feeling they have included you, so your physical visits to them are less compelling.

of June by the time we were provisioned and ready to set sail southbound. The day before, my mother and sister had driven down to the boat with a load of farm fresh vegetables. They'd invited me to join them for one last "girls" lunch.

"Bonnie and I are worried. Are you sure Larry is up for this voyaging?" Mom said even before we sat down. "He seems to be depending on you more and more, all the time. He seems to get tired pretty easily. He did have that stroke last September."

"It wasn't a stroke. It was just a TIA[2] ," I reminded them. We are lucky one of our sailing friends is a top neurosurgeon at the UCLA medical school. He had arranged for his clinic to do a full assessment of Larry and said there was no damage. I tried to reassure my mother. "If you could have seen what Larry was like in New Zealand, seen him putting the roof on the boatshed, watched how he handled *Jonquil* and got us into trophy positions in the last race series, you wouldn't be concerned at all."

All this was true: the only thing that TIA did was convince Larry his age increased the risk that something could happen to him. Then, I might have to take care of him and sail the boat too. He had become concerned I'd be too busy to take sights if that came about. And so, to put Larry at ease, I agreed to bring the GPS back from New Zealand with us and bought a second as a backup.

I told all this to Mom and Bonnie, even the part about us now carrying the handheld GPS. I saw how they listened quietly as I tried to assure them. "Mom, you know I can sail that boat by myself if I must," I said. "I don't want to. But please don't worry."

Mom made us laugh by saying, "A mother's job is to worry. So call me whenever you can."

———————•———————

The next morning, we set sail. As we worked south, we experienced a mixed bag of weather, winds at first from the northwest then gradually backing to the northeast, rarely over 30 knots, rarely so light we couldn't keep moving. And until this morning, Larry had been right about the hurricanes. Because the waters along the Pacific coast had not yet warmed

---

2   A transient ischemic attack (TIA) is a short period of symptoms similar to those of a stroke. It's caused by a brief blockage of blood flow to the brain. A TIA usually lasts only a few minutes and doesn't cause long-term damage. In Larry's case, he awoke confused and unable to speak for about 20 minutes and felt tired for a few days afterwards. Otherwise, he seemed to have no lasting effects.

to their summer temperatures, the three different depressions that formed in the Caribbean Sea and crossed the Mexican mainland seemed to stall then fade away, near the coast of Baja California, long before they could cross our track.

But now, the low, long swells I'd noticed earlier in the day, the ones Larry was now feeling when he awoke after our leisurely afternoon "date" on the foredeck, were an ominous sign.

The WWV weather warnings that evening confirmed a tropical depression was deepening several hundred miles to the east of us. By morning, the depression had a name, Hurricane Boris. It was packing 85 knots of wind. We agreed to change our course and head farther towards the west, hoping Boris would follow the usual track of early cyclones and turn towards the northwest.

For the next three days we tuned our shortwave radio to WWV every six hours, plotting Boris's progress and potential track. I did my usual bit of worrying, listing the preparations we should start making. Larry was his usual pragmatic self, saying, "We'll handle things when we have to." I did bake some extra loaves of bread plus a casserole when the frontal band of Boris was within 250 miles of us, and Larry pulled the parachute anchor out from its storage spot under the light air sails and put it in the bathtub where it was within easy reach. Otherwise, our normal onboard routine continued as *Taleisin* reached southward on a 20-knot northeasterly wind and the skies began to cloud over. By the morning of the third day the increasing swells made it obvious: Boris was tracking right towards us. As the winds increased to 25 then 30 knots, I turned on WWV to learn both the good news and the bad news. The bad? The frontal bands of Boris were now just 90 miles east of us. The good? Boris had been downgraded to a tropical storm with winds at only 50 knots, gusting 55.

Larry lowered the reefed mainsail and set the trysail in its place. I secured all the locks on the floorboards and installed and tightened the cushion retaining straps that ensured nothing could come flying out of the lockers under the pilot berths or saloon seats. Six hours later when I tuned in to WWV, there was no longer any mention of Hurricane Boris. I tapped my barometer. Until a few hours earlier it had consistently been moving downward. This time, when I tapped the glass, the needle jumped upward three millibars.

"What's the latest report?" Larry called down from the cockpit.

"Boris is gone. Seems to have dissipated," I called back.

"Not surprised to hear that," he replied. "I already noticed the swell seems to be laying down and I spotted some patches of blue sky just to the south of us. Guess changing our course to head west was the right call. Give me a new course, I'll adjust the vane." I replied with the new course and watched as Larry adjusted the windvane. As he came below he gave me a quick squeeze, grabbed a handful of trail mix from the canister in the snack locker, then he said, "Really glad we have that behind us. Hope our luck holds all the way home."

By dark the skies had cleared, the swells had laid down, the wind had steadied to give us a fast downwind run. When I came out on deck for my watch, for the first time on this passage, I spotted the stars of the Southern Cross rising just above the horizon. As *Taleisin* surged along I settled on the cockpit seat and glanced below to where a single oil lamp cast its glow to show Larry sleeping soundly. I thought about the fleeting sense of disappointment I'd experienced earlier that day when I realized Hurricane Boris was no longer a threat. I realized I had been disappointed that I hadn't had a chance to once again feel the screaming winds of a storm at sea, or watch storm waves marching towards us, and it was not the thrill I was missing — no, I was disappointed that I probably would never again work alongside Larry setting the parachute anchor, or feel *Taleisin* rise and then settle to each passing storm-generated sea as she lay hove to, because we took the right steps to prepare ourselves and the boat. I scanned the horizon, then looked once again at Larry comfortably sleeping in the bunk. I listened to the water racing under our hull, then turned to contemplate the glowing trail of bioluminescence in our wake — and I realized there were few preparations we could make, no course we could choose, to carry us unscathed through the emotional storms that now lay directly in our path.

17

New Friends, New Memories

2008 - South Pacific Ocean, bound for Samoa

This voyage from Southern California towards New Zealand encapsulated the best of cruising experiences. Two factors influenced our choice of routes. First, we would be setting sail when the hurricane season in Mexico was already at hand — thus, we wanted to get south to within a few degrees of the equator and beyond the hurricane danger area as quickly as possible. Secondly, I had a strong desire to visit at least one place we had never seen before. That left us with only one choice, heading directly towards Kiritimati in the Line Islands due south of Hawai'i. What we hadn't expected was the wonderful variety of experiences this route would add to the journey.

We were 120 miles from our first landfall when Larry said, "According to the pilot book, pretty strong, variable currents can be found in the approaches to Kiritimati Island." He marked our position on the detail chart for the Line Islands, then added, "GPS indicates we're being shoved south about 1½ knots. Don't want to accidentally be swept into this big bight on the northeast of the atoll — name is ominous:: Shipwreck Bay." Then Larry suggested we take a round of star sights before he turned in for his first off watch that night. My logbook entry for that evening still makes me chuckle. It reads: *took sights on five stars, to check GPS.*

With the star sights confirming our position, we changed course. Now we were no longer running wing and wing, but on a beam reach to counter the set from the current. Twenty hours later we had rounded the north end of Kiritimati and were reaching down the calm water to leeward of one of the largest atolls in the world. "There's not one other boat here," I commented as we reached the open roadstead anchorage indicated on our chart.

Just after midmorning the next day, when no officials had come out to give us inbound clearance, we rowed ashore to find the customs and immigration office. We were also hoping to locate a laundry or at least a communal washing spot where we could clean up the month's worth of dirty clothes we'd brought along with us in the dinghy. We didn't find either.

We secured the dinghy well above the surf line and walked up the beach to the only building we saw, a small, bright blue concrete house. A young man was waiting at the door ready to greet us. Fortunately, he, like many of the islanders we met, spoke English. "Customs officer is out fishing in the lagoon," Karau explained. "No need to see him. He already knows you are here. Just write the info he might want on a piece of paper and leave it with me. Harbormaster goes past here on his way home." When I asked if there was any internet or phone service on the island, Karau walked along with us towards the "Commercial district." He explained we were headed towards the center of London, the smallest of the three villages on the island.

A small fish freezing plant, a tiny shop, and the unmarked café stood next to a shallow fishing boat harbor and rickety wooden landing just inside the entrance to the lagoon. The café, home of the only computer and internet connection in the village, opened for five hours each weekday, Karau explained. Larry and I ordered lunch and asked him to join us, but Karau gracefully declined, saying he had people to see. Before leaving, Karau brought over the internet sign-up sheet. I added my name for a half-hour internet slot for that afternoon and for each of the next five days.

By the time we returned to the dinghy a few hours later we had learned we were the only foreign visitors on the island. Karau was waiting on his porch, and immediately came over to help us relaunch *Cheeky*. Just when I thought he'd forgotten my question about laundry he lifted the sail bag containing our dirty clothes out onto the rocky beach and announced, "My aunt would be pleased to take care of your clothes for you. She wants to earn some money so she can buy two more chickens."

Tired as we both were from the voyage, from the hours we'd just spent on shore during the heat of the tropical day, we put off retreating below for dinner. Instead, we sat watching as the sun dipped towards the horizon. Just when half of the sun had been swallowed by the sea, I noticed a disturbance in the waters astern of us. I pointed it out to Larry. "Could be a few whales," he said. I went below and got the binoculars. A minute later I didn't need them. We sat in awed silence as, just a few hundred feet from where we lay, a large pod of spinner dolphin began circling, chasing fish, leaping high into the air, twisting and turning as the tropical sunset painted their bodies gold and red.

After that first foray ashore, everyone we met greeted us by name. And soon, each person we encountered asked if we had any plans to sail onward. Six days after we'd first sailed in, I mentioned to one of the local women that we planned to leave in a day or two. "You can't," she exclaimed. But she didn't say anything more. Late that afternoon, a fisherman brought his rugged-looking outboard-powered boat carefully alongside *Taleisin* and handed me a small woven basket. Nestled on top of a hand of bananas was a printed invitation. Tears clouded my vision as I finished reading the note. "How did Teretia know my birthday is this week?" I asked.

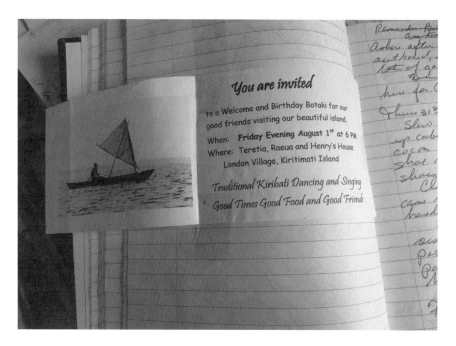

I taped Teretia's irresistible invitation into my logbook.

"Everyone knows," the fisherman answered. "The customs man told us. He knew you would need us to help you celebrate."

Three nights later 22 Micronesian[1] voices ring out in exquisite harmony, accompanied by a trio of musicians. A freshly made crown of local flowers

---

1   Kiritimati (also known as Christmas Island) is part of the Republic of Kiribati, a chain of small coral islands 2,000 miles from the home islands in the Western Pacific. Though the majority of island people in the Eastern Pacific are of Polynesian descent, the majority of Kiribati's population is of Melanesian descent.

adorned my head. A dozen women encouraged both Larry and me to join their dancing while children darted in and out of the big front room of the blue house too quickly to be accurately counted. We'd not known one person when we sailed into Kiritimati. Ten days later we had a village full of friends — friends who had worked much of the day gathering and preparing clams, crayfish, and crab, plus one of Teretia's chickens, then stringing festive lights and keeping the wood fire going to create a feast and properly celebrate my 64th birthday.

Adorned with a fragrant floral lei and headdress, I felt like a princess as my new island friends helped me celebrate my birthday.

By the next morning, when we were preparing to set sail and head farther south, the ITCZ had shifted. Instead of being a few hundred miles to the west of us, it now lay in a line that extended across Kiritimati and south along the exact track we intended following towards Penrhyn, the northernmost of the Cook Islands. We had felt the winds increasing during the night. By morning rain showers and gusting winds greeted us when we came on deck. Ever since we arrived at Kiritimati there had been a slight swell rolling through the anchorage. Not enough to be uncomfortable, but enough to ensure we didn't leave any glasses standing loose on the counters. But now the ever-increasing swells gave us irrefutable proof it was time to move on. The anchorage was becoming untenable. As Larry sheeted in the staysail and pushed the helm over to reach offshore, I looked back towards the crowd of islanders who had come down to the beach to wave farewell. What good fortune we'd had. If that ITCZ had moved over us even a day sooner, I'd have missed the most memorable birthday celebration in my life.

The strong winds made for a fast passage as we reached 700 miles due south to Penrhyn. Unfortunately, the same winds prevented us from getting ashore to experience a second place that would have been completely new to me. We arrived at the narrow pass at the height of the incoming tide. As the surge of water tried to rush through the narrow pass into Penrhyn's generously sized lagoon, it was turned into a maelstrom of overfalls by the 25 to 30 knots of wind that blew directly against the flow. Instead of trying to beat into the lagoon in these conditions, we decided to wait in the shallower waters our chart showed, just a short distance away in an area protected by a cove-like curve of the coral reef. There the water was relatively calm and clear enough that we could easily see our anchor and chain as it lay across the white sand 30 feet below us.

"This is just fine for now," Larry said. "We can work our way into the lagoon tomorrow at the change of tide when things should be calmer."

Within an hour I was delighted we had been forced to wait. Just at the height of the outgoing tide, we were treated to a sight almost as impressive as the daily display of spinner dolphins that had livened our cocktail hours at Kiritimati. Here the dolphin seemed to be practicing gliding as they surfed through the crests of four- and five-foot-high overfalls. As they reached the last of the overfalls, the dolphins continued onward, zooming through the water until they were within a dozen feet of us. There we could clearly see them, looking just like racing swimmers in indoor pools, doing underwater backflips to head into the pass for another round of surfing.

Late that afternoon, when the tide turned to flow with the wind, the pass quieted down. A large open-decked work boat motored out of the pass towards us. The helmsman introduced himself as the preacher from the village closest to the pass. He then turned to introduce the chief of the village and one of the local fishermen. "This wind is too strong for you to come ashore, if you did sail into the lagoon and anchor near our village. It is better if you wait right here until the wind grows quieter. But don't worry. I have some fresh fruit and a fish for you. Is there anything else you need?"

We waited three days more. The wind didn't abate; instead, it increased, often gusting to near-gale force. The wind and occasional rain showers kept us below deck. But Larry had worked to ensure Taleisin rode comfortably. He had rigged the anchor snubber line through a block attached to the lower edge of headstay fitting at the end of Taleisin's 8-foot bowsprit. He then led the one end of the line to the anchor chain and attached it with a rolling hitch and brought the other end back to the cleat behind the anchor windlass. Once this was done, he let out a bit more chain so the snubber took all the strain. Rigged this way, *Taleisin* didn't yaw or charge about, nor did the chain clatter against the windlass when each gust hit. To counter the slight roll from the swell that wrapped around the southern end of the atoll and made its way into our anchorage, he had set the storm trysail and sheeted it flat amidships.

Time slipped by easily. In the months leading up to this voyage, we had gathered a generous selection of books. And just before we left California, I'd hidden a dozen of the most enticing titles at the bottom of the food storage locker. I brought them out now. As we waited for better weather both of us spent hours at a time, lost in their pages. I also spent part of each day writing while Larry edited what I'd put down on paper. And just before dusk each evening the local work boat arrived, half a dozen villagers on board — ostensibly to deliver some of the island bounty, but obviously eager to know more about who we were, where we came from. I was glad my sister Bonnie, a life-long teacher, had suggested we buy several reams of brightly colored construction paper[2] and a few dozen sets of colored pencils as gifts for people we might meet in the islands. For when I offered to pay for the fresh produce and seafood the Penrhyn islanders brought to us, our greeters would not accept anything in return. They refused money, beer, wine, even sweets. But they were pleased to accept something for their children's school.

"Looks like these winds aren't going to go die down any time soon," I said to Larry on the fourth day. "Barometer hasn't shifted. I think we should head to Suwarrow."

"Lin, how about skipping Suwarrow?" he replied. "These reinforced trades are probably blowing down there too. Not a great anchorage. Why don't we head straight for Western Samoa?"[3] I was already thinking of the quiet of Suwarrow, where we'd spent a wonderful week two decades before, when Larry said, "I'm ready for some bright lights, a chance to take you out for dinner instead of watching you cook all the time. Besides, we've been at sea or in rolly anchorages for more than two months. I remember the anchorage at Apia is completely landlocked, safe and calm."

As he was speaking, I continued laying out our course to Suwarrow,

---

2   Called card stock in some countries.

3   Samoa, an independent nation. It is sometimes called Western Samoa to differentiate it from American Samoa, an unincorporated US territory which lays just 80 miles to the east.

memories of our time there flooding through my mind. I had relished being at anchor at this isolated atoll, rarely visited by anyone but cruising sailors. Though I am not much of a swimmer, I had spent part of every day snorkeling in the clear waters of Suwarrow's fish-laden lagoon. I often dove in wearing just fins and a mask to meander through colorful coral gardens where I could almost touch the small sharks that swam alongside me. Now, I hesitated before readjusting my parallel rules and laying out a course towards Samoa. But as soon as I did so, the decision became simple. With these winds, if we headed to Suwarrow we would be in for a bouncy, wet, 455-mile close reach, then another 500-mile run, dead before the wind, to reach Apia. The course directly towards Samoa would put us on an 850-mile broad reach, with the seas rolling comfortably on our stern quarter. Along with the bright lights, there would be a bonus waiting for us there:: two months' worth of forwarded mail.

⬩

Though most visitors extoll the quiet gentleness of Apia, after our time at Kiritimati and Penrhyn, we were almost overwhelmed by the abrupt change from the quiet of island anchorages to the noise of a bustling little city, the crowded sidewalks, the abundance of cafés, markets full of fresh local produce. There also was a brand-new marina[4] where we could forget about how our ground tackle was holding and enjoy being where the boat lay absolutely still and we could step ashore right off the side of the boat. This meant that, instead of having to load jugs of water into the dinghy, fill them on shore, then cart 85 gallons of water back on board, we could just turn on a tap and run a hose directly into our water tanks. There also was the camaraderie of being in the midst of a diverse crowd of voyaging sailors once again, sailors eager to include us in a constant round of socializing.

Our cruising over the previous years had taken us mostly away from tradewind cruising routes. Since leaving Bermuda bound for Argentina and Cape Horn almost seven years before, we hadn't been around more than two or three long-distance voyagers at the same time. Now we were

---

4   The marina was so new, there were still large coral heads that had not been removed from the area that was awaiting an additional section of floating docks. Unfortunately, as we were tacking through this area towards our assigned berth, we got our keel stuck between two coral heads which had not been marked. This was most embarrassing as our lead keel made a clunk that brought a few dozen cruisers out on their decks. A bit of kedging accompanied by shouts of encouragement from our audience, and we were able to sail free. Later inspection showed a bit of paint missing from the side of the keel.

surrounded by voyagers from a dozen different countries. We were meeting people who had attended seminars we'd presented in previous years, people who had read our books or viewed our videos. I must admit I enjoyed being a bit of a celebrity. I also liked hearing each person's stories, having a look through their boats. But most of all, I loved being able to refute my mother's warning as I watched Larry, full of energy and eagerly heading off to check over a mainsheet arrangement that was giving one of our marina neighbors problems, then across the marina to help trace the source of a leak in another cruiser's deck.

He came back on board from his leak-tracing mission with a suggestion that went on to become a topic of conversation throughout the Apia cruising fleet. "Lin, you said you planned to update the *Capable Cruiser*. I think you have a great opportunity for a new chapter right here," Larry said. "A lot of the folks we are meeting had never crossed an ocean until they set sail for Polynesia. That was the first time they encountered the realities of long-distance voyaging."

His suggestion: Interview as many people as possible and ask them what they worried about that *didn't* actually happen. Within one day I had lined up a dozen interviewees, and rekindled my plan to use this voyage to gather new information I could add to the third edition of *Capable Cruiser*.

Halfway through our stay in Apia, I had sent an email to a couple we'd met a few years previously when we had been cruising Desolation Sound in British Columbia. We'd enjoyed encouraging them as they organized their life, sold their house, and prepared their handsome 28 foot Bristol Channel Cutter for a long cruising sabbatical. We last exchanged emails at Kiritimati so I knew they were planning to leave French Polynesia bound westward as we were sailing towards Apia. I had been expecting to find them or at least an email from them as soon as we arrived in Apia. When neither was waiting, I'd written, "Where are you now? Still on for our rendezvous in Tonga?"

The next day I almost cried as I read, "We are so disappointed. After sailing all the way from Seattle we are stuck only 75 miles away from you. We broke our mast."

The email described how they had been running through the convergence zone between Bora Bora and Suwarrow. As the wind increased almost to gale force, they decided to heave to. By then they were running under just a scrap of jib held out by the spinnaker pole. They decided to take that down before they turned into the wind to heave to. Unfortunately, just as they prepared to roll in the last of the jib, a steep wave sent the boat into a broach. The force of the spinnaker pole hitting the water shoved it against the mast so hard, the mast developed an eight-inch kink. Under vastly reduced canvas they had carried on to Pago Pago in American Samoa, where they tried to get a new mast shipped in. Once they replaced the mast they planned to continue their journey. Their email ended with, "Can't find any guaranteed way we can get a replacement mast to let us carry on and reach New Zealand before the cyclone season sets in. Looks like this is the end of our cruise. We are searching for a way to ship the boat home."

I immediately wrote back. "Send some detailed photos of your mast. Maybe Larry can come up with a way to fix it."

In my eyes, Larry deserves a hero badge for his actions from that moment forward. When I showed him the email exchange, he immediately said, "Check out the price of some airline tickets. I know I can fix that mast!"

The force of the spinnaker pole hitting the water during the broach had bent the mast almost eight inches out of true.

Emails flew back and forth. By the end of the day, a five-foot-long section of aluminum mast and two sets of aluminum splines, built to Larry's specifications, had been ordered from the spar builder in California.

Our friends had one bit of good fortune in this situation. On almost every other island throughout the South Pacific, packages can sometimes take as long as a month to arrive, even those sent via express courier. But Pago Pago has daily plane service from the US mainland. Courier packages sent from the West Coast take only two days to arrive.

Three days later, we were on a plane from Apia, Western Samoa (the *real* Samoa, according to locals) to Pago Pago. By the time we arrived, our friends had their mast out of the boat and lying in the local boat yard, along with the parts that had been made by the same people who originally built the mast. I watched in awe as Larry set to work. Using a skilsaw, Larry cut the mast into three sections. Just 48 hours after we arrived in Pago Pago, the mast, with its supporting splines riveted in place, was now perfectly straight and only 1/8th of an inch shorter than it had been when it was built. And now it was being hoisted back into the boat, and we were on a plane back to *Taleisin*.

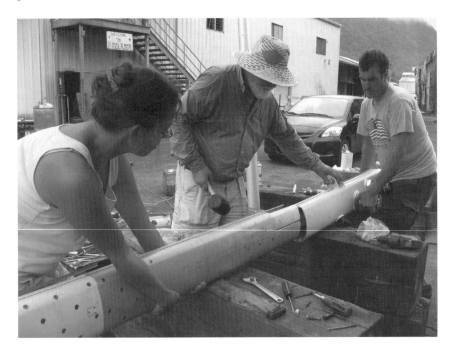

First the spar was cut into three separate pieces, then two replacement sections with internal splines were riveted in place. Renamed Frankenmast, the spare served well for several thousand miles of sailing.

18
Return to the Happy Kingdom

2008 - The Kingdom of Tonga

"Are you sure this is a good idea?" I asked Larry when the peak of Tafahi rose over the horizon.

Just a few miles south of this towering, steep-sided volcano lay our destination, the island where the finest memories of our first South Pacific crossings were born.

I really appreciated Taleisin's wide, clear foredeck and eight-inch-high bulwarks.

"I am looking forward to being anchored in a quiet place," Larry answered. "Nuiatoputapu is the best anchorage in the South Pacific and, even if there are a dozen yachts there, it won't feel crowded." Then, for the third or fourth time he reminded me, "Just don't expect things to be the same."

Twenty-three years previously, the captain of the port at Nuiatoputapu (he was also the chief of police, head radio operator, health inspector and postmaster) informed us *Taleisin* was just the second cruising boat to anchor in the lagoon and we were the first cruising visitors to come ashore at this isolated island, which is home to about 1,200 Tongans. Up until a few weeks before we arrived, there had been no way through the barrier reef for boats drawing more than three feet. Nuiatoputapu is separated from the rest of Tonga by almost 200 miles of ocean. Supply ships, which arrived approximately every six weeks, lay offshore and transferred cargo and passengers using barges. The only possible anchorage for yachts was on a small ledge on the outer side of the reef. Unfortunately, this ledge is also a favorite breeding and nursery area for migrating humpback whales, and their migration coincides with the safe cruising season.

When we had been in Apia, Samoa, during our first foray towards Tonga, we'd struck up a friendship with the captain off an Australian cargo ship. During a meal onboard his ship, the captain mentioned the Australian Navy had just finished blasting a pass through the reef at Nuiatoputapu. Armed with a paper sketch of the pass the captain had drawn, we'd ventured slightly off the normal cruising route and experienced an amazing reception which convinced us Tonga deserved the name bestowed upon it by Captain Cook, "The Friendly Isles."[1]

Fortunately, Larry's warnings had been unnecessary. As we sailed in for the second time, things were very much the same as they'd been 23 years before, maybe even a bit better. Despite being just 40 or 50 miles to leeward of a rhumbline course between Western Samoa and VavaŠu, Tonga, I was surprised to see only one cruising boat at anchor near the landing at the eastern most of the three villages on Nuiatoputapu. On shore, we could see a few new concrete houses, and a new covered meeting area near the boat landing alongside a fish sorting shed. Just as had happened many years previously, soon after we anchored, two youngsters rowed towards us waving wildly. But this time, instead of bringing us gifts and telling us we would have to walk to the capital to find any officials, the youngsters yelled in heavily accented English, "The customs ladies saw you sailing in.

---

1   In my book, *Taleisin's Tales, Sailing towards the Southern Cross*, I have written in much more detail about that first visit to the Friendly Isles.

They will be here as soon as they change into their uniforms. You must row ashore and pick them up."

Even from a few hundred yards away, I could hear the giggles and shrieks as three tall, fulsome Tongan women were helped into our eight-foot dinghy by a crowd of youngsters. I had cookies and canned soft drinks waiting, along with the guest book we had used on *Taleisin* since the day she was launched. As soon as we'd filled out the obligatory forms, I opened the guestbook and pointed to an entry. "Do you know Molokeini Lolohea? Does she still live here?" I asked. "She was just 17 years when we visited your island."

An uproar ensued — laughter and exclamations of surprise. It took several minutes before the officials slowed down and explained why they were so excited. "You won't believe it. Molokeini hasn't been home for two years. She just arrived back on the island two days ago. She lives in New Zealand now and has brought her two boys to stay for the next six months."

I rowed ashore on my own soon afterward, while Larry took a "catch-up snooze." I was sitting on the grass next to the dinghy, putting on my walking shoes when I noticed a tall, elegant lady walking towards me. Even though she was now almost middle-aged and no longer a gangly teenager, I immediately recognized Molokeini.

"Are you the Pelangi (non-islander) who is looking for me?" she asked. I began singing the first lines of "Grandma's Feather Bed," the song I'd taught some of the island children many years before. Keini let out a shriek and threw her arms around me. "Linnie, I knew we'd meet again!"

Molokeini Tollemach, the vibrant, laughing teenager I'd met 23 years before, now was an elegant and warmhearted woman.

*Here is Molokeini (Keini) with her arm around Larry. Her sisters and mother
stand next to her. In the front row are Keini's two sons, Fred and Daniel with their cousin.*

*By the time we'd walked the length of the island and given each of the nearly 400 school
children and teachers on Nuiatoputapu three ball point pens, I was relieved to be offered a
ride home in the island's only school bus.*

Two weeks later, as we were negotiating our way past the pod of whales which frolicked and slapped their tails just outside Nuiatoputapu's reef entrance, I recalled our concerns about revisiting a place that held such fond memories. Just as she had all those years ago, Keini once again wove us into the island social life. Two other cruising boats arrived during our stay, each carrying people we knew well. They too were enfolded into our "family" and included in forays to the family plantation, where everyone brought home baskets of fresh tropical fruits, plus treks along the spine of the rugged interior hills, fishing expeditions, shared meals, weaving sessions with a half-dozen local women trying to guide the feeble efforts of cruisers who had never made a basket before. A real highlight for both Keini and me came about when I asked her how I should share the reams of multi-colored construction paper, the colored pencils we had stashed in the lazarette, plus the 1,500 ballpoint pens I'd been given by my book distributor as I helped him pack up after the national publishers book fair I had attended just a month before we set sail from the US. After careful consideration Keini declared, "You realize the children must buy their own school supplies. Pens cost more than a dollar each here. That is a heavy burden on a family that might earn only $40 or $50 cash income in a month. I counted and there are enough to give three pens to each child in the primary and secondary schools. The card paper and colored pencils should go to the teachers to use for their art lessons."

Fortunately, when I was getting everything out of the lazarette, I had found one extra box of 300 monogrammed pens hidden under a sail bag. In the excitement of unloading everything from the dinghy into a wagon Keini had brought along, I'd forgotten to tell her about the extras. At the first school we visited, as I was handing each child their allotment of pens, I noticed two of the teachers intensely conversing with Keini. She came over to me and whispered, "The school doesn't have enough money to buy pens for the teachers. The teachers were hoping they could have a pen too. But I told them you have only enough for the children." But because of that extra box, everyone was happy that day. Each of the nearly 400 school children and each of the teachers in five different schools on Nuiatoputapu had three pens. By the time we said farewell at the last school, we had walked the length of the island. I was relieved when the headmaster suggested Keini and I be driven back to my dinghy in the island's one and only school bus.

Two days later, just after the sun rose, Larry and I cranked in our anchor and set sail. I stood on the foredeck, waving back towards where I could still see Keini watching from the shore. She had been up at daybreak to say one last farewell and bring us yet another gift, an intricately woven basket brimming with fresh fruit to share with cousins who lived 200 miles south in Neiafu, VavaṠu.

We received many gifts during our stay in Tonga. Only a few of them were material. We had forged a firm friendship with Keini and her two sons, 10-year-old Daniel and 12-year-old Fred, a friendship that would help me through the storms that were waiting just beyond the horizon. I'd been reminded that wealth comes in many forms, one of which is being part of a caring community like we'd seen in this and other Polynesian islands where cash was limited. And, I'd learned that, as much as the cruising fleet has grown since Larry and I first set off several decades previously, by being willing to venture just a short way off the beaten track, by slowing right down and forgetting about calendars, there are still places where you can find the magic that accrues into unforgettable cruising memories.

We pulled up our anchor and slowly sailed towards Neiafu, the capital and port of entry for the VavaṠu archipelago.

We'd spent three months here during our last visit, and back then, we had also arrived with baskets of fresh produce Keini's family had sent along for her cousins. From the moment we delivered these gifts, we were adopted into the boisterous, generous Hausia family. We kept in touch after we left, exchanged letters and occasional gifts through the years. Before we set sail from California, I'd written to say we might be coming to VavaṠu on our way through Tonga as we sailed towards our home in New Zealand. In the mail package we'd received on our arrival in Apia, I was delighted to find I'd finally meet my 23-year-old goddaughter Linlarry in person, not just in photographs. When she heard we were headed towards Tonga, Linlarry had decided to fly from her current home in Brisbane, Australia, with her two-year-old daughter Vasali.

As we walked up to her family home in the quiet village of Pangaimotu, just a few miles from Neiafu, she was standing in the doorway, holding her daughter, Vasali. "I have a big photo of the two of you on the wall at home. Everyone wants to know why it is there and why I have Pelangi godparents. I tell them what my mother told me: I am here because you gave her too much wine when she was having dinner on your boat."

The bright red summer dress I'd bought for Linlarry in Apia, Samoa, had seemed quite modest to me. I had to guess at the correct size based on a photograph she had sent me. As I was shopping, I looked around the store to find someone I hoped was the right size and asked her to model it for me. A few nights after we sailed into Neiafu, the port of entry for the northern most group of Tongan islands, I realized I'd misjudged the customary mores of my local family.

Linlarry had appeared delighted with the gift we'd given to her the day we arrived. Now she walked alongside me looking stunning in the red dress and holding my hand as we headed towards the café where visiting cruisers gather to dance to the music of a local band. She looked into the window of the crowded café and surveyed the crowd. Then she stepped back and let go of my hand to reach into her handbag. She pulled a white summery jacket out and quickly slid her arms into it and said, "Sorry, but there are people who know me and my parents in there. I don't want them to see me in a public place with my shoulders bare. It would embarrass my family."

My goddaughter Linlarry and her daughter Vasali.

VavaŚu had changed. But, only on the surface. Now there were moorings which we learned were lifted each year and professionally maintained, plus a greatly enhanced assortment of businesses and technicians offering special services for the large fleet of cruising boats that congregated here. There were a dozen cafés, whereas before there had been three. Instead of just one small resort, there was an array of small resorts on several of the small islands scattered throughout the archipelago, which catered to a contingent of overseas tourists hoping to swim with the humpback whales which, during the winter months, frequented VavaŜu's clear waters. But the underlying relaxed and welcoming nature of the local people was the same. Just as in the past, Larry and I looked forward to Sunday church services with our family, and we hummed along with the elegant harmonies as the whole congregation joined in, hymn after hymn. The same relaxed activities filled our days as we sometimes met at the family plantation, sometimes on board *Taleisin*, and sometimes on one of the small islands where a dozen or more members of "our family" gathered to swim, snorkel, and spear fish to cook over an open fire we built on the sand. The biggest difference was that now, Linlarry was always there to ensure we were comfortable, included, and treated as someone important and dear to her.

Only one change bothered me. After a few weeks of being secured to a mooring I felt like finding a quiet place to ourselves for a few days, a place where I could spend a few days writing and where I would feel no obligation to join in each gathering or event our Tongan family and other cruisers proposed. I was surprised by Larry's reaction when I suggested setting sail and heading off to one of the anchorages that lay just a dozen miles from Neiafu. He shook his head and said, "I like it right here on this mooring. I know it is safe. Don't have to constantly worry about squalls, wind changing direction, anchor dragging."

In the past it had always been Larry who became restless after just a few days in a busy anchorage. I was surprised to realize he appeared to be hiding his anxieties from me, so I pressed him until he finally blurted out, "You're not the one who has to try to row out an anchor when the wind gets up. You're not the one who has to get in the water and dive down to see if the anchor is properly set or untangle the chain if it snags on a coral head. I just don't think I can do it anymore."

His outburst left me sleepless that night. Up until that moment, I had probably been fooling myself by thinking Larry wanted to get home to New Zealand because he had satisfied his desire to cruise to new places, that he wanted to settle where he could once again use his hands and skills building beautiful things out of timber. Now I had to face a bigger reality. My hero was fading.

———————

About four weeks after we sailed into Neiafu, I began consulting my favorite weather sites each morning in the computer lounge at the Coconut Café just inshore of us. Each time, as I was leaving, I'd been approached by one or another of the other voyagers who, like me, were watching for a break in the weather to head south at the end of the southern hemisphere winter and before the start of the tropical cyclone season. "What do you think of this weather pattern? What are you looking for? When do you plan to leave?" I was asked. Never before had I been amidst such a large gathering of relatively new voyagers. As the number of cruisers who were interested in my decision grew, I felt a mantle of responsibility land on my shoulders.

I could appreciate the concerns these cruisers felt. Though the voyage from Tonga to New Zealand is relatively short, just 1,100 miles if you sail a rhumbline course, this would be the first time most of them would be crossing out of the tradewind-warmed tropics and towards the gale-prone waters in the approaches to New Zealand, the first time that they could not count on following winds and seas and might have to go windward in potentially fresh breezes.

With the realization that Larry was less confident than I was used to, I was doubly concerned as I watched for the right weather window for our departure. That is when I decided to call Bob McDavitt, friend and highly respected New Zealand weather forecaster who had made a name for himself as a weather advisor in yacht racing circles. Now he offered his services as a weather router for yachts transiting the Pacific. Bob laughed knowingly as I explained my predicament. "Bob, if I contact you when I see a window I like, can you let me know if I am missing something. We've been across this sea several times before and are probably more willing to put up with going to windward in heavier weather than these newer cruisers."

"Sure," he replied immediately.

Four days later I was on the phone again with Bob.

"So what are your plans?" he said when I suggested we'd be setting sail in two days.

"Head down to about 30 degrees south, then turn west," I replied. "When we get due north of Cape Reinga, turn south." To give him a chance to consult his array of magic weather models I waited at the phone exchange and called him back an hour later.

"Looks like a pretty nice window for you," he said. "But I think there could be a brisk southwesterly forming in the Tasman about ten days from now. I'd consider keeping on your westward track and sailing an extra 50 or 60 miles past the north tip of New Zealand before turning south." I couldn't see any downside in taking his suggestion. If the wind shifted to the west, we'd be able to reach down to New Zealand instead of having to go to windward. If it didn't shift, but continued to blow from the east, we'd just have to tighten up our sheets a bit for the last few days of our passage.

I shared this information with a few of the cruisers who had been asking about my plans. At their suggestion, I joined in on the morning cruisers' network using our handheld VHF radio and explained why I was choosing this time to leave, plus I noted our intended track and what Bob had suggested.

Larry pointed astern as we sailed into deep water a few hours after setting sail from Neiafu. There, a dozen sails could be seen, heading south just as we were. I thought of these sailors often as we contended with squally winds and hove to for 10 hours just three days out. The air temperatures began to drop more each day as we sailed south. When we reached 30 degrees south latitude we turned due west, and I got out another blanket and our winter sweaters. The winds steadied and carried us relatively swiftly towards our next waypoint.

When we were about 250 miles from New Zealand, I picked up a shore station on my shortwave radio and heard, "Thursday, winds shifting to SW 20 knots, gusting 25." Bob had called it perfectly. Thursday would be exactly 10 days after we'd departed Neiafu. We carried on past the longitude of New Zealand for another 50 miles as he suggested, before turning south. I'll always remember the rambunctious fun reach we had then, about 15 degrees off close-hauled, staysail and reefed main eased and pulling well, *Taleisin*'s taffrail log spinning at seven knots, Larry looking well rested and eager as spray flew across the foredeck and occasionally spattered against the companionway hood.

Eleven days out of Neiafu, the distinctive rocks at the entrance to New Zealand's Bay of Islands came clear on the horizon. I dug out my New Zealand cellphone and attached it to our solar charger.

"Can't you relax and enjoy this nice sailing?" Larry said. "Wind's eased off enough we can have breakfast on deck.

"No, I wanted it charged because as soon as we get reception, I need to call Mom," I told Larry.

"Need to or want to. She won't know the difference if you wait until we actually get into Opua."

I couldn't explain my gut feeling to Larry. Something within me made me want to call immediately.

An hour later I had a signal.

"Lin, I am so glad you called," Mom said. "I had a great time taking Cami's kids to the San Francisco Zoo yesterday. I flew home this morning because I had a doctor's appointment."

Then, as casually as if she was talking about needing a haircut or a crown for a tooth she said, "I knew there was something wrong when I felt all achy, but the doctor ignored me. Now he tells me I have bone cancer and I'm dying. But don't rush around buying airline tickets. Get Larry and that boat of yours home first. Doctor says I'll be around for another three or four months."

Part Five
Home and Beyond

19

The Trajectory of Our Lives

2009 - New Zealand

When Larry and I first met, I was an insecure, lonely, somewhat frustrated 20-year-old university drop-out, working at jobs that paid a bit more than the minimum wage. I had little idea of what I wanted to do next. But I was determined I didn't want to lead "a normal life." Unfortunately, I had no idea of how to achieve that. Larry, on the other hand, knew exactly where he was headed and, at 26, had already acquired the skills he needed to make his dreams a reality. He was rarely concerned about earning money because he had an array of skills that were uniquely suited to his chosen life. He also had a nice lump of money set aside for emergencies. Thus, in our nascent relationship, he had power on his side, power he used gently to entice me into his world as he taught me to sail, to create things using my hands and, to be willing to leap into the unknown.

As we worked side by side building *Seraffyn*, and then headed off cruising, I became, under Larry's guidance, not only a competent sailor but a more confident person. Within a few years I was able to assist as well as any paid crew when we delivered boats, and able to do the finish work as he repaired boats. Gradually my writing income increased. That's when I began to see a shift in the power dynamics of our relationship. Within a few years of publishing my first story, I began earning as much or more from my writing as Larry from his boatbuilding skills. One day I asked if this bothered him. "Hell no, makes me proud as hell. Makes me feel freer," Larry replied. "I am the one who helped you find something to write about. Now I know you can take care of both of us if anything happens to me."

By the time we finished our first circumnavigation on board *Seraffyn* and began building *Taleisin*, our relationship felt like it was on a completely equal footing. We had always tried to share decision making, but now comfortably accepted which one of us should have the final say on certain aspects of our life: me on financial matters, Larry on construction decisions. As Larry worked most of the day building the new boat, while I spent many of my hours at my desk, we began joking that he was earning our capital while I was earning the cash.

We set sail from North Cove on Kawau Island, planning to sail to Australia to restore a 117-year-old boat there. It was, 21 years and a circumnavigation ever westward via the southern capes, before we sailed her back home again.

It wasn't until we sailed past Cape Horn and on towards Canada that I noticed this power dynamic gradually shifting the other way. As Larry began to feel the first signs of aging, I began taking on more and more of the decision-making, more of the financial responsibility. With the confidence and skills Larry had helped me gain through the years, this didn't feel like a burden, but an opportunity to shape the next stages of our life, as Larry had shaped it in the beginning.

With encouragement from my sister and brother, I boarded a plane to California a day after arriving in Opua, the northernmost yacht clearance port in New Zealand. "Forget funerals, come now," both Bonnie and Allen had urged me when I called. I am so glad I rushed. While I was on the plane, enroute to Los Angeles, my mother took a fall as she was getting out of bed. By the time I landed in California, she was just coming out of emergency surgery, which had been performed to stabilize a shattered hip. By the time I arrived at the hospital, Mom was conscious and by evening, eager to recall how much she had enjoyed dancing with Larry just before we set sail five months previously. We cried together, we laughed together. I was able to hug and thank her one last time for not killing me when I was a totally contrary teenager. And I didn't laugh when she insisted, "The most important thing I've done is make sure you and Allen and Bonnie are there for each other. If you ever fall out, I'll come back to haunt you."

I had told Allen and Bonnie I was a bit concerned at how tired Larry had seemed once we arrived in New Zealand. With their full encouragement, I didn't stay once Mom faded into a comatose state; we knew her death was imminent. And so, I was on a flight back to New Zealand only five days after I'd flown to see my family. All the way across the Pacific, my hand reached for the gold and opal pendant my brother and sister felt I should take with me as a reminder that Mom was delighted with the choices I'd made through the years. She wore the pendant almost every day. And Allen and Bonnie reminded me Mom often said, "Lin is having the kind of life I could only dream of."

When I arrived back in New Zealand, Larry was at the local airport accompanied by our close friend Doug Schmuck. Since sailing from the USA and settling in New Zealand almost 20 years previously, Doug had relocated from Kawau Island to the Bay of Islands and bought a small boat yard near the customs dock in Opua. *Taleisin* was secured on one of his moorings. I was surprised to learn Doug and his wife, Helen, had insisted Larry move off the boat and stay with them on their small farm, 10 miles from the boat yard.

"I didn't feel comfortable leaving him on his own," Doug told me when we had a quiet moment. "Do you realize how helpless he is without you? Couldn't even figure out how to take money out of the ATM, got lost when we were in Kerikeri for dinner."

I was able to hide my annoyance as I explained I always used the ATMs, not Larry. I handled our only cell phone, and the computer, because Larry had no interest at all in electronic "stuff."

"Give him a break," I told Doug, "He's 70 years old and we just got in from a long season of voyaging and the last few days of sailing were fun, but pretty rambunctious. Larry's not confused, he's just tired. Larry and Mom were very close. So he's probably upset about that too."

"Might be right," Doug said. Then he laughed and added, "He was down at the boat yard working with me every day, alert, full of good ideas, not confused at all. He sure does know how to move boats around. Teased me about having the most labor-intensive yacht haulout system in the world."

Looking back at the three or four years that followed my conversation with Doug, I now see I was guilty of hiding from reality. Probably, had I considered Doug's observations more carefully, or mentioned Larry's occasional memory lapses to our doctor, or mentioned some of the other small changes that were happening, we would have learned Larry was experiencing the early signs of Parkinson's disease. But I didn't. And that meant, instead of treating Larry as somehow fragile or needing constant medical attention, instead of searching for cures, instead of Larry or me visualizing and worrying about the tragic downhill slide facing him, the two of us just got on with life. It is a choice I would make again because the next few years of our life together, though quite different from the previous ones, were truly memorable.

Within a few days of sailing alongside the jetty at our island home, Larry was contentedly hard at work sketching up plans for a guest house he wanted to build at the far side of our property. I was excited about this too. Our house, though beautifully renovated and exactly what the two of us wanted and needed, is small, with only one bedroom and one bathroom. We often suggested our mainland visitors stay for the night on the sofa in my office rather than rush to catch the last ferry of the day at 6 pm. But now that we wouldn't be off cruising as much, I knew we would enjoy having more overnight visitors. The money my mother had left to me would cover the cost of buying materials and hiring an apprentice builder to help Larry and speed the project along.

Soon Larry was handing me ever-growing lists of the materials he would need. At the same time, he was also working on the final details that would ensure the unique birthday gift he'd given me was in perfect working order.

Through our years together, Larry had not been much of a gift giver. Maybe that was because the first surprise he gifted me, a puppy, promptly bit my hand so hard I ended up in hospital. In any case, instead of surprising me with gift-wrapped packages, he'd notice me looking at a dress or blouse and suggest, "Why don't we buy that for you?" I always felt his pragmatism and his tenderness when he'd admit, "I never know what to get you so let's call it a birthday gift." And then, after years of knowing this was Larry's approach to gift-giving, there came the unexpected surprise of two significant gifts.

During the previous three years, when we were enjoying endless summers by commuting between North America and New Zealand, we had been custodians of *Jonquil*, Each time we arrived back in New Zealand, we'd sail *Jonquil* from her mooring in Auckland near Sarah's place to our Kawau home, where we prepared her for the season and continued to upgrade her. After a summer of regattas interspersed with local cruising on *Taleisin*, we would sail *Jonquil* back to her Auckland mooring. The previous season, when we'd contacted Sarah to say we were flying back to New Zealand and would retrieve *Jonquil* and prepare her for summer racing, I had been disappointed to learn I'd done my job too well. Sarah's daughter Sybil had enjoyed racing with us and gained the confidence to take charge of *Jonquil* by herself. By then Sybil was 18 and had gathered a group of friends who liked sailing with her. "Sybil wants to keep *Jonquil* here right near our home," Sarah said. "But she says you are welcome to crew for her in some of the big regattas."

Though we had *Taleisin* waiting at the jetty, ready to take us cruising among the myriad islands nearby, I'd come to love the camaraderie found by being part of the very active classic boat racing fleet. I loved the challenges of learning how to control a gaff-rigged lightweight centerboard boat, of coming to terms with *Jonquil*'s 120-feet of mainsheet when it was time to gybe jibe the boom, a boom that extended several feet beyond the transom.

And I soon had further proof Larry felt the same when, a few weeks after learning *Jonquil* was no longer part of our life, he mentioned he had been asked to visit a boatbuilding friend on the mainland. "You've got a deadline to keep," Larry reminded me. "Neil wants me to look at some boat that needs repairing. So, I'll head over on my own."

Two days later he came sailing into North Cove on a tatty-looking, 34-foot gaff-rigged sloop with an elegant but dainty profile. On board with him was Lynn Shrewsbury, the boat's owner. "I know it's a few months late," Larry said as he stepped ashore and gave me a hug, "But Happy Birthday — that is, if you like her and if we survey her and don't find too much wrong."

I helped guide *Thelma*, a 114-year-old beauty, onto our tidal grid, then secured her lines. Then I climbed on board and began noticing the details

Thelma *is dried out on the tidal grid next to the boatshed so Larry can repair the scrolling on her trailboards.*

Reefed down in 28 knots gusting to 32, Thelma *averaged close to 10 knots as we raced around Rangitoto Island, just outside Auckland Harbour. photo - Jill Dingle* that would shine once I got out my sandpaper and varnish brushes. I had my fingers crossed all during the three hours we had to wait for the tide to recede so Larry could go over every inch of her. A few hours later, she was mine. I walked along the shore a short distance to admire *Thelma*'s sleek, handsome underbody, her lovely clipper bow. As I was standing there admiring *Thelma*, a neighbor came walking along the foreshore.

"Beautiful boat," she said. "Do you know anything about her?"

"Yup, designed by C.W. Bailey. Built in Auckland in 1895. She's mine. Larry just gave her to me as a birthday gift."

"Doesn't he know about jewelry?" my neighbor chuckled.

"Well, to a sailor she is probably the ultimate piece of jewelry," I said — and found myself smiling the rest of the day.

Thelma had cost Larry very little, about the same as a five-year-old car because a portion of her stern had serious rot issues, and her rigging needed upgrading. But within two days, Larry had taken a chainsaw to her transom and opened the affected area to expose the inside of her lazarette. Six weeks later *Thelma* and the two of us were out racing.

Thelma proved to be an excellent gift. She let me once again watch Larry at his best, confidently shaving off the edge of a plank so it slid perfectly into place, or carefully chiseling out a damaged section of carving in the beautifully scrolled decorative trailboards adorning her clipper bow. By the time he inserted a sliver of wood and I'd added a coat of paint, the century-old scroll work looked like new.

An extra bonus of owning *Thelma* was the new friendships she drew into our lives. This included the two generations of previous owners who were delighted to see her out on the water again, and the other classic boat owners who were glad she hadn't ended up abandoned and rotted. "So good to preserve these truly old classics," Chad Thompson, the commodore of the Classic Boat Association, said when he came by to visit. "Only 150 are now left sailing in all of New Zealand."

By the time we had *Thelma* shaped up enough to enter our first races together, we had found a building assistant to work with Larry, and the timber to frame up the guest house had arrived. At the same time, the seed I'd planted when I realized our offshore cruising days were coming to an end had sprouted, far more quickly than I expected.

At the first Kawau Island residents committee meeting I attended after we arrived home with *Taleisin*, I had been asked if I would stand for election as the political representative for the community. I learned that meant attending occasional meetings of the local council at the nearby village on the mainland, and occasionally the district council 40 miles to the south in

Auckland City, to ensure the problems faced by a small, isolated community on a unique roadless island were addressed. I have never been elected to anything, never taken part in what usually turns out to be a popularity competition, knew nothing about what councils did, and had little grasp of New Zealand laws and regulations — and said so.

"But you know how to write, and you aren't the least bit afraid of standing up and speaking in front of people," the retiring representative said. With that Lyn Hume and Michael Marris, the other two people who had previously worked together in this position and had put their hands up for the election, immediately decided I should become the chairman of the Kawau Island Advisory Committee and they, the two members.

"Sounds like you have volunteered to be the dog catcher," Larry joked as, over the next few evenings, I began working my way through the three large folders of council business that might affect Kawau. But slowly he became a willing sounding board and supporter as part of each day I worked with my "team" to defeat a mainland government's scheme to increase the fee islanders paid to park their cars at the ferry landing on the mainland from $200 a year to $1,800. What I'd learned from our previous legal battle helped me overcome my frustration with bureaucrats. I became fascinated by the intricacies of working with local government, then eventually town planners, while at the same time learning how to work with the differing factions that exist in most communities.

My world of writing expanded dramatically. This was the period when I turned my attention to adding books written by other people to the list of books published by L & L Pardey Publications. We had originally set this informal company up to distribute the videos we made with Roy Blow in Australia. Then it had expanded to include the books we wrote. This expansion was prompted by the fact that our previous publishing house had shut its doors on the sailing books that were a minor part of their list.

Timing had seemed to be on our side, almost always — in sailing, and in publishing. We had been lucky with our books — allowing us to share our growing knowledge and reach an audience of cruisers and sailing enthusiasts. For 17 years, each one we wrote was published by W.W. Norton, a highly reputable New York publisher noted for serious academic tomes and books like *Helter Skelter* and *The Ugly American*. Its vice chairman, Eric Swenson, had acquired those illustrious titles and was a keen, and successful, racing sailor. To add spice to his life, Eric decided to create a nautical line of books. Larry and I had been amazed when he wrote and suggested we let him publish our second book, *Seraffyn's European Adventures*. We would be joining Eric's stable of some of the best-known nautical writers of our time.

236

Larry insisted we actually go to New York, just for the thrill of signing our first book contract in person. Eric made it feel even more momentous as he laid the paperwork out on the same round table at the famous Algonquin Hotel where literary giants like Noel Coward, Edna Ferber, Harpo Marx and Dorothy Parker had once shared boisterous lunches.

Seven books later we were disappointed to learn Eric was retiring. In 1996, we had flown from South Africa to present seminars in 20 different cities and introduce the first edition of *Storm Tactics Handbook*. While we were there, we learned no one else at W.W. Norton was interested in continuing Eric's nautical book line. "People still want your books, but we don't have any editors who want to take over getting them reprinted," the chairman had told us. Then he suggested we join the growing trend towards independent publishing and begin publishing our own books. I doubt we would have tried this on our own, but we were offered the help of W.W. Norton's staff to shepherd us through the intricacies of publishing. This was the start of an exciting new journey.

I found learning about publishing was mind-expanding and exciting. Though it was time-consuming, though we had to foot all the costs of hiring editors and designers, and though we had to finance the printing of 2,000 books at a time, the financial returns were many times higher. Larry, who seemed to thrive on risk, and always preferred feeling he was in control of his own financial life, loved it. He relished being able to choose the cover picture and design we wanted, relished being able to set the book's price and track the actual sales. "I really didn't like other people being in control of our retirement fund," he stated as we went through the process of finding a book distributor, a book designer, or editors. But soon we had the first edition of *Storm Tactics Handbook*, with our own logo on the spine, sitting on *Taleisin*'s bookshelf (and fortunately on many others too). By the time we were preparing to set sail from the Pacific Northwest, several years after becoming self-publishers, we had successfully launched two new books, plus new editions of four of our previous books.

And then, we did a little more. In 2006, just before we left Port Townsend bound for New Zealand, we had visited Herb Payson, another well-known sailing writer. Several years previously, Herb had written what is probably one of the funniest cruising books I've read, telling about the cruise he and Nancy took through the Pacific on a leaky 36-foot-long wooden boat with four of their six children on board. The book, *Blown Away*, had been a rousing success and been reprinted several times. As we were chatting, Nancy mentioned how sad it was that *Blown Away*, after selling out the latest edition, was now out of print, had never been offered as an eBook, and there were no copies left to give to their grandchildren.

"Why don't you self-publish it?" I suggested. "I can coach you through the process."

Herb immediately replied, "Why don't you publish it for me?"

Larry didn't hesitate. "Why not?"

By the time we headed home, I had finished updating Herb's book and it was almost ready to go to the printer and be uploaded as an eBook, complete with our new logo – L and L Pardey Publications.

 Now I could actually call myself a publisher. To top everything off, income from our own books had increased enough that I felt I could finally afford to spend a year or more writing a book I had been putting aside, a memoir that I sensed would interest only a small portion of our sailing readers because it was set on land, not the sea. I made ten photocopies of the six chapters I'd written several years previously. Then I asked the members of the Kawau Bookworms readers group for their honest opinions. "Dump the first three paragraphs and go for it," was the consensus. With the bookworms and Larry encouraging me, I set to work on my first memoir, a project that I found far more challenging than writing narratives about sailing. The resulting book, *Bull Canyon*, eventually gained the subtitle, *A Boatbuilder, a Writer, and Other Wildlife*, as well as my first literary award.

For most of the four decades since Larry and I launched *Seraffyn* in 1968, I had spent only a few months each year working for money, the rest of the year meandering around under sail. Now, just when I reached the age of 65, I found myself fully employed and fully involved in a world that reached beyond sailboats. Each day I dedicated four hours to writing, two to publishing and another hour or two – sandpaper, varnish, or paintbrush in hand – to adding the final touch to Larry's current project. Any spare time I had left was consumed by my ever-expanding role as chairman of the Kawau Island Advisory Board, followed by a walk to inspect progress on the cottage that now we had named The Heron's Nest. I couldn't have felt better about this new routine. It also seemed to suit Larry as he lovingly built a handsome 150-square-foot guest cabin on a 500-square-foot raised platform 150 feet beyond our boat shop and almost 600 feet away from our cottage. Each evening, he was eager to read and edit whatever I'd written or discuss "community business."

When we had successfully rounded Cape Horn, Larry stated he finally fulfilled every dream he had ever had. But as we had been cruising through the Pacific towards New Zealand, the books we carried included several biographies and added a new dream, a wish to someday relate his story, or more accurately, our story, to a skillful writer, then see it in print. His dream unexpectedly came true soon after he finished the final details of the cottage. The genesis of this was an article written by a relatively new sailing journalist, Cindy Rogers. Cindy had interviewed us when we were in Chicago to present seminars at a boat show a year before. Her flattering and well-written article appeared in *Good Old Boat* magazine a short time later. Paradise Cay is a small nautical book publishing and distribution company. They had, since we began publishing our own books, handled our book storage and the business of filling orders for the books we published.

We took a break from being interviewed by Herb McCormick and headed out for an afternoon of winter sailing on board Taleisin. *Photo Gail Carpenter*

Jim Morehouse, its owner, noticed Cindy's story and wrote, "I'm thinking of asking her to expand that article into a biography of the two of you. It could be an interesting title to add to my line."

I barely had time to consider this proposal before Larry firmly stated, "Great idea. But the only person I'd ever let write my bio is Herb McCormick." Larry listed his reasons:

1. Cindy's article had been highly flattering and indicated she liked us too much, thus she might not be able to show us as we truly were, warts and all.

2. Her sailing experience was relatively limited. And she had, at that time, only written a few articles. Herb, on the other hand, had been writing and editing for sailing magazines for 28 years by that time.

3. Herb had written two books, sailed right around the Americas. He had covered several thousand miles voyaging on at least two dozen different boats.

4. Through the years we'd spent a lot of time with Herb, and he actually sailed with us several times.

5. He seemed to know everyone in the sailing world.

6. Herb had a good sense of humor.

7. We knew he wouldn't be reluctant to seek out the less flattering aspects of our lives.

By good fortune, the bio project fitted well into Herb's life. It fitted well with Jim's publishing schedule. And when Herb suggested he come to New Zealand and spend three weeks interviewing the two of us, it fitted right into our lives. Especially as now we had a comfortable, self-contained place for him to stay.

The cold winter days we spent with Herb were especially memorable and often filled with laughter. Each morning he would interview Larry and me together for a few hours. Then I'd go off to my office, in a tiny building separate from the house, while Herb interviewed Larry on his own. After lunch I'd spend a few hours with Herb, answering his questions, providing lists of people who might be worth interviewing. Then he would disappear to the cottage to work through his notes and prepare more questions for the next day. Evenings were a delight as the three of us sat around the woodburning stove and shared sea stories. The day before Herb was preparing to leave, we all went out for an afternoon of sailing on *Taleisin*. The next day when he came over to my office for our last interview session, Herb said, "I am sure glad we are doing this right now. Larry seems to be having a difficult time remembering stories about some of your more recent sailing adventures, keeps saying I should ask you about this or that. He looks exhausted after we've talked for a few hours. But get him on that boat, and he's fully with it, completely in tune, just like the old Larry."[1]

Sadly, Herb was one of the few people to enjoy our Heron's Nest. About five months after interviewing us, Zelia swept out of the tropics and stalled over the north of New Zealand for two days. Rain came pummeling down,

---

1   Before Herb began the process of writing *As Long as It's Fun*, we agreed in writing that we could review the manuscript but had no veto rights unless something he included was either incorrect or could hurt someone's feelings.

winds gusted over 70 knots. Then Cyclone Zelia faded away. Only a few days later, while the ground was still soggy, an even stronger cyclone swept in. Wilma gusted to 100 knots at times, but even worse, the downpours of rain that fell as Wilma stalled over the country caused massive landslides. throughout the north of New Zealand. She was rated as one of the top ten cyclones to ever hit the country. She didn't spare us. We woke up the morning after she headed off to sea to find the hill behind the Heron's Nest had collapsed. The wonderful cabin Larry had crafted was now a broken shell resting in the sea, covered in mud and trees. Ours was a small loss compared to many others throughout the north of New Zealand. And, only a few weeks later, the massive earthquake that struck the South Island of New Zealand and leveled much of Christchurch dwarfed all previous cyclone losses. We never rebuilt the cabin.

It was a year and a half after Herb had stayed with us that we joined him in Toronto to help launch his book, *As Long as It's Fun*, and at the same time, my book, *Bull Canyon*. Ever since our first book had been published and we began getting invitations to present seminars at boat shows and for various sailing organizations, both of us had looked forward to doing a tour every three or four years. Along with topping up our cruising kitty, these tours gave us a chance to meet up with our far-flung array of sailing friends, meet new ones, share evenings with editors or other writers we'd worked with through the years. Each of these tours had generally been hard work but good fun. The time we spent with Herb at the boat show in Toronto, and a few weeks later at the Chicago Boat Show, was memorable for several reasons. There was the wonderful reception we all received. There was the champagne-fueled celebratory dinner the three of us shared after a boat show attendee handed Herb a copy of the *Wall Street Journal* – the paper was opened to show Herb a highly complimentary half-page review of *As Long as It's Fun*, written by Angus Phillips, one more of Herb's old sailing mates.

Soon after Herb had come to interview us for his book, I realized Larry was tiring more easily and having ever more trouble walking. He'd begun suggesting he stay behind when I headed over to the mainland for our weekly shopping trip, usually saying he had a project he wanted to work on, a book he wanted to read. Then my "political" position began requiring that I go to meetings in the city a few times each month because, due to a realignment of several local towns into one "Supercity," a complete overhaul of the zoning plan was required. The changes proposed for Kawau Island threatened to drastically impinge on islanders' use of their land. That forced me to quickly learn about town planning, assisted and guided by three other islanders: John Sinclair, a well-respected architect; Michael

Marris, a diplomatic psychologist who had years of experience dealing with bureaucrats; and Lyn Hume, the most determined researcher I have ever met. As I dove deeper into the concerns of our local community and felt energized by the idea of helping, Larry seemed to grow more tired. At first he had relished the excuse to spend a few nights at a friend's house or hotel in the city, eating at nice cafés, seeing first-run movies or a live performance. But gradually he began suggesting he stay behind. A visit to our family doctor, who also had a home on Kawau, was, as usual, filled with laughter and a bit of island gossip. Larry was perky, alert. The only outward sign of his declining health was his slow-paced walking. Maybe I should have mentioned he wasn't always this perky at home. But I didn't. Warwick pronounced Larry healthy but aging, then, just as we were leaving, he quietly said to me, "If his walking gets worse, might pay to see a specialist."

About the same time, a young boatbuilder approached us to say he was in love with *Thelma*. Matt's timing was perfect. We settled on a price he could afford, one that covered the time and cost we'd put into repairing and upgrading *Thelma*. A few weeks later she sailed away from our jetty, her tiller in the hand of her new owner. Larry turned to me with a relieved look on his face and said, "Sorry to disappoint you but I just don't have the competitive spirit to do right by her anymore. She needs someone young like Matt."

I was secretly pleased. Larry had developed a shoulder problem while he was hammering in all the nails as he finished the extensive decks surrounding the guest cabin. Thus, the task of varnishing her mast each year had fallen to me. Taking care of her mast and *Taleisin's* far higher mast at the beginning of each summer required hauling myself aloft using a gantline for at least a week of hard work. "Don't be concerned," I said to Larry as *Thelma* headed towards the entrance to the cove. "If we feel like it, we can take *Taleisin* out racing. She's easier to sail and she'll do well in the modern classics division."

But as relieved as I was, as I watched the lovely old gaffer that had been Larry's special gift to me sail slowly out of our life, I knew I was saying farewell to something I'd come to love: the hold-my-breath feeling of charging down towards the starting line under a full spread of canvas to sneak through an advantageous gap, the excitement of gybing to cover another competitor, the thrill of sometimes crossing a finish line and looking back to see the whole fleet behind me, the fun and laughter of the after-race gatherings. And more than that, I was losing one more part of the life the two of us had built together.

20

Facing Reality

2013 - Kawau Island, New Zealand

"What do you think of this name?" Larry called from the far side of the shed.

"Give me a minute while I climb off this scaffolding," I shouted. "I'll come and take a look."

We had spent the past hour acting like tourists as we admired the array of beautiful classic boats stored at the Cape Cod Shipbuilding company. Now he was directing me to something that I'd come to see as a new turn in our life together.

A few months after *Thelma* sailed out of our life towards her new home in Wellington, winter storms began blasting our Kawau Island home. That is when we received an invitation to fly to the USA and spend a week racing on board *Seminole*, a beautifully restored, 47-foot gaff-rigged ketch built in 1917. Her owner, Elizabeth Meyer, thought I'd enjoy being navigator during a series of classic boat races starting at Camden, Maine and ending with the famous Eggemoggin Reach Regatta. I explained that Larry was experiencing some difficulty moving around on boats. "No problem. Larry can be tactician," she'd suggested. "That will keep him busy, in the cockpit and away from grinding winches."

If the New Zealand winter weather had not been so harsh that year, if the idea of summer sunshine in the northern hemisphere hadn't been so tempting, if the latest edition of *Storm Tactics Handbook*, launched just a few weeks before Elizabeth's call, hadn't brought in an unexpected windfall, I doubt we would have agreed. But three weeks later the two of us arrived in Connecticut. The truck and slide-in camper we used for seminar tours a few years previously was stored in a Peter's workshop there . With our rolling home cleaned, fueled, and provisioned, we meandered north towards Maine to join *Seminole*.

Everywhere we sailed with Elizabeth, we seemed to encounter fleets of Herreshoff 12 ½s.[1] These charming daysailers had been designed by Nathanial Herreshoff in 1914 when he was 70 years old. "I want to keep sailing as long as possible," he had written, "and this will be the perfect boat, even when I'm 90."

The Herreshoff Manufacturing had built 400 wooden versions of these long-keeled, well-ballasted open-decked daysailers. They became cherished collectables. Just before his death at the age of 90, Herreshoff authorized Cape Cod Shipbuilding to build a fiberglass version, the Bullseye. By the time we were sailing on *Seminole*, over 1,000 Bullseyes were added to the original fleet, a fleet kept ever popular by frequent summer regattas all along the US East Coast. Everyone we encountered over the month we spent in Maine, everyone who raced with us on *Seminole*, seemed to have learned to sail on an original wooden 12½ or the Bullseye version.

Now, after a fine time in Maine, as we meandered slowly south towards Groton to store our truck away before flying home to spring, Larry suggested we break up our trip by stopping at the Cape Cod shipyard. "Heard there are some wonderfully restored original 12½s there," he'd said. And he was right. Scattered among a dozen of the more modern fiberglass versions were several of the wooden ones built by the Herreshoff company, each sitting in glowing splendor on their specially designed launching trailer. I'd glanced at one or two of the glass versions but was more interested in studying the elegant woodwork of boats that had obviously been cherished by three or four generations of owners.

Now I walked across the shed, wondering what had caught Larry's eye.

I walked around the stern of the tidy little fiberglass Bullseye. Larry simply pointed at her transom. "Felicity," I read. "Sweet name for a sweet boat."

"Whew, so glad you like it. I just bought it for your birthday."

My first reaction: "How do you expect to get it from here to New Zealand?"

"That's your problem," he replied. "Happy 69th. Now you can keep sailing until you are 90."

---

1   The actual length of these sloops is 15 feet on deck. The waterline length is 12½ feet.

Felicity is a rarity here in New Zealand, with her classic underbody and substantial lead ballast keel.

We often headed out with a picnic lunch and anchored for lunch and a quiet siesta in one of the other bays around the island.

Felicity turned out to be a wonderful and easy-to-care-for addition to my life (and fleet of boats.)

———•———

Getting *Felicity* home turned out to be far easier than I had imagined. Soon she was in a container and on board a ship headed for New Zealand. And only a few weeks later, we too were headed home, arriving just a week before the ship carrying our new toy docked in Auckland. *Taleisin* was soon displaced from her marina berth alongside the end of the jetty by *Felicity*. Secured on a mooring in front of our house, *Taleisin* sat unused day after day.

This was a turning point for us. Only when friends came to visit and helped Larry climb into our dinghy, then get on board, did we take Taleisin out sailing for a few hours. Each month, it became more difficult for Larry to walk to the end of the 220-foot-long jetty, but his face lit up whenever I suggested we head down to the marina berth and take *Felicity* out for a meander around the waters surrounding our home. His surehanded helmsmanship, his ability to work this little mini-yacht to weather — these were a welcome reminder of our finest sailing times together.

Larry suffered another small stroke not long after *Felicity* entered my life. The scans and tests no longer left room for doubt: Larry was diagnosed as having the early signs of dementia with Parkinsonian features. Over the next four years Larry's physical abilities slowly ebbed until eventually, a year and a half after we bought *Felicity*, he needed a wheelchair if we left the house. His decline into dementia became ever more evident and he could not safely be left on his own for more than a few hours at a time.

"That must have been a terrible time for you," many people have commented. But I remember those last four years before Larry required full-time professional caretakers differently. Yes, they were challenging years. There were times when I felt lonely as Larry slowly lost his ability to communicate beyond a yes or no until, eventually, he didn't utter a word or move from his favorite chair for hours at a time. Now we had a new rhythm, and days passed with him watching the tide come in and the tide go out for hours at a time. I know I was fortunate in that Larry never suffered the hallucinations nor tremors of full-blown Parkinson's disease, but became ever more gentle, ever quieter, as his dementia deepened. I also saw those years as deeply interesting ones, often filled with laughter, music, and some sailing too. This was a time when I came to appreciate the warmth of deep friendships, the rewards available by becoming deeply involved with community efforts and, most important, the strength and determination Larry had fostered in me.

Felicity was just one of the reasons I could say that. There were many others. But by far the most important reason was a friendship that had been rekindled on our last voyage through the Pacific. When we stopped at Nuiatoputapu in Tonga and I asked the customs ladies if they knew what had happened to Molokeini, the young girl we'd encountered there 23 years before, I could never have imagined how important that young girl, now a woman known to everyone as Keini, would prove to be.

———————

Not long after we'd arrived home from our last long voyage on *Taleisin*, a bright orange 26-foot sloop named *Taheke* sailed alongside our jetty. I was delighted when I realized Keini was on board with her two sons and New Zealand-born husband Rafe Tollemach. Within a short time, their home in Auckland became almost as familiar to Larry and me as our island home, and vice versa. Winter visits to the city usually became overnighters for us as we spent time with "our family." Summer weekends saw Keini and her family diving off the end of our jetty, sailing on *Felicity* or *Taleisin* or heading out fishing on our 14-foot runabout. Keini became known throughout the cove for her fishing abilities and laughter. Our friendship deepened ever more when she was faced with the failure of her marriage and asked for my assistance with the legal wrangling needed to ensure a fair financial separation.

Keini was part of our family and became deeply attached to Larry. With her skills as a professional caregiver for seniors, and with the warmth towards elders ingrained in the Polynesian culture she was raised in, Keini was wonderful with him. As Larry's decline accelerated, she became almost like my caretaker too. Keini coached me on how to ensure Larry always felt safe, how to help him move around. She developed an ever-increasing rapport with Larry, and he with her. And it was Keini who knew, at a certain point, that it was no longer sensible for me to take Larry along when I flew to the US or England to introduce a new book. Then Keini insisted I leave him in her care, sometimes coming over to stay for three or four weeks at a time at Kawau, other times taking him home to the city where the whole family welcomed and pampered him. "It's not an imposition," she said time and again. "I love Larry and he loves me."

The income from the books Larry and I had written together, plus the ones I wrote myself, became far more important as I realized Larry would, in the not-too-distant future, require nursing home care, and probably for several years. The financial burden for that would fall on me. This concern led to one more big project that challenged my brain and introduced me to

three special cruising sailors. Sara Dawn Johnson had sailed into North Cove
on board *Wondertime*, a Benford 38 sloop, to share Thanksgiving dinner with
us. She and her husband Michael and two daughters were three years into
their cruising life. They were headed into Auckland for the winter where
she hoped to enroll her girls in "real" schools for the first time. Sara asked
if we could meet for coffee the next time I came into the city.

"Three of us are thinking of pooling our knowledge and writing a
book about sailing with kids," Sara Dawn explained over a cup of tea. She
was hoping I might be able to help her as she considered how to write and
then publish the book. Larry and I have always enjoyed seeing families out
cruising together. I liked the sound of the book she and her potential co-
authors proposed. During one of my forays into the city on island business,
we scheduled a meeting.

We talked for two hours as I explained how they could go about their
project, Sara Dawn wildly taking notes about editors, distributor costs,
finding a publisher vs. self-publishing. Then I left to head to Keini's house,
where Larry was comfortably ensconced. I had driven just two blocks when
I actually slammed on the brakes. I turned the car around and rushed back
to the café. I caught Sara just as she was leaving. "How about letting me
publish your book?" I blurted out. Just a few weeks later I was shepherding
the biggest book publishing project I had ever handled through its truly
international journey. Sara Dawn, along with her two co-authors Behan
Gifford and Michael Robertson, had each spent several years cruising with
their children. Each was currently in a different country. So were the copy
editor and proofreader. This meant juggling six different time zones as we
all worked via internet in a time before there were apps set up for online
sharing like SmartSheets, WorkZone, or Google Projects. *Voyaging with
Kids* took two years to reach completion and helped fill any empty spaces
in my life and mind. To try to add more variety to Larry's days, I'd take my
computer into the house and show him the pictures we planned to use, or
the pages as they arrived from the designer. Though he rarely commented,
Larry did seem to enjoy the picture show. And, though I had to work
through a few of the inevitable problems of creating a project with three
different authors, Behan, Sara Dawn, and Michael each assured me they
were pleased they hadn't tried to self-publish the book.[2]

A question I have been asked by several cruisers is: What makes someone

---

2   Along with the books written by Larry and me, I eventually published three books for
other nautical writers along with five for the Kawau Island Bookworms. But I found the
responsibility of ensuring authors earned the best possible returns for their efforts left me
little mental space to continue with my own writing projects.

a publisher? The simple answer, the publisher puts up all the money and takes all the financial risk. I had to pay the editors, the designers, and the proofreader. I had to take charge of the publicity plus the cost of printing and storing books. By the time that book was available in both print and eBook formats, I had risked a large portion of our savings. As publisher, I also had to guide the content which, in this case, was a particularly enjoyable task. But then came the more difficult part: ensuring people knew about the book — i.e., the publicity. I found it far easier to promote *Voyaging with Kids* than the books I had written. I am not comfortable "bragging" about myself. And to me that is what publicity releases do. But I was really proud of the work the three authors had done, so it was easy to brag about them during podcast interviews and in the press releases I wrote. With Keini caring for Larry, I was able to fly to the USA to promote this book, along with my own new book, *Taleisin's Tales*, at the Annapolis boat show and several other venues. Though it took a few years before I recouped my investment and began making a profit on *Voyaging with Kids*, my efforts also helped promote my own books.

The sun shone and the water glistened as I helped Larry clamber on board *Felicity*. This was in November 2015, soon after I had returned from the book promotion tour. I had wheeled Larry down to the end of the jetty, then helped him climb on board. I hoisted the sails and untied her mooring lines. With Larry at the helm, we began skimming towards the entrance to the bay. Suddenly, he pulled the tiller towards him and headed into the wind. We came to a stop just astern of *Taleisin*. Larry pointed towards *Taleisin's* upper spreaders. Then for the first time that day he struggled to gather the words and said, "She needs you."

He was right. The varnish on the timber around the bronze spreader fittings was beginning to deteriorate. "I'll do something about it," I said to reassure him.

As we continued out of the cove and into the open waters of Kawau Bay, I managed to hide my frustration and guilt as, for the first time ever, I really felt pressured by the need to maintain a boat that sat unused, serving as a daily reminder of a life that no longer existed.

A half hour later, Larry pulled the tiller to tack as the afternoon sea breeze began to freshen. I trimmed the sheets. He deftly caught each wind shift, a slight smile lighting his face as *Felicity* heeled and raced onward, water occasionally sloshing along her leeward deck. Then Larry pushed the helm over to tack again and at the same time tried to move from one side of the cockpit to the other. I reached out to steady him but was a second too late. He lost his balance and let go of the tiller. *Felicity* swung into the wind, her boom flailing madly, her headsail flapping as I tried to help Larry up from the bottom of the boat.

But I couldn't.

Just as Keini had taught me, I soothingly said, "Just lie there for a few minutes."

Larry looked up from the bottom of the boat and smiled meekly. I hid my tears as I stepped around him and dropped the jib, then got the boat under control and slowly beat into the cove using only the mainsail.

Once I had *Felicity* secured alongside her pontoon and her mainsail down, I was able to help Larry struggle up from the bottom of the boat and onto her cockpit seat. A neighbor had noticed us sail in and came over to see what was wrong. Together we helped Larry out of *Felicity* and into his wheelchair, then up to the house. Through all this, he had not appeared agitated. Instead, Larry had been quietly and calmly expecting that I would take care of his problems.

With assistance, Larry was able to get on board Taleisin *for a final sail before Annie and Eben became her owners. The minute he took the helm, he was the Larry I remembered so well, catching every little windshift, confident and serene.*

It was a moment of clarity. I said, "I think it is time to find someone else to love *Taleisin*." Larry nodded in agreement.

I helped Larry take a shower to get warmed up, then made him a cup of hot soup. I helped him climb into bed. He was almost instantly asleep. I went out to my office to continue working on "island business." I came back to the house a few hours later to see Larry sitting in his favorite chair next to the front window, staring intently out to where *Taleisin* lay.

"Talk to Davey Jones," he said. "Tell him she needs someone young who will take her sailing."

The next day I contacted Davey, a specialist classic yacht broker we'd met during one of our forays to Maine. Six months after contacting him, soon after dawn, I stood on the foreshore next to Larry as Eben and Annie Bruyns hoisted *Taleisin*'s mainsail to take her away from North Cove towards the berth they had secured in an Auckland marina. I had taken Eben and Annie out on sea trials. We brought Larry along and he seemed to like the two of them. Once Annie and Eben became *Taleisin*'s new owners, I took them out for two more afternoon orientation forays.[3] Now they were headed towards a date I had arranged and paid for. Awaiting their arrival in Auckland was one of the best mast varnishers in New Zealand. He promised to call me once he had *Taleisin*'s mast gleaming again. Only then would I feel I'd done the best I could for that wonderful little ship.

Larry watched as *Taleisin* sailed slowly out of view and said, "She'll take care of them." I thought of how successful *Taleisin* had been. For 23 years she had been a wonderful home and adventure machine, and now the funds from her sale, when the time came, would cover several years of nursing home expenses for Larry. Just before I turned to help Larry back up the steps into the house I replied, "She definitely took good care of us."

———————

As Larry's memories slid away and his ability to express himself faded, I encouraged friends who had held him in high regard to come and visit while he might still recognize them. A dozen different friends from overseas did so. Larry seemed to enjoy these four- or five-day visits. I know I did. Ashley Butler had come under Larry's wing when he was a 16-year-old student at

3   Eben has written an interesting story of why he and Annie bought *Taleisin* at http://www.unlikelyboatbuilder.com/2016/04/why-did-you-buy-taleisin.html. Ten years later she is still where I can see her, on a mooring across the cove from me. Eben and Annie still live on board *Taleisin*, which they have sailed to Tonga and back. They hope to sail farther afield over the next few years.

the Falmouth England Boatbuilding School many years ago, and was able to sneak away from his very busy classic Cornwall boatbuilding yard for a two-week visit. The day before he left us, I wheeled Larry down to the boatshed to show him the two boxes of small, specialized boatbuilding tools I had set out on the workbench. Many of these tools had helped build *Seraffyn*, others had been gifts from retiring boatbuilders who came to encourage us as we built *Taleisin*. These were the tools I suggested Ashley take home with him; I was sure Larry would like Ashley to have them. Some were ones Larry had built, some were more than 100 years old. It was good to find a top-rate boatbuilder who would use them and also appreciate their value, their history. Larry ran his hands over the tools, then indicated he wanted me to open a wooden tool chest at the far end of the shed. He reached in and lifted out a large chisel, then pulled off the leather sheath he made to protect its cutting edge. "Ashley needs this," he quietly whispered to me.

Larry had far more trouble recognizing Kenny Thorall, who had spent more than a year sailing with Larry and working together delivering boats just before I came on the scene more than five decades before. When I met Larry, Ken was there, too. The three of us had palled around together for another nine months, until Kenny set sail on an 85-foot Bahamian schooner, the Double Eagle, to run charters in the Caribbean. We hadn't seen him in 50 years. Facebook brought Kenny back into our lives just when I was beginning to realize I might not be able to care for Larry at home much longer. It happened in the way these things often do, one unlikely thing leading to the next.

I always left a few current magazines on the table where Larry spent most of his day. He usually just turned the pages and looked at the pictures. Recently, he had begun tearing out pictures of Arctic and Antarctic fjords and icebergs in cruise ship advertisements. I was a bit confused by this; cruise ships had never interested either of us. Then it dawned on me.

"We've never been up close to a glacier, never heard an iceberg calve, or watched bergy bits float past us," I said, looking over his shoulder at the images on the table. Larry nodded in agreement. "Would you like to do that now? We can't do it on a sailing boat, but I could take you on a cruise ship."

He nodded vigorously.

As it was mid-winter, the cruise ships that visited the Antarctic during the summer months had moved north, to warmer waters. I booked a trip on board a 2,000-passenger, modestly priced cruise liner from Vancouver to Alaska.

A few weeks later, as I was packing for our cruise, I received a message on Facebook. "My brother Kenny says you and Larry were the most important people in his life. Would you be willing to give him your email address or phone number? He doesn't use Facebook."

The next day Kenny called me from his home in Alaska and we talked for an hour. Kenny had lived an adventuresome life, first as a motorcycle racer, then race car mechanic, before signing on as engineer on large charter yachts. That lead to him meeting Larry and teaming up to deliver yachts and eventually buying the Double Eagle. After a successful few years chartering in the Caribbean, he became a small plane engine repair specialist, which led him to Alaska, where he became a bush pilot, raised his son, and, as a hobby, built small airplanes.

We laughed, we cried. As we were saying goodbye, Kenny said, "This is so sad. I finally catch up with you two after all these years and I won't ever get to see you because you live in New Zealand, and I live in Alaska."

"Oh yes you will," I immediately replied. "We are headed to Alaska next week."

Though the flight from New Zealand to Vancouver, where we boarded the ship, had been difficult for him, Larry seemed more comfortable once aboard. He spent hour after hour on the tiny balcony of our equally tiny shipboard cabin, watching contentedly as the ship cut through the water, smiling as we floated through the bergy bits at the head of long, icebound fjords. Though I wished we could have been in these waters on our own boat, I'd found the nine-day interlude pleasant, the vistas beautiful, and Larry's contentment satisfying.

Then we arrived in Anchorage and Kenny was standing on the dock waiting for us.

The reunion was wonderful for me. Kenny had arranged for his son to take me flying in the miniature Mustang aircraft the two of them had built. On our second day in Anchorage, I set off flying with Patrick. He piloted the powerful little plane just above the surface of huge rivers of ice, and through deep valleys cut by glaciers. We chased after half a dozen moose as they ran along the glacial rivers towards the sea. Meanwhile, Kenny drove Larry along the winding roads below us until eventually we came to a landing strip at the convergence of two rivers, where we all stopped for lunch together. When I rejoined Larry in Kenny's car, Larry whispered to me, "Who is this old man? He seems to know all sorts of stories about what Kenny Thorall and I did together."

Six months later, Kenny flew to New Zealand. "I wanted a bit more time with the two of you," he told me. A day after he arrived, Kenny said, "Never enjoyed working or playing alongside anyone as much Larry. He was good to both of us. Now I want to pay for some sort of memorial that

Kenny provided enough funding to construct a platform and small storage building plus four Skywatcher 10-inch telescopes and 12 pairs of specialist stargazing binoculars.

The plaque at the Larry Pardey Memorial Observatory.

might help other folks remember him. Any ideas?"

One came to mind almost immediately: Camp Bentzon. It is a 28-acre camp directly across the cove from our home on Kawau Island, run by a trust for the benefit of the school children of New Zealand. We had become involved with the camp almost immediately after buying our property here. A youngster had floated up against our seawall with a broken mast on one of the camp dinghies just a few days after we arrived. Larry towed him back to the camp. "Offered to fix it for them," he told me. Over the years we'd helped fix dinghies for the camp and participated in fundraising events, and I was briefly on the board of trustees. And best of all, we became friends with each of the camp managers. Several years ago, during one late-night discussion, the current manager, Peter Hyde, had said, "Sometimes during the winter I wish there was something more for the kids to do out here to get them outside at night." Larry had immediately answered, "Wouldn't it be nice if there were some telescopes they could use — a mini observatory, so to speak. Night sky is often clear and bright here. No city lights nearby to dull it down."

As soon as I told Kenny my thoughts, he was in full accord. "The Larry Pardey Observatory — perfect. Larry always used the stars to navigate. Let's do it."

The $20,000 Kenny donated paid for the materials to build a viewing platform high up the hills and clear of trees, plus a small building to house four portable but substantial telescopes and a dozen pair of stargazing binoculars. The local Lions Club did the construction work. Within a year, many of the 5,000 children who visited the camp had climbed up to Larry's observatory for a close-up look at the moon, the stars, and the planets.

Who knows when it is the right time to put someone in care? As I had ignored Larry's first signs of age, I tried to ignore this approaching reality. When they asked about him, I told my family, my close friends, "Taking care of Larry isn't that much work." And it was true. He spent most of the day sleeping or sitting, looking out the window. I would take him for a ride around the property or out the jetty in his wheelchair most afternoons. Neighbors took care of him when I had to go to town. He could still walk a bit if there was something to hold onto, which meant I could still get him on and off the ferry for doctors' appointments. He still liked it when I read to him or cuddled up next to him on the couch while we watched a video. "I will put him in care when and if I can't handle things." I replied each time. "Right now, I'm doing just fine."

One day, soon after Kenny's visit, I was reading a chapter of *Seraffyn's European Adventure* to Larry. I had learned people with dementia like Larry's lost their most recent memories first, but often retained memories from their distant past, though those slowly fade away too. I was reading about Paul Lees and his wife, Vicky, and the 500-year-old house we'd shared with them during a cold and snowy winter in the south of England. As Larry rarely spoke by this time, I was surprised when he said, "I wonder what happened to them? Are they okay?" I was able to tell him I had recently seen an advertisement for their sail loft in a sailing magazine. Then I noticed, for the first time in several months, how Larry appeared to be fully engaged, smiling slightly, nodding.

I asked, "Don't you wish we were planning one more crazy adventure together?"

Larry appeared to carefully consider this question. Then he gave me yet another wonderful gift. He looked me directly in the eyes, shook his head and clearly stated, "That would be downright greedy."

I carried his words, his sense of satisfaction with me as I flew to the United States a few weeks later. I'd left Larry at Keini's home on the way to the airport. She and her sons, almost grown by this time, were planning to take him back to Kawau in a few weeks where, Keini assured me, she would enjoy fishing, caring for Larry, and "a holiday" from her work at a large retirement community near her home.

Maybe I was greedy, maybe I just don't know how to say no, maybe I was trying to run away from the sad reality of caring for Larry, but instead of scheduling just three weeks for my yearly overseas seminar visit, after conferring with Keini, I accepted dates that required I be away six weeks. I rationalized the seminar fees, and the extra books I'd sell, would earn more than the costs of covering the wages Keini was giving up. In reality, I was relishing being away from the sadness that was becoming hard to ignore and in a world of laughter and boat talk, relishing being surrounded by friends and compatriots plus the people Larry had always described as "friends we haven't met yet." Just as important, I admit to loving having this time to myself, how I was only looking after my own needs.

But as the last few weeks of my tour ran down, reality finally struck. "Lin, this is too long," Keini said on the phone one night. "I am getting too tired. Larry is waking me up all night long," I could hear the strain in her voice. Then she said, quietly, "I think he is looking for you."

The day I arrived home, Keini said, "Lin, you have to find a home for Larry. You can't take care of him anymore." She had found him lying on the floor several times when he decided to get out of bed by himself. "I can barely lift him," Keini said. "And I am twice as strong as you. You are going to hurt yourself if you try."

Keini was right. Larry's worsening dementia kept him awake every night. I couldn't lift him when he accidentally slid out of the bed onto the floor. I had called one or another neighbor three times over the next two days to help me lift Larry up off the floor. On the third day after I arrived home from my tour, I had called the small dementia home I'd visited earlier that year, one situated on a farm about 20 minutes' drive from where the Kawau Island Ferry landed and just a few hundred feet away from a beautiful estuary where Larry could be wheeled down to watch fishboats and sailboats skimming across the water. Though they had room for only 23 residents, they did have one available for Larry, a room under the government-controlled program, which ensured I had the funds to keep our home and know Larry was in a well-managed, safe environment. I knew there was no choice but to accept it.

Four days later, the ferry skipper helped maneuver Larry on board for his final voyage away from the jetty. This was the jetty he had salvaged and rebuilt, the house he had turned from an abandoned, badly painted little box into an elegant wooden jewel of a home. This was the place filled with love and laughter.

The staff invited Larry into the room where he would be staying in a caring and gentle way. They told white lies when they said, "a nurse will help you settle in. You are here so we can help you be healthy." This seemed to calm any fears he had. I left — as I was told to — as soon as he was in bed and dozing off.

I tried to hide my tears when I boarded the ferry home. "Was he frightened at all? Does he know he won't be coming home?" the driver asked me. I had no idea how Larry felt, but I was frightened. Frightened I'd made the wrong decision. Frightened because I would be going back to an empty house.

Late in the afternoon, on a stunningly beautiful spring afternoon, I walked slowly, almost reluctantly, up the jetty, past the sweet little sailboat Larry had given me, past the boatshed where he and I had worked side by side for hours at a time, and into the little cottage. I sat down in the chair Larry had always favored and looked around the quiet house. Suddenly I realized, instead of feeling lonely, instead of feeling twinged with sadness, the home Larry had found for us all those years ago had fulfilled his dreams. This little house no longer held the ghost of what Larry had been, but the wonderful memories of what we had been together. And now it felt like a welcoming refuge.

21
Making the Hardest Decision

2017 - Kawau Island, New Zealand

"All you want to do is ride around Sally…"

Hundreds of people were singing along to the rousing chorus of "Mustang Sally." The grounds of the old Governor Grey's Mansion House, two miles from my Kawau home, were alive with dancers. I could hear dozens of additional voices echoing the music from the flotilla of anchored boats filling Mansion House Cove. For the first time that day, I was standing still, hiding away in a relatively quiet spot behind the big portable stage, taking a break from my responsibilities and scanning the hundred or more dinghies and tenders that lined the beach in front of me. Keini came around the corner of the stage, obviously looking for me. She walked over, put her arm around me and said, "Larry would have loved this."

That was exactly what I had been thinking. Four years previously, one of my neighbors came up with the idea of Music in the Gardens. "A nice way to get people from all over the island to bring their summer visitors for a picnic lunch and listen to a local jazz band," she had said. The first year about 250 people turned up. Since then it had grown to a full-day event, with 1,200 ticketed attendees and three different bands, plus locally produced food and wine and a silent and live fundraising auction. Two years previously, I had become the main coordinator of a festival that now required the assistance of 50 volunteers, two barges, two large ferries, and six security guards. I relished the challenge, and the connection it gave me to people around the island. Even as his dementia deepened, Larry had enjoyed coming along with me during the year preceding each event as I sought out new performers. Together, we'd visit weekend markets and small music venues to listen to various musical groups before choosing the bands who would be featured in the following year's lineup.

Now, I heard the last band of the day begin playing the song that signaled the end of their current set. I returned to the front of the stage to ensure the performers had cold drinks and food waiting when they took their break. On the way, I glanced over to where Larry usually would have been ensconced with Keini and her two boys, surrounded by an array of friends who had sailed over to join us for the whole weekend. The blankets were there. Our friends were there. I was momentarily expecting to see Larry there too, even though it had been more than four months since I had uprooted him from the life we'd shared for half a century.

I had been riding an emotional rollercoaster in the months since I had left Larry at the dementia care home. The first three weeks had been the easiest. The psychologist who met with me when I arrived at the facility explained Larry would adjust more quickly if I stayed away until then. A daily phone call with one or the other of his caretakers had eased some of my discomfort. When I tried to talk to Larry on the phone, he was confused and didn't understand who I was.

Fortunately, the projects I'd taken on to help me connect with other people all seemed to need my attention at the same time: planning this music festival; learning about town planning so I could properly represent the island population as Auckland city changed the zoning codes; being committee member and secretary for the local boating club. Summer and the approaching holiday season brought sailing visitors and friends from the mainland most weekends. At the same time, I'd taken on the challenge of writing the first narrative I'd written about our sailing adventures in almost 20 years, *Taleisin's Tales*. My decision to create a new book was partially for the extra income, but just as important, it gave me something special to look forward to after the holiday hustle was over and the autumn nights began to grow long and cold. I welcomed the quiet peace of my writing time and I knew launching the book would bring me a good reason to run away from winter to visit my USA friends and families.

Soon after *Felicity* had come into our lives, Larry urged me to take her out myself. "Sure, it's fun to sail together," he'd said. "But there might be times when you feel like going out on your own. So take a break. Go see if there is anything you need to make singlehanding easier."

A few hours later, I'd carefully led *Felicity*'s mooring lines around the base of the pontoon cleats, then back to where I could release them from the cockpit. I hoisted the mainsail, tightened it in, and cleated the mainsheet. Then I hoisted the jib, ran the leeward sheet around the small snubber winch on the back edge of her small cuddy then back to where I'd be sitting. I left the jib flapping loosely in the 10- knot breeze. Deftly, I released the mooring lines and pulled them on board, then slowly sheeted in the jib as *Felicity* sweetly skimmed clear of the pontoon. I was feeling quite proud of myself as *Felicity* picked up speed. A neighbor motored by in his small workboat and teased me about running away from home. I may have been grandstanding a bit as I sailed towards the large ketch that lay on a mooring near the entrance to the cove. I waited until I was within a few feet of the ketch before I prepared to tack. I pushed the tiller hard over, let go of the jib sheet, stood to move to the other side of the cockpit, and, as the boom came across, reached to grab the other jib sheet and wrap it around the snubber winch. But things didn't go to plan: I couldn't reach the winch unless I let go of the tiller. I couldn't let go of the tiller or I'd hit the boat I was trying to avoid.

I was lucky. Lucky *Felicity* had been moving quickly and still had way on, lucky she was willing to respond to her rudder, lucky I thought to pull her mainsheet clear of the cam cleat and push the boom out to help her pay off. She did pay off just quickly enough. I avoided a collision by inches. And despite knowing my neighbor probably was still watching, I sailed right back to the pontoon, secured *Felicity*, and stomped off the pontoon and up the jetty.

"Wasn't expecting you back so soon," Larry commented when I charged past his workshop towards my office.

"You were right. I need a tiller extension stick before I can sail her on my own."

The next time we headed over to the mainland, I bought a tiller extension. I lashed it to *Felicity*'s tiller and waited for a quiet day, one when I didn't think any of my neighbors would be out on the water to notice my latest screwups. Then I headed out on my own again. *Perfect*, I thought as I short-tacked around the moored boats inside the cove, tiller extension stick in hand, able to sit right forward where I could easily control the jib sheets. Then I worked clear of the cove and was enjoying a lovely beam reach in the open waters of Kawau Bay. Sails set and pulling well, I settled back into the comfortable curve at the aft end of the cockpit and found it just as easy to hold the tiller as the extension stick. Then a gust of wind heeled *Felicity* sharply. I pushed the tiller to head her into the wind. The extension stick, which I'd left hanging free, jammed itself against the leeward cockpit coaming. Fortunately, the gust eased before much water had slopped over the cockpit coaming. Lesson number two: Use one of my ponytail bands to secure the extension stick along the tiller if I am not using it.

When I had mastered the tiller extension stick, I enjoyed occasional solo excursions, but found I preferred sharing my sailing time with Larry. As Larry became ever less able to sail with me, I'd sometimes wait until he had settled in for a long afternoon snooze. Then I'd head out on my own. Still, the sailing was bittersweet. I got better at handling *Felicity*, and I enjoyed the time on the water, but I was alone.

⸻

Once Larry had begun requiring ever more care, *Felicity* rarely left her pontoon. Now, as he was no longer at home, I found time to sail again. I didn't have to be concerned that Larry might need my help at any moment; whenever I saw a nice breeze filling in, I didn't hesitate. I took a few hours away from my phone and desk and headed out across the bay. I rationalized this by reminding myself, *if I am going to write about sailing, I should get out sailing.* I'd throw together a few nibbles, something to drink, and head off on *Felicity.* I relished being on the water under sail again, learning how to get her to lay hove to so I could roll a reef into her mainsail, figuring out the best tactics to use when I had to bring her alongside the pontoon with winds gusted to 20 or 25 knots.[1]

These sailing sessions were a balm. Soon, I also found freedom in inviting visitors to stay long past when Larry would have needed my help to settle him in for the night. I ate when or if I wished without having to consider Larry's dietary requirements. I found greater ease in caring for our small home without the additional work added by the needs of an invalid. All this made those first three weeks seem to flow quickly.

Skimming across the bay on *Felicity* also planted the seeds of my next adventure, and I began glancing at advertisements for small, affordable cruising boats that would let me range farther afield. Larry's voice always seemed to be there as I googled the specs for one boat or another. "Townsend's designs are sweet," I'd hear him saying. "Elliott? Great in light winds, but a handful when it breezes up. When three weeks had passed, I headed for the mainland for my first visit with Larry since he had gone into fulltime

---

1 You might enjoy watching this short video showing Felicity and I under sail. https::// www.youtube.com/watch?v=Dj2rplrfKRI It was produced in 2017 by TVNZ for a weekly program called Neighbourhood.

care. I had prepared for this by cooking up his favorite treats, packing a few books I thought he would like, some photographs to help decorate his room, a selection of the videos he and I had created together. What I could never have prepared for was the emotional jolt I felt upon seeing him again, one I can still picture today.

I am not sure if Larry had really dwindled during those three weeks since I had last seen him, or if I was just seeing him as he truly was. It may have been the gauntness of his face that was more visible, now that his caretakers had trimmed his beard far closer than he normally wore it. Or maybe it was seeing him sitting absentmindedly in a large room, staring at a TV monitor and surrounded by a dozen other people in varying states of dementia. I was further discomfited by his look of confusion when one of the caretakers whispered to Larry, "Your wife is here to see you. Larry, look over here, it's Lin."

Suddenly I broke down, and had to turn and leave. I stood in the flower-filled front yard of the care home, crying and thinking of how selfish I had been to leave him here. The facility nurse came out and led me back into the quiet sitting room at the front of the home. "We know how hard it is for someone to bring their partner here," she said.

"But I don't need to. I just made a rash decision when I was tired from a long flight home," I replied. "I have to take him back home. I can care for him there."

"That's not what I heard," the nurse stated. "My sister-in-law lives near you. She said everyone on the island thought you should have brought Larry here months ago." I wiped my nose and listened. "She told me you had to go to the doctor a few days after you left Larry here. She said you started having fainting spells." This was true. I had been taking pills to control my high blood pressure. But without the complications of caring for Larry, my high blood pressure had dropped like a stone. I no longer needed the medication. The nurse gently said, "The stress of caring for Larry was taking a real toll on you."

I had shared this information with two of my neighbors. And I had taken the doctor's advice and stopped my daily dose of blood pressure pills, and that had solved my problem. Though tears still ran down my face, I almost broke out laughing at this example of life in a small community.

The nurse put her arm around my shoulder and said, "You spent most of your life being a wife, a partner. You've done your job well, from what I hear. But you are not a trained caretaker. It's time to let us do our job. It is our turn to take care of Larry."

———— • ————

I never found it easy to see Larry in these surroundings. Despite being a nicely appointed homelike building surrounded by flower and vegetable gardens in the middle of a small farm, despite the warmth of the caretakers, I still felt like I had consigned Larry to a prison. At first, I chastised myself because I used living on an island as an excuse to visit just once every week or 10 days, and in those visits I rarely stayed more than an hour. But slowly I came to realize that visiting more frequently or staying longer would not have contributed to Larry living a better life. Though he sometimes appeared pleased when I arrived, within minutes he became distracted by someone passing by and forgot I was there. When stormy weather made it impossible to visit for almost three weeks, he didn't seem to have noticed my absence. The same warm-hearted nurse told me time and again, "A minute or two after you leave, he doesn't remember you were here." But still, I'd find myself having bouts of guilt that I wasn't doing more for him.

John Sinclair, who had a home across the cove from me, noted my emotional struggle and suggested I meet Di Edwards. "Di lost her husband the same way," John told me. "When he finally died, she married a good friend of mine. She spent her working life as an ordained minister, but that's not why I suggest you talk to her. I just think she might be helpful."

Di invited me to visit her at her home any time I came into the city. A few weeks later, I did. I listened intently as she spoke of her own experience. "Watching your husband slowly fading away, knowing he will possibly be in care for years, it is especially hard," she said. "You can't truly say farewell and begin the grieving that could help you move on freely with life. You are coping with an ambiguous loss." She generously spent the next few hours putting into words thoughts I'd been trying to formulate. As I was leaving, Di gave me one last bit of advice. "Do not worry about what your friends or your family think. As long as Larry is safe and being cared for, there is no right or wrong way to handle your situation, no right or wrong time to start moving on with your own life."

The quickly approaching holidays, the rash of Christmas gatherings, the inevitable overseas visitors who fled winter to enjoy summer holidays in New Zealand, the final countdown for Music in the Garden — these activities left me little time to consider what "moving on with your own life" would mean for me.

Then Ty Ebright arrived. He was an old friend, and he came to Kawau Island from Santa Cruz, California. It was the middle of December and Ty was here for a three-day stay. His exuberant energy and enthusiasm made his visit fly by. Despite the fun of reliving the weeks Larry and I spent with him a few years previously, meandering up the Burgundy canal in France in his river boat, I was relieved when Ty packed up to continue his tour of New Zealand. I needed to get back to work. On the last morning of his visit, I gave Ty a short tour of the island in *Jay Dee*, my 14-foot runabout, then said farewell to him at the Mansion House Reserve, where he could have a walk around before catching the ferry to the mainland.

He called two hours later. "Great time, thanks. I'm on the ferry," he said. "I had a chat with a nice Australian singlehander in the park. He didn't know you lived here. I want you to do me a favor. He's really shy. Call and invite him over for a drink."

I didn't give Ty a chance to say another word. "Too darned busy right now," I stated.

"You owe me a favor," Ty answered. "He's got your storm book and I think he'd like it signed."

I did owe Ty a favor. Several years earlier he had given Larry and me some excellent financial advice, and then helped us implement it. So, I did call and invite the "shy Australian singlehander" over for a drink the next evening. I also called my neighbor, Leanne, a very successful IT businesswoman, around 40 years old, who had recently bought the rambling house across the cove from me. We had quickly become friends when she decided I should not have any chance to languish on my own. Now I asked her to ring me at 7 pm the next evening and pretend she needed my help so I could easily call my drinks date to an end.

I took little notice of the bright red cutter that came to anchor near the entrance to the cove early the next afternoon. When I saw an aged and multi-patched inflatable dinghy approaching soon afterwards, I went out to greet the "shy Australian singlehander."

"Just checking the time for this evening," David Haigh said.

"I'll need a break about 5:30," I answered. "Come by then."

I was pleased when he left immediately.

Within a few minutes of sitting down to share a drink with David that evening, I was reminded how much I missed talking with someone who had actually voyaged across an ocean, how much I missed laughing — laughing until tears ran down my face. David had taken early retirement from his work at James Cook University in Townsville, Australia, where he had been a senior environmental law lecturer and environmental campaigner and embarked on a leisurely 10-year circumnavigation. New Zealand was his last intended stop before closing the loop by returning to the country where he had three daughters and loads of friends. I roared with laughter as he described the antics of various young people he met by posting notes in backpackers hotels when he wanted crew to help him cross another ocean. David seemed entranced as I described the wild scenes Larry and I experienced when we joined three million Brazilians on the beaches of Copacabana to celebrate their World Cup Football victory.

On and on went the story sharing until my phone rang.

"Thanks, Leanne," I said when she called to ask if I needed to escape from a lonely, boring singlehander looking for a free meal. "No, I don't think that needs to be handled tonight. We can get together tomorrow and work on it." Then I threw together a light dinner for David and me.

Five hours after he had arrived, David said farewell. He set sail early the next morning to meet two of his daughters who were flying into Auckland from Australia to help celebrate his 70th birthday. The enjoyable interlude with a fellow cruising sailor had been a warm reminder of the life I'd shared with Larry. It gave me a chance to talk about the man I'd loved, who was now lost to me. And for the first time I'd aired my desire to search for a boat that would get me out cruising, beyond Kawau Bay. By morning all of this was swept from my mind as the music festival and my book deadline marched ever closer.

Dozens of potential catastrophes might have spoiled Music in the Gardens that year: rain, strong winds; stages or freezers not arriving in time to get on the barges; portable toilets falling over when we had to wrangle them off the barge and transport them across a rocky beach. But not one major thing went wrong, and I was now savoring the last hour of the highly successful music event I'd helped create. The skipper of the local coast guard boat, which had been on hand to help transport people from anchored boats to the jetty, came over and gave me a hug. "Great day. Just wanted you to know, if you ever consider finding someone to go out with when Larry passes on, I can introduce you to a friend I think you'd like. Lost his wife a year ago. He's a sailor too."

His comment caught me by surprise. Up until that moment, I hadn't thought about "someone else." I was enjoying learning to be "just me." I truly loved the home Larry and I had built and decorated with our favorite artwork and mementos. It took me a long time to get over feeling guilty when, soon after Larry moved into care, I removed the large, beautifully framed oil painting of the square-rigged clipper ship, the *Cutty Sark*, hove to in a storm. It had been painted several years previously by Roger Morris, a well-known New Zealand marine historian and artist, as a gift for Larry, and had graced the feature wall opposite the dining table. I had always found the painting to be too gray, too threatening to be the focal point of our otherwise bright, small home, but Larry had loved it. Though I had a few twinges of discomfort when I looked at the now bare spot on the wall, I gradually came to realize this small change was not about being disloyal to Larry, but about becoming a new, single person. The same held true for gradually consigning boatbuilding books to the downstairs bookshelf, adding a hand-stitched brightly colored quilt to replace the more subdued one Larry had chosen for the bed that stood in the corner of our open-plan house. As the weeks passed, I began slowly putting away some of Larry's favorite Tijuana Brass CDs. Soon a pile of opera CDs topped the pile next to the machine.

It wasn't until several months had passed that opera made me revisit the casual comment the coast guard skipper had made. I'd begun going into the city every few weeks since Larry had moved. Guitar concerts, festival films, an ABBA tribute band. Sometimes Keini or another friend joined me, but often I was on my own. My neighbors on Kawau Island jokingly called me "a culture vulture." When I came back from a weekend that included attending a well-presented version of the opera *Carmen*, Leanne asked, "Have a good time?"

"Yes, but I miss having someone to share it with. Really miss turning to someone to see how they are reacting to an especially stirring aria."

"How about going on a dating site and saying just that?" Leanne asked. "Isn't it about time?"

I approached this idea gingerly — like anyone, especially anyone my age, new to dating sites. Over the next few months, I had slightly boring lunch dates with three different men. Though each man I met was pleasant, I was surprised at how sedate their lives appeared to be, how rarely they showed any interest in what my life had entailed, how each hoped I would immediately step into the shoes of the partner he'd recently lost. My adventures in dating did provide a new, often amusing topic of conversation with Leanne over a glass of wine. I also shared them with the nurses and helpers at Larry's care home. I enjoyed sharing stories from my life with them, and found the best thing I could do for Larry during my visits was to befriend and encourage the hardworking and unbelievably gentle people he depended upon.

Three months after I had signed up, just when I was ready to opt out of the dating site because I soon would be heading overseas to introduce *Taleisin's Tales*, I was contacted by a man who loved heading out into the wilds in his specially adapted 4X4 truck. It was when I arrived home after our fourth evening together that Leanne came over.

"Well?" She stood there waiting for an answer.

"Nice, but you know he hasn't made me laugh once," I said. "Chuckle, but not actually laugh."

"So, when's the last time you met someone who made you laugh?" Leanne asked.

"*Really* laugh? Not since that Australian sailor came for drinks months ago," I answered. Then I turned and began putting some nibbles on a plate to go with the bottle of French champagne Leanne had brought with her.

She meandered over to the far side of the room. "His name was David, wasn't it?"

A few minutes later Leanne came over to where I was standing, holding my cellphone. "Found his number in your guestbook," she said. "I'm inviting him to grab a ferry and come over for dinner on Friday." And she put her thumb on the send button.

I tried to grab the phone before she pushed the button. But I was too late.

"Leanne, you can't do that," I said. "If he does come over, he's stuck here for the night!"

"Soooo?" she replied.

I felt a terrible sense of embarrassment but reminded myself David was probably no longer in New Zealand and had set sail for Australia. He'd told me that was his plan after he'd hauled and repainted his boat in Whangārei, a day's sail north of Kawau Island.

My phone rang a few hours after Leanne had headed back across the cove to her place.

"What a nice invitation," David said as we seemed to launch right back into the conversation we'd been having when I'd last seen him seven months previously. I understood the frustrations he must have experienced as he described the setbacks that turned his quick refit into a five-month saga, and how he was just now, after six months of hard work in the shipyard, preparing to relaunch his completely sandblasted and repainted steel cutter. I was surprised when David said he'd been thinking of sailing back to Kawau to see if I felt like going out for a few days of sailing when he relaunched *Sahula*, and before he set sail to explore the fiords of southern New Zealand and then headed on to Australia.

"I would enjoy joining you for dinner," David said. "But one of my daughters is expecting my first grandchild next week, so I am planning to fly to Melbourne to be with her. Can we postpone the invite for about three weeks?"

"Unfortunately, just under three weeks from now, I'm headed overseas for three and a half months. Maybe our paths will cross some other time," I said as we wrapped up our conversation.

An hour later, just as I was dozing off, my phone rang. "Been thinking. My daughter is going to be surrounded with family and grandparents," David said. "Probably better to wait a few weeks and let her and the baby get home and settled before I fly there." I didn't have time to weigh in when he quickly added, "Thought I'd enjoy a break from cleaning up the boat. I'll see you on Friday."

———————•———————

There was an important factor that made it easy for me to accept our almost immediate connection. David is so completely different from Larry, not once did I fall into the trap of comparing the two men. Larry was built like a bulldog; David is built more like a greyhound. Larry had a wide face that looked cheerful, even in repose, with a gentle smile that reminded people of their favorite Santa Claus image; David's thin long face is far more stern looking but his frequent smiles seem to cut it almost in half. Larry was a born craftsman with hands that seemed to easily, even naturally, fit around any tool; David introduces himself as a professional pen pusher and handles tools like they are unfamiliar necessities. Larry quickly, *quickly* grew tired of deep political debates; David thrives on them. Larry loved maintaining boats and naturally kept every inch of any he sailed on shipshape and in Bristol fashion; David considers boat maintenance a chore and is casual about the details of his boat's appearance. The two men did have certain important things in common, namely: Both seemed to find me special, and both felt the same about *Felicity*. "She's delightful," David exclaimed when we headed out for a sail together that first long weekend. "*Felicity* feels like a little ship. I'd love to get her out in a bit of a breeze."

During the 17 days between our first night together and my scheduled departure, David and I spent nine with each other, three of them on board *Sahula*, just relaunched and glistening brightly in her fresh red topside paint. The cabin lights were low when I arrived on board for the first time. The seat cushions plumped up to perfection. Candles lit her table. There were flowers too. David had prepared a simple but tasty meal to make me feel welcome. I had forgotten how much fun being romanced could be, the excitement of discovering common interests and intriguing differences, the warmth of figuring out how to nestle against a body that at first was completely unknown, but within an amazingly short time grew to feel like a perfect fit.

———————

Four days before I boarded my plane bound for meetings with an English publisher, followed by boat shows, family visits and seminars in the US, I found myself thinking of both Larry and David. I considered how I'd come to feel comfortable with David so quickly, while still so deeply invested in Larry. I had made sure Larry's care was well handled — and by then, after ten months, his life at the home had become a pattern that was familiar to us all. Keini had insisted she or her boys would visit Larry's care home frequently and let me know how well he was being treated, and I knew he wanted for nothing. But still, I found myself growing anxious about my departure and the time I'd be away. And then it hit me: I was not worried over Larry anymore; I knew he was in the very best hands. What struck me was that I didn't like the idea of leaving my quickly deepening feelings for David.

I spent several hours going over my schedule, looking for a way to shorten my time away. But I'd made too many commitments. Then I spotted a possible solution. "David, how about flying over to Boston six weeks from now and touring around the East Coast in my camper truck?" I said when he telephoned that evening. Just a few weeks before, when I'd been going out with men I met on the dating site, I would not have imagined such a proposition, but now I said, "I have two weeks without any set dates during that time. Then you can come along to the Annapolis boat show, meet some of my friends."

He reluctantly declined, citing his plan to finally fly to Australia and meet his new granddaughter, the drained state of his savings after a costly refit, the need to finish sorting *Sahula* so, when spring arrived, she would be ready for her voyage to the Fiords, then on to Australia — hopefully with me on board.

I was sound asleep when the phone rang just before midnight. "I think it's important to learn more about your world," David said. "When should I fly to Boston?"

———————

Six weeks later, the Wooden Boat Festival was over, and I found myself sitting quietly in a café in Port Townsend, Washington, waiting for Kenny Thorall, who had surprised me by announcing he was flying from Anchorage, Alaska, just to see me.

"I've got something important for you," Kenny had told me. "Has to be done in person."

The business part of my tour had gone well. I'd found a British publisher to take over a project I realized I didn't have the resources to handle. *Taleisin's Tales* was being warmly received. I'd enjoyed my time with enthusiastic audiences, new and old friends in six different cities. The Port Townsend Wooden Boat Festival flew by. Each of the close friends I'd visited along the way had generously put up with my (probably overwhelming) chatter about this new man I had met, the risk I was taking by jumping so suddenly into the relationship, the fear that maybe I was in some way denigrating the wonderful relationship Larry and I had shared. Some said, "Larry would want you to go for it. At your age, no time to waste." Others commented, "Wouldn't it be a good idea to have more time enjoying being on your own?" Only a small handful of people implied I was shirking my responsibilities by limiting my visits to Larry at his care facility or getting involved with another man before Larry died.

Now, with just three days before David was due to join me, I was caught between the fear that I was pushing the relationship too quickly, had been too hasty in inviting him to move into the tight confines of an eight-foot-long, slide-in camper for three weeks, and the desire to be wrapped in his warmth again.

Kenny walked into the café carrying a large envelope. We shared a hug, then he sat down opposite and said, "Brought you some New Zealand cash I had left over from my trip down to see you. Probably $1,000 in there. Didn't want to risk sending it by post. Use it for Larry's observatory. I hope you'd like to have those photos, too." I glanced at the pictures of Kenny with the long, curling golden locks of his distant youth. Then I looked up to see he seemed to be tearing up.

"Lin, you know I haven't too long to live," Kenny said. I knew this as, over several phone conversations during the previous months, he'd mentioned his mounting health problems. But I did not expect what came next. He began, "I couldn't feel good unless I finally tell you the truth about what happened the night I left without saying goodbye back in 1966."

A sense of nostalgia instantly flooded over me. I had been introduced to Larry and Ken at the exact same moment when, as a naïve 20-year-old, I drove to Newport Beach, California, to begin my quest for a small boat so I could learn to sail. For six months Ken and Larry had both crewed on *Double Eagle* (the one Ken later bought and sailed for himself), then formed a working partnership, delivering yachts between Mexico and San Francisco, repairing boats together, playing pool late into the night. The day after I'd been introduced to the two men, I encountered Larry on his own when he invited me to join him for a cup of coffee. Three weeks after we met, Larry and I moved in together. From the start, Kenny was a comfortable part of our lives, coming by most mornings to plan whatever job Larry and he were working on, eating dinner with us two or three nights a week in the rented cottage opposite the shed where Larry and I were in the early stages of building *Seraffyn*. Sometimes Kenny would join us when we headed out for an evening movie. Eight months into our new relationship, Larry decided to fly to Vancouver on his own to spend Christmas with his family and retrieve some of the hand tools he'd left there. The night before he left, just before I dozed off to sleep, Larry said, "You know, I'd never planned on meeting someone like you, especially at this time in my life. My dream was to get a cruising boat, any way I could, and sail off, looking for that proverbial girl in every port. I'm going to have to do some serious thinking about our relationship while I'm up in Vancouver."

I'd been a bit confused about his declaration, but in the rush to get him on his plane very early the next morning, there was no time to continue the conversation.

Kenny was waiting at the cottage when I got home from work late that day. "Been talking to my dad and brother. They agree, you shouldn't be on your own for Christmas. I'll come by tomorrow and we can drive up to their place and stay for the whole weekend."

During our two-hour drive the next day, Kenny blurted out, "Larry told me he thinks you are wonderful, but he is having doubts about committing to a life with you. Implied he's ready to move on. You deserve better than that, Lin."

Ridden with the insecurities of youth, I never considered Kenny might be slanting his interpretation of Larry's words. The warmth of the holiday season I shared with Ken and his small family, the fun of racing through the back roads of Orange County on a big black motorcycle, clutching Ken's lithe strong body, my disappointment that the dreams of sailing the world Larry had offered me were now evaporating all led to the inevitable.

Two weeks later I was on my own when Larry's plane landed. On the ride back to the cottage, I explained that, since Larry wanted to move on, Ken and I were now an item.

Larry fell silent until we arrived back at the cottage. Ken was sitting on the porch waiting.

"Lin, I want to have a talk with Ken," Larry told me as he carried his bags into the cottage. A minute later, the two of them drove off in Larry's little MG TC.

I heard the two men arrive an hour later, then the sound of a car leaving. Larry walked in the door and said, "I should have taken you with me when I went to Canada. Would have avoided this mess. But I asked Ken if he was serious, if he intended to marry you. He said he was just enjoying a fling. He's decided to leave in the morning and deliver the *Double Eagle* to the Caribbean. Now let's talk."

The rest is history. Larry had not wanted out of our relationship, he told me; he wanted to decide if it was time to suggest it should be a permanent one. "I just wanted time to think and be sure before I said that to you." Though I sometimes felt a bit embarrassed at that interlude with Ken, in some ways, it probably helped Larry and me firm up our commitment to each other. And — maybe for that reason — I could never get too angry with Ken and always carried fond memories of that holiday I'd spent with him.

Now we were sitting together in a diner, two cups of hot chocolate and an envelope of NZ dollars on the table between us. Ken said, "I don't know what Larry told you about that night. But when we sat down at the Anchor Cove Bar and ordered a drink he asked if I intended to marry you. He said, 'Are you really serious about Lin?' I hesitated. Then Larry said, 'If you aren't serious, get out of town. Because I am.' "

Ken paused, "Can't say for sure what made me choose the way I did. Maybe I was afraid of the responsibility, maybe I was thinking Larry would be a better bet for you than I would. But whatever the reason, I made the worst mistake of my life. I said I'd just been leading you on."

Ken reached across, took my hand, then said, "It took me years to realize you were the only woman I ever really loved."

Tears splashed from my eyes as I heard this. I was stunned to think that I'd been so admired by not just one man in my life, but two. I moved over to sit next to Ken and put my arm around him. I couldn't think of a good response so said nothing at all, and after a few moments I realized that was the only possible answer. Our silence turned to laughter only when the waitress came by with a handful of tissues and asked if we were okay.

Just before we said farewell, I told Ken about my discomfort with jumping into a new relationship, almost as quickly as I had jumped into the one with Larry.

"Lin, that's what Larry and I both loved about you. You know your own mind. You aren't afraid of doing something risky. He would be thrilled to know you liked being with him so much you are ready to have another go. Just check that boat of David's out well before you go to sea. Don't want to worry about you."

———————

The following day I was at the arrivals terminal when David's plane landed. I had flown into Boston, where my truck and camper were waiting for me at Logan Airport. The reunion was as good as I hoped it would be. But it was a small moment the following day that confirmed the next passage I'd embark upon.

As David had never handled a rig as large as my Toyota Tundra and camper, and since he was used to driving on the opposite side of the road, I drove us to Scituate Harbor, just south of Boston, where I'd arranged a small surprise. When we arrived and parked my camper in the tree-lined parking lot of the Mill Wharf Marina, George Dow, the current owner of *Seraffyn*, was waiting. Together, the three of us walked down to the landing and climbed aboard the water taxi that took us out to where she lay on a mooring, her paintwork sparkling, her varnish work glowing. As she made a slow circuit around *Seraffyn* before laying alongside so we could climb on board, the water taxi driver told us everyone was in love with this jaunty little boat.

I sat on the cockpit seat, taking in David's reaction as he walked around *Seraffyn*'s generous side decks, running his hand over the smoothness of her beautifully varnished hatches. I watched as he went out onto her uncluttered foredeck to look up along her network of shrouds towards the handsomely tapered spreaders and graceful masthead fittings, then climbed below to admire the rich patina that years of love and use had laid over the varnished interior. David seemed fascinated by what he saw, admiring the clever way Larry had built special storage spaces for the companionway boards, the beautiful joints that, after 50 years, were still as tight as when he first created them, the ash countertops that had turned a mellow gold color as they aged. He came out into the cockpit to sit beside me and, despite his long lanky limbs, settled comfortably onto the cockpit seating that had been tailored to a much different frame. Then he quietly said, "I can see why you love this boat. You look completely at home here. I have never seen you look so happy."

I nodded in agreement. Bringing David to see the boat that was the genesis of the wonderful life Larry and I shared, seeing his appreciation and understanding of my past, removed any doubts I had. I was fully ready to accept the chance he was offering, a chance to come home to the world I knew best, one filled with love, adventure, and sailing.

This is still David's favorite photo of me, the one he took of me sitting in the cockpit of Seraffyn *in Scituate, Massachusetts.*

Only a day after I arrived home from the United States, David sailed in to begin sharing my life.

I suggested he bring Sahula alongside the boatshed and remove every single thing he had on board.

Epilogue

Summer was fast approaching when I arrived home from the USA at the end of my book tour. I woke to see David securing Sahula on the mooring in front of my cottage. He quickly launched his tender to row ashore and into a full-time life with me.

Once we settled in together, David set to work cleaning up the last of the sand, dirt, and dust that had invaded every nook and cranny of *Sahula's* interior during her refit. I watched his struggle for a few hours, then suggested he bring *Sahula* up onto the tidal grid next to the boatshed. Within two days the boatshed was filled to overflowing with cushions, provisions, tools, spare parts, plus a 10-year accumulation of books, art supplies, camping gear, and souvenirs.

When the boat was an empty shell and David had scrubbed and vacuumed her from stem to stern, I suggested he give me a complete tour. Early the next day we climbed through the empty hull, from the lazarette to the chain locker, inspecting every inch of the interior, including the prop shaft alley and engine room. We opened every locker, every floorboard. David pointed out each seacock, showed me where each hose and electrical cable ran. He commented on my keen interest in the workings of the boat.

But he never suspected I was taking Kenny Thorall's advice. Nor did he realize my interest in his boat, my inspection of every detail, was a way of weighing up my next steps before I made a commitment. By the end of the day, my doubts were gone. For, beyond the condition of the boat, his inspection had also shown me how much more I could look forward to learning, not only about this boat, but about this new man in my life.

Appendix I

———•———

Incident Statement

Date: 9/6/18
By: Gordon Gregg, Master, sv Ms *Murphy*, NZ 2129

After arriving into Suva Harbouron Wednesday 6 June and being given practique, I moved to the small yacht anchorage off the Royal Suva Yacht Club. My anchorage was approximately 18 07.357 S and 178 25.351 E in seven metres of water. My anchor was a 60-pound CQR, and I had 30 metres of eight-millimeter chain out. I was the only person on board Ms *Murphy*.

At about 19:30 on Thursday 7 June 2018 the wind suddenly started increasing rapidly from the south due to a thunderstorm over Suva Harbour. I became concerned about the strength of the wind — estimated to be well in excess of 30 knots — and started the engine in case I needed to move. After starting the engine and putting on foul weather gear, I came on deck to find that I was about to be hit by two vessels that were fouled together and dragging anchor.

The two vessels were the mv *Princess Civa* and sv *Second Wind*. The master of *Second Wind* told me that the *Princess Civa* was dragging her anchor and in the process hit *Second Wind* and took her along. When the two vessels hit Ms *Murphy*, *Second Wind* was pressed under the starboard quarter of the *Princess Civa* at a severe angle of heel and unable to free herself. The point of impact for Ms *Murphy* was directly on her bow and against *Second Wind*'s starboard quarter. Ms *Murphy* was unable to slide past *Second Wind* and was dragged along with *Princess Civa* and *Second Wind* for approximately three minutes before *Princess Civa* slipped forward enough to let *Second Wind* and Ms *Murphy* pass behind her stern.

Once free of *Princess Civa*, it immediately became obvious that the anchors and chains of *Second Wind* and Ms *Murphy* had become entangled. Both vessels attempted to lift and separate their anchors without success.

During these attempts, both vessels were slowly dragging northward toward the shallows.

After less than 10 minutes, I noticed that *Princess Civa* had run aground and was laying broadside to the wind with her bow pointing westward. *Ms Murphy* and *Second Wind* were slowly dragging down directly on top of *Princess Civa*. To avoid ending up lying on the windward side of *Princess Civa* and pounding against her, I attempted to motor into the wind at full throttle and drag *Ms Murphy* along with *Second Wind* into clear water. Progress was made until the anchor chain wrapped around the propeller on *Ms Murphy* and stopped the engine. At that point, *Ms Murphy* was adrift and being blown northwards toward the shallows.

I deployed my second anchor – a 45-pound Manson Supreme with 10 meters of eight-millimeter chain and 30 metres of 14 millimetre nylon rode. This slowed us down but could not prevent us from going aground. Eventually, *Ms Murphy* touched at approximately 18 07.146 S and 178 25.275 E. *Second Wind* was about 20 metres to *Ms Murphy*'s north-northeast.

The wind and waves had the vessel pounding and grinding on the coral bottom quite severely. The impact was on its keel and rudder. Over the course of the rest of the night, I set about trying to kedge *Ms Murphy* off into deeper water with my third anchor. I dived down and freed the chain from the propeller. I buoyed and dropped my primary anchor and began to motor off into deeper water when a fishing net became wrapped around the propeller. I was unable to remove the net before receiving an offer to be pulled off by a powerboat at approximately 8 am.

With regards to the other vessels that *Princess Civa* collided with, I only observed that she was headed toward sv *Sahula*. I could see *Sahula*'s anchor light on the leeward side of *Princess Civa* as she drifted northward towards the shallows. I could not see the impact but felt that it was going to happen given their relative positions.

Damage report. *Ms Murphy* suffered the following damage:

1. 1) The bow roller chain retaining rod was destroyed during the contact with *Second Wind*.
2. 2) The blades of the Kiwi feathering propeller were severely damage by the chain when attempting to avoid drifting down upon *Princess Civa*.
3. 3) The rudder bushes were damaged when pounding on the coral after grounding.
4. 4) All paint on the bottom of the keel and rudder has been ground away.

Repair Estimate:

F$13.50   Tug charges to haul *Ms Murphy* to deep water
F$150   Diver charges to retrieve anchor (to be confirmed)
F$200   Bow roller welding (estimate — to be confirmed)
F$1,000   Propeller blades (estimate — to be confirmed)
F$1,000   Rudder bushes (estimate — to be confirmed)
F$1,000   Haulout to effect repairs (estimate — to be confirmed)
$3,213.50   Total + anchor retrieval charges to be confirmed

In my opinion, all damage done to *Ms Murphy* and the other four yachts was caused completely by *Princess Civa* dragging her anchor. *Ms Murphy*'s anchor was holding firmly until it was dislodged upon impact by *Princess Civa*.

Signed,
Gordon Gregg, Master
sv *Ms Murphy*
NZ2129

Appendix II

The Boats I've Sailed

When I look back over my sailing life, I realize how many different boats I've had the privilege (and sometimes the pain) of being on at sea. Most of my sailing time has been spent on the two boats Larry and I built, boats that were like magic carpets, carrying us across thousands of miles of ocean waters. But I crossed oceans on almost two dozen more, and ventured out for shorter forays on many others. From yacht deliveries to races, and sometimes on easy and pleasant excursions with friends, each different boat taught me something new. Sometimes it was a trick to keep our own boat sailing better, other times it was an idea to make life afloat easier. Many times we discovered a new reason to be glad we'd built and outfitted our own boats the way we did.

The most beautiful boat I ever sailed on must have been the 51-foot Starling Burgess- designed schooner, *Rose of Sharon*. She had been built in 1931. In the early 1980s, Byron Chamberlain, a friend from the earliest days of my time with Larry, invited Larry and me to race to Mexico with him. Beautifully restored, well maintained, elegantly designed, in the light winds of Southern California, *Rose of Sharon's* huge spread of canvas kept us gliding southward while far lighter modern race boats sat motionless in the late-night zephyrs. I loved my stints behind her varnished steering wheel. No bimini hid the sweep of her spars, spars that towered so high they seemed to almost touch the brightest stars of the Milky Way. No doghouse kept me from watching the end of the long bowsprit as I pointed towards the flash of the light on San Clemente Island. Not once did I have to glance at the compass to keep on course during my two-hour helming stint.

Beating to windward in the open ocean in fresh winds is rarely fun. But there was one boat Larry and I delivered that made the upwind voyage from Mexico to California enjoyable, almost exciting. The Cal 39, designed by Bill Lapworth for racing and coastal cruising, pointed high and ate up the miles yet rode comfortably over the northwest swell driven by constant

20-knot winds. Unlike her bigger sister, the Cal 40 (we delivered three different ones up this coastline while we were building our two boats), the Cal 39 did not slam into waves, but seemed to ride over them.

From 90-footers, like the ketch *Sea Diamond*, which we helped sail down the coast of California to Mexico, to half a dozen brand-new cruising boats we moved from their Florida-based builders to owners in various parts of the Caribbean, from the two different 50-footers we delivered from the Mediterranean to the USA and the two shrimp trawlers Larry and I crewed on (one out of Mexico, the other out of Costa Rica), each forced me to learn new skills and consider new ideas.

But none taught me as much as the two boats Larry and I built together, the two he gave me as gifts and the one I now share with David, boats you have read about in this book. I hope the following overview offers you a little more insight into these remarkable sailing vessels.

Details of the Boats that Shaped my Life

———◆———

Seraffyn of Victoria

Designed by Lyle C. Hess, 1954

The hull was originally designed for Hale Field of Newport Beach, California. Lyle Hess built the hull and deck, Hale built the interior and gaff-rig then named the boat *Renegade*. She was raced successfully. That is why she caught Larry's eye.

Lyle created a new rig for Larry and me after we had sailed on Hale Field's *Renegade*.

It took us 3.5 years to build the boat, which we launched in 1968. We voyaged more than 47,000 miles on *Seraffyn*.

Length on Deck: 24'7"
Waterline length: 22' 2"
Length overall : 32'
Beam: 8'11"
Draft: 4'8"
Ballast: 2,780 pounds
Displacement: 10,686 pounds, loaded for cruising
Working sail area: 461 square feet
Construction: Mahogany planking. Double sawn mahogany frames every 30 inches with two steamed oak bent frames between each sawn frame. Solid teak decks. Hollow Sitka spruce spars.
Interior: varnished mahogany

SAILS					
	MATERIAL	LUFF	FOOT	LEACH	AREA
MAIN	7 OZ. DAC.	30'-0"	15'-0"	31'-9"	200
JIB	7 OZ. DAC.	33'-0"	16'-0"	22'-6"	156
STAYS'L	7 OZ. DAC.	22'-3"	10'-4"	20'-3"	105
GENOA 150%	6 OZ. DAC.	33'-0"	25'-6"	31'-6"	356
STORM TRYS'L	6 OZ. DAC.	12'-0"	10'-3"	18'-0"	83

Taleisin of Victoria

Designed by Lyle C. Hess 1978

In 1977 we asked Lyle to design us a larger version of *Seraffyn*, one that was less than 30 feet in length and could be driven downwind at hull speed without developing a heavy helm. That had been one of the problems with *Seraffyn*, as she developed a heavy weather helm when moving over five knots. We also wanted this boat to drive to windward better in stronger breezes, so we asked that she carry more ballast. We were delighted with the results. It took us three years to complete building *Taleisin*. She was launched late in 1983. On her we voyaged almost 85,000 miles.

Length on deck: 29'6"
Length overall: 42'6"
Waterline length: 27'6"
Beam: 10'9"
Draft: 5'3"
Ballast: 6,600 pounds
Displacement for cruising: 17,800 pounds
Working sail area: 740 square feet
Construction: teak planking over sawn black locust double sawn frames, bronze floors and hanging knees, bronze cross strapping. Solid teak decks. Hollow Sitka spruce spars
Interior: varnished teak with ash counters and tabletop, black walnut trim. A special feature of this boat is a sitz tub under the companionway.

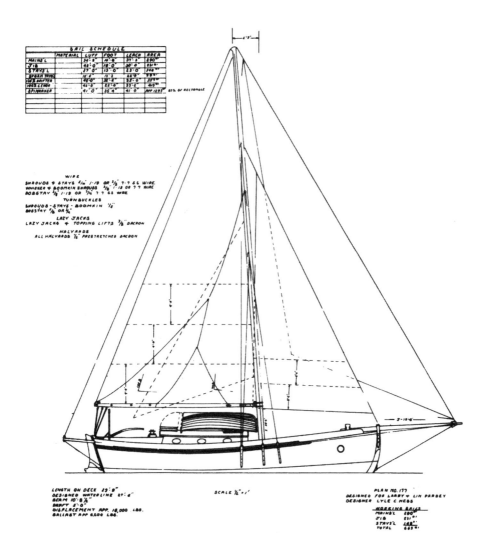

Thelma

Designed by C. W. Bailey to the-then current 2-1/2 rater handicap rules and launched in 1895 in Auckland, New Zealand. She was commissioned by a racing syndicate in Dunedin. A few days after she was launched she took part in the Auckland Anniversary Regatta and won her class. The next day she was shipped to Dunedin where she continued to be actively raced for almost 60 years. In 1984 she was moved to Auckland.

Length on deck: 34 feet
Overall length including spars: 46 feet
Beam: 7 feet
Draft: 4'6"
Displacement: 8,000 pounds
Ballast: 3,500 pounds
Sail area: 840 square feet with topsail set, 740 without
Construction: kauri diagonal planking on longitudinal stringers. Three skins from keel to waterline, two skins above. Two layers of kauri for decking. Solid Douglas fir spars.
Interior: painted kauri with varnished kauri trim
An unusual feature of Thelma is her bulb shaped lead keel. At some stage in her life, an 8-horsepower diesel engine was installed with an offset propeller.

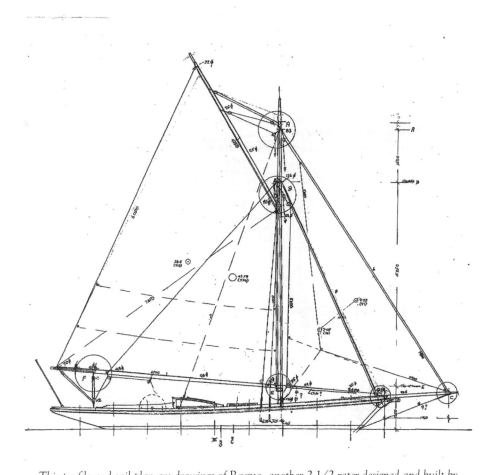

This profile and sail plan are drawings of Rogue, *another 2-1/2 rater designed and built by C.W. Bailey in 1894, just six months before* Thelma.
The rig and profile is identical other than the boom length. The boom on Thelma *is three feet longer. Drawing provided by Pheroze Jagose.*

Felicity

Originally designed by Nathaniel G. Herreshoff for his own personal use and called the Herreshoff 12½. In 1937 Herreshoff gave Cape Cod boatbuilders license to replicate this boat in fiberglass. The only modifications they made were to strengthen the rig so the boat could be sailed in heavier weather.

Length overall: 15' 8 1/2"
Waterline length: 12' 6 3/4"
Beam: 5' 10"
Draft: 2'5"
Lead keel: 750 pounds
Displacement: 1,350 pounds
Sail Area: 140 square feet
Fiberglass hull and deck, aluminum spars

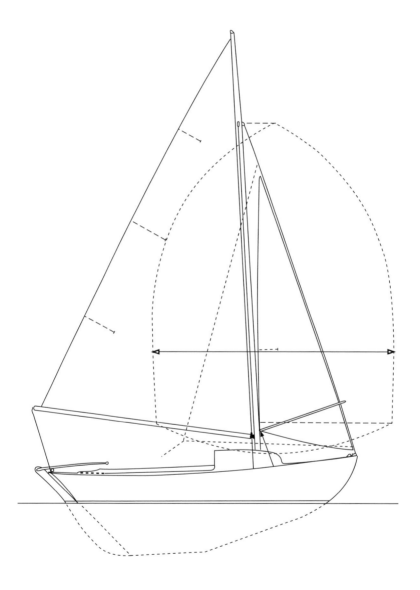

Appendix II

293

Sahula

Designed by E. G. van de Stadt

Originally built as a steel version of the shoal draft Seal 36, not long after her launching, *Sahula* was modified with the addition of a 4-foot-long lazarette drawn by van de Stadt to provide extra storage at the builder's request.

At age 60 David Haigh decided to take early retirement and set off cruising. To keep from being overwhelmed by choices as he shopped for a cruising boat, he decided to only look at boats designed by van de Stadt. Several factors influenced his choice of *Sahula*; these included his height (slightly over six feet tall), his preference for long cockpit seats on which he could lounge comfortably, plus a relatively shallow shoal draft as he wanted to explore up rivers as well as cross oceans. Other factors were a limited budget, a non-technical bent, and the probability that he would spend a large portion of his cruising time sailing singlehandedly.

His eventual choice, *Sahula*, was built and outfitted in Sydney by an amateur and launched in 1991. David purchased the boat in 2004, and immediately replaced the original engine with a Yanmar 54-horsepower diesel. David sailed *Sahula* approximately 36,000 miles during a 12-year circumnavigation, which included voyaging up the Danube and up the Rhine Rivers through Europe by way of Romania. Together, David and I have sailed her an additional 14,000 miles.

Length on deck: 39'6" including the added lazarette
Load waterline: 28'6"
Beam: 11'7"
Draft: 4'11"
Displacement: 20,600 pounds
Ballast: 7,275 pounds
Sail area: 754 square feet
Construction: Hull — four millemeter steel plating on frames (no stringers). Deck — three millimeter steel. Insulation throughout is removable.
Interior:: painted marine grade plywood with varnished wood trim
You can learn more about my current cruising home here - https://www.youtube.com/playlist?list=PLDECIBcuk_M9bAfBoiN2vSMNU1Z2Tc1b7

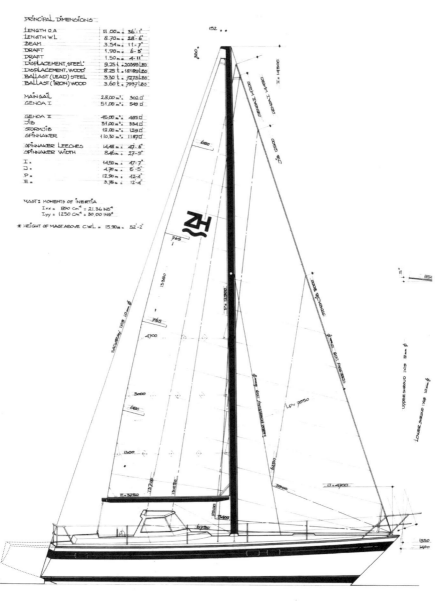

PRINCIPAL DIMENSIONS

LENGTH O.A	11.00 m.	36'-1"
LENGTH W.L	8.70 m.	28'-6"
BEAM	3.54 m.	11'-7"
DRAFT	1.90 m.	6'-5"
DRAFT	1.50 m.	4'-11"
DISPLACEMENT, STEEL	9.25 t.	20595 LBS
DISPLACEMENT, WOOD	8.25 t.	18189 LBS
BALLAST (LEAD) STEEL	3.30 t.	7275 LBS
BALLAST (IRON) WOOD	3.60 t.	7937 LBS
MAINSAIL	28.00 m².	302 ☐
GENOA I	51.00 m².	549 ☐
GENOA II	45.00 m².	485 ☐
JIB	31.00 m².	334 ☐
STORM JIB	12.00 m².	129 ☐
SPINNAKER	110.30 m².	1187 ☐
SPINNAKER LEECHES	14.48 m.	47'-6"
SPINNAKER WIDTH	8.46 m.	27'-9"
I.	14.50 m.	47'-7"
J.	4.70 m.	15'-5"
P.	12.90 m.	42'-4"
E.	3.76 m.	12'-4"

MAST: MOMENTS OF INERTIA
 Ixx = 890 Cm⁴ = 21.36 INS⁴
 Iyy = 1250 Cm⁴ = 30.00 INS⁴

* HEIGHT OF MAST ABOVE C.W.L. = 15.90 m = 52'-2"

NOTE:
 HEADROOM UNDER DOG HOUSE 1.52 m = 5'-0"

Acknowledgements

Hundreds of the people encouraged me to write this book, from Facebook friends to the cruisers I met when David and I were sailing around the Tasman sea, then on to Vanuatu and New Caledonia together. They, along with others I met at boat shows asked when I would write more about *Taleisin's* adventures. I hope *Passages* meets your expectations.

Mariette Baldwin has, for more than 40 years, been a close friend and first reader. I couldn't have kept going through the sadder sections of this book without her shoulder to lean on.

Once again, I have had the pleasure of working with two of the most encouraging editors I can imagine. One was Michelle Elvy, who helped me shape my ideas as I contemplated this project, then edited each new chapter as it was written. She was there to encourage me on down days. The other, Elaine Lembo, despite her heavy load as editor of *Caribbean Compass* magazine, she offered to take on the task of final proofing this manuscript.

Steve Horsley of Outline Design worked his usual magic in changing a manuscript into a handsome book. Jim Morehouse and his team at Paradise Cay Publications have once again made my writing life run more smoothly. Tom Doherty and the crew at Cardinal Publishing Group helped get the finalized book out the gate. Then there were the friends and David's family members who understood and encouraged me as I sneaked away from summer gatherings for several hours each day to keep writing: Annalise Haigh, Emily Haigh and Lachlan Pigott, Nichola Haigh and Chris Burke, Di Mah and Ben Boer. Thank you to each and every one of you.

The elegant cover image was created by Michael Bell, a sailor and artist from Tacoma, Washington. We met just after Larry and I had sailed around Cape Horn from east to west. Michael gifted us a set of four pastel drawings representing each of the southern capes we had weathered.

I also wish to acknowledge the two men who helped shape my life. I can't believe how fortunate I was that Larry was playing pool at the Anchor Cove in Newport Beach just when I decided to learn about sailing. I got far more sailing than I bargained for and loved it all. Though Larry is no longer with me, almost every day something reminds me of our wonderful years together. David Haigh, thank you for being a thoughtful first reader and also knowing when I needed some extra quiet time by myself. I doubt anyone could have helped get this book finished as much as you have. I am glad you sailed into my life.

About the Author

In 2022 Lin and Larry Pardey were inducted into the US Sailing Hall of Fame. For Larry it was a posthumous induction. At the ceremony, Lin was introduced as "The woman who launched 50,000 dreams." For more than 50 years, through 12 books and literally hundreds of magazine articles, both Lin and Larry encouraged thousands of potential sailors to set sail and find their own adventures. Working alongside Larry, Lin helped build two capable engine-free wooden boats then voyaged on them to more than 77 countries during extended east about and west about circumnavigations including sailing against the prevailing wind westward around the great southern capes. When age took Larry, Lin continued sailing and eventually met David Haigh, an Australian circumnavigator. Together they continue voyaging on *Sahula*, David's 40-foot steel cutter. Currently they are preparing for a voyage west towards Australia's Great Barrier Reef.

Lin and Larry often said they would continue cruising for "As long as it's Fun." With 58 years of voyaging under her keel and with a new partner, Lin has now amended this to, "As long as we're able."

You might enjoy viewing more about my life in this 93 minute long video which was created by Mike Anderson as a tribute to Larry.

Streaming is available on Vimeo or Sailflix.com.

USB or DVD versions are available from thesailingchannel.tv.

All profits from *The Real Deal* go towards maintaining the Larry Pardey Memorial Observatory at Camp Bentzon's Children's Outdoor recreation center here on Kawau Island, New Zealand

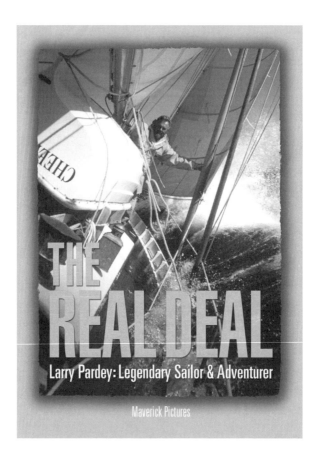

A big Thank You to all of my friends, and to all the friends I haven't met yet for the generous donations you sent when Larry passed on to Fiddler's Green on July 27, 2020. Because of your generosity, there is now a covered picnic area and fireplace just below Larry's Observatory at Camp Bentzon. More than 5000 children enjoyed these facilities and the observatory during the past year. (http:://campbentzon.co.nz)